Trapped

Trapped

Modern-day Slavery in the Brazilian Amazon

BINKA LE BRETON

Kumarian
Press, Inc.

Trapped: Modern-day Slavery in the Brazilian Amazon

Published 2003 in the United States of America by Kumarian Press, Inc.
1294 Blue Hills Avenue, Bloomfield, CT 06002 USA

Published in Great Britain in 2003 by
Latin America Bureau
1 Amwell Street
London EC1R 1UL

ISBN 1-899365-56-7

Portuguese edition: Vidas Roubadas, Ediçoes Loyola, São Paulo, 2002.

Copyedited by Lora Jorstad.
Design and production by Joan Weber Laflamme, jml ediset, Vienna, Va.
Index by Barbara DeGennaro.
Proofread by Beth Richards.
The text of this book is set in 10.5/13 Velijovic.

Printed in the United States of America by Thomson-Shore. Text printed
with vegetable oil-based ink.
♾ : acid free.

Library of Congress Cataloging-in-Publication Data

Le Breton, Binka.
    Trapped : modern-day slavery in the Brazilian Amazon / Binka Le Breton.
       p. cm.
Includes index.
    ISBN 1-56549-155-6 (pbk. : alk. paper) — ISBN 1-56549-156-4 (hard : alk.
paper)
1. Peonage—Brazil. 2. Ranching—Brazil. 3. Cattle trade—Corrupt practices—Brazil. 4. Amazon River Valley—Social conditions. I. Title: Modern-day slavery in the Brazilian Amazon. II. Title.
    HD4875.B8 L4 2003
    305.5'63—dc2003

            2002014319

12 11 10 09 08 07 06 05 04 03   10 9 8 7 6 5 4 3 2 1   First Printing 2003

Contents

Foreword

The Universal Declaration of Human Rights states that *All human beings are born free and equal in dignity and rights*. Yet UN figures estimate that the trade in human flesh moves more money than any other trade—except for illegal dealing in arms and drugs.

All across the world millions of men, women, and children are being bought and sold into slavery, yet most of us don't even hear about it, and wouldn't believe it if we did. Think of slavery at all and you think of black slaves forced to work in the plantations of the New World. Today's slavery is equally obscene—and far more subtle. Of the estimated twenty-seven million people who live in slavery today, you will find people from many races: Asian, European, Native American, African, and the mixed-blood peoples of South America.

Trapped tells the little-known tale of the thousands of men held in slavery in the far-flung cattle ranches of the Amazon jungle, working under appalling conditions and destroying their own lives as they destroy the last great forests. Migrant laborers from within Brazil, they move from contract to contract in an endless cycle of debt slavery that frequently ends in death. Leaving home to make their fortunes, they fall easy prey to the labor contractors who promise them good work and plenty of it. Eagerly they climb aboard the truck that will take them many hundreds of miles to their promised land. They little realize they are on a one-way journey to slavery and few, if any, of them will ever go home. Conditions in the labor camps are harsh, malaria is prevalent, all expenses will be discounted against the promised wages—which seldom materialize. Imprisoned by debt, secured by terror tactics, they will be lucky to finish the contract with any money at all, and if they do, it will be a matter of days before they will have to sign up for the next one.

But there is hope. All across the region brave people are working to make potential slave workers aware of the dangers, to shelter the pitifully small number who manage to escape, to summon help for those trapped in the distant jungle. What has all this got to do with us? No man is an island, we are all part of the continent, and how much more so in the days of globalization, quick profits, and bottom lines.

The bottom line is that it must stop. And we must help to stop it. Slavery is too important to be left in the hands of governments and international institutions; we too need to play our part. Make sure that people know about it, support those who work for the victims of slavery, those who work to provide just alternatives to slavery, lawgivers and lawmakers. Support fair trade and goods that are justly produced, lobby our families, friends, and neighbors, lobby our governments and the United Nations to work so that the brave words of the Universal Declaration of Human Rights become a reality.

—Archbishop Desmond Tutu

Preface

It is hard for a country to face up to slavery. No government, no society, likes to admit that slaves live inside its borders, feed into its economy, and suffer terrible violations of their rights. Around the world nations display split personalities when it comes to slavery: denouncing it to the world, unable to look it in the face at home.

It is denial, and if it is practiced by the majority of those in power, it is deadly.

Brazil has a long history of living in this state of denial. When Europeans, mostly Portuguese, first came to Brazil, they brought large-scale slavery with them. Eight years after Columbus "discovered" America, a Portuguese sailor named Pedro Alvares Cabral "found" Brazil, and soon the new owners began to realize the riches they could make from growing sugar there for the European market. The indigenous peoples were quickly conquered and enslaved to serve the new masters, but they proved neither numerous nor durable enough to supply the labor needs of the growing plantations (the Europeans carried diseases that exterminated many tribes). This wasn't a crisis for the settlers since the Portuguese had already begun capturing slaves on the coast of Africa. Shipping them to Brazil was an easier, shorter trip than sending them to the Caribbean or North America. Soon all the settled parts of Brazil were practicing legal slavery and a national economy grew up on the backs of slaves.

From the beginning of colonization until late in the nineteenth century slaves were transported from Africa to Brazil in huge numbers. As many as ten times more Africans were shipped to Brazil than to the United States, something on the order of ten million people. But because the death rate on the sugar plantations was so high, the slave population of Brazil was never more than half that of the United States. In the eighteenth century the discovery of gold helped carry slavery deeper into the interior and the Amazon. By the nineteenth century Brazil was locked in a struggle over slavery, but unlike that in the United States, it did not lead to civil war. For Brazil the key antislavery forces were the British, upon whom the Portuguese had become increasingly dependent for economic support and protection. From 1832 the British navy patrolled the oceans off Brazil intercepting and freeing African slaves. Inside Brazil the slaveholders worked constantly to whip up the racism and fear necessary to preserve slavery, and in government, ineffective, largely unenforced laws were enacted *para inglês ver* (for the English to see), a phrase Brazilians still use to mean doing something by subterfuge. In 1854 the importation of slaves and the international slave trade was abolished, but not slavery within the country. The power of the British had its limits, and in the end it was the Brazilian antislavery movement, led by Joaquim Nabuco, that forged a coalition of nationalists, anticolonialists, and liberals that defeated the landlords and slaveholders after twenty years of political conflict. When full emancipation came in May 1888, Brazil was the last country in the Americas to abolish legal slavery.

It is hard to know if slavery ever completely disappeared in Brazil after the emancipation of 1888. The great plantations of the coastal regions, the areas nearest government inspection, converted from slavery within a few years, but in the remote areas of the Amazon and the far west, there was little enforcement. These distant parts of the country were relatively untouched until the 1950s, and then exploration and exploitation began in earnest. Big changes began when Brazil experienced an economic boom in the 1960s and 1970s. Lower infant mortality and immigration led to a population explosion, the cities grew and filled, industry expanded, and the pockets of poverty grew deeper and deeper. The military government courted foreign investors with promises of cheap labor and loose environmental and tax laws. But mechanization drove more people from the countryside to the cities than the new industries could absorb, and enormous slums ruled by gang lords grew up in Rio and São Paulo. The military rulers also borrowed heavily to support nuclear power and mining projects. When the bust came in the 1980s, in spite of a return to elected governments, the uneven development of twenty years crashed. Hyperinflation wiped out savings, and servicing the foreign debt, now equaling $120 billion, crippled the economy.

The stage was set for the mushrooming of slavery. With a greatly expanded population of poor people pressed deeper and deeper into desperation and vulnerability, and with corrupt police turning a blind eye, potential slaves were ready for harvest. Around the country, and especially in the far west, where the rule of law is tenuous, those with power and guns could take total control of the workers they had "recruited." Wherever profits could be made from human sweat, slavery grew like a cancer. In agriculture, land clearances, mining, charcoal production, and prostitution men, women, and children lost their free will and sometimes their lives to the slaveholders.

Denouncing slavery at the United Nations, condemning it in the European press, assuring the U.S. government of their earnest efforts, the Brazilian government dodges their responsibilities at home. Their protests and assurances are just another case of *para inglês ver*. It is true that the Special Group for the Suppression of Forced Labor (GERTRAF) has had its resources slightly increased. It is true that its four squads have increased the number liberated to sixteen hundred in 2001, doubling the number they freed the year before. But if the whole neighborhood is full of cockroaches, four cans of insecticide won't go very far. Four squads in a country the size of Brazil, with many thousands in slavery, simply isn't enough. The government is losing the war against slavery.

How can we be so sure that the government is falling behind? A key measure is the fact that the government cannot even protect the human rights workers who are doing their work for them. Between 1997 and 2001 human rights workers were assaulted in large numbers. Twenty-three were murdered. Murder attempts, beatings, disappearances, and death threats affected hundreds more. A report submitted to the United Nations in 2002 called this "a national trend." The very people whom the government should be supporting in a fight against slavery are being left to confront the criminals alone.

The failure to protect human rights workers is a problem; the failure to protect the most vulnerable in society is despicable. Slavery would be hard to find in Brazil if the estimates provided by the government were true. As Binka Le Breton demonstrates in this book, slavery is easy to discover in Brazil. And when it is found, it is not discovered in the exploitation of isolated individuals; slaves are found in the hundreds. The CPT estimates there are at least fifteen thousand Brazilians in slavery today. I suspect there are more.

To eradicate this slavery requires a large increase in the resources brought to bear on the problem. It is important to remember that people are enslaved in order to make money. No slaveholder enslaves someone just to be cruel; slavery rides on the back of greed. In Brazil, and especially in the western states, there are vast profits to be made. Three of Brazil's most important exports are steel, timber, and beef. They account for billions of dollars in foreign earnings. All three are tainted with slavery. Leave aside for a moment the cost of human suffering, and consider the great financial risk Brazil is taking by letting slavery pollute its exports. The United States, for example, has a law that forbids the importation of any goods that have slavery anywhere in their production. Which would be cheaper, enforcing existing laws against slavery in Brazil or dealing with economic collapse following a ban on Brazil's most lucrative exports?

There are five simple steps the Brazilian government could take to eradicate slavery:

1. Form a national task force on slavery and trafficking headed by an energetic, incorruptible chief, with the power and resources to bring change.
2. Reform the law to allow prosecution at the federal level of any traffickers and slaveholders, further reform the laws to allow any investigators to "follow the money"—thus holding liable those whose financial records show returns from farms, mines, charcoal camps, etc., that are using slave labor.
3. Increase the number of squads in the Special Group for the Suppression of Forced Labor (GERTRAF) to at least twenty.
4. Punish corruption of police and officials severely. When the Special Group for the Suppression of Forced Labor (GERTRAF) makes raids to free slaves they often find that the slaveholders have been warned. Clearly, bribes are being taken.

5. Put significant resources, in the millions of *reais,* into eradicating slavery and its prevention through public education. That expenditure would still be only a fraction of what it costs Brazil in export products every time the *New York Times* publishes an article about slavery.

The enslavement of thousands of Brazilian citizens is an insult to a society that calls itself a democracy. That this enslavement has continued for years points to both the bravery and the importance of this book. Binka Le Breton roamed Brazil and looked slavery in the face. It is a highly personal book, one that peels away the layers of lies, the clouds of smoke, that criminals use to conceal slavery. Yes, Binka is a skilled investigator and interviewer, but she is not a magician; were the slavery not there to find, she would have searched in vain. The regular denials of extensive slavery by government and business are collapsing under the weight of investigations like this one.

Every person who cares about human dignity owes Binka Le Breton a vote of thanks. We should not forget the human rights workers who have been murdered and assaulted. Binka put herself in harm's way to bring us the truth, and now that her work is published she may suffer denigration by those who deny slavery's spread. We can reward her with our admiration and support, but undoubtedly the greatest reward would be for the Brazilian government to take the steps outlined here and end this abuse forever.

—Kevin Bales

Glossary and Abbreviations

Glossary

alqueire	4.84 hectares
Amazon	Generic term for the entire Amazon region that comprises parts of Venezuela, the Guianas, Brazil, Bolivia, Peru, Ecuador, and Colombia.
Amazonas	The largest state in Brazil.
Amazônia	The term given by the military government in Brazil to define the boundaries of the Amazon region, *Amazônia Legal*. The region covers over half of the entire landmass of Brazil and includes areas of natural grassland and some savanna, as well as swampland and forest.
cativo	system of hiring; higher wage with supplies discounted
caboclo	forest people of mixed blood
cabaré	brothel
companheiro	fellow worker
fazenda	large estate
favela	slum
feirinha	market
gato	contractor
hectare	2.74 acres

latifúndio	very large estate
livre	system of hiring; lower wage with supplies provided
machismo	male superiority
peon	rural worker
pistoleiro	gunman
real (s); *reais* (pl.)	approximately forty cents U.S.
usucapio	squatter's rights

Abbreviations

BASA	Amazon Bank
CEJIL	Center for Justice and International Law
CPT	Pastoral Lands Commission
EMBRAPA	Brazilian Agricultural Research Institute
FIDAM	Fund for Investment and Development in Amazônia
GERA	Executive Group for Agricultural Reform
GERTRAF	Special Group for the Suppression of Forced Labor
GETAT	Executive Group for Araguaia/Tocantins
IBRA	Brazilian Institute for Agricultural Reform
INCRA	National Institute for Settlement and Agricultural Reform
INDA	National Institute for Agricultural Development
IPES	Institute of Economic and Social Planning
MST	Landless Movement
SPVEA	Agency for the Economic Valorization of Amazônia
SUDAM	Agency for the Development of Amazônia
UDR	Rural Democratic Union

Acknowledgments

Many people had a part in the publication of this book, and without their help and encouragement it would never have been successfully concluded. Brother Xavier was the instigator, reviser, unfailing enthusiast, and a great source of inspiration. Among his colleagues in the Pastoral Lands Commission I would like to thank Trindade, Brother Henri, Aninha, Airton, Brother Jean, Brother Carlinho, and Amarildo. (Xavier, Henri, Jean, and Carlinho are affectionately known locally as the Dominicans on the Frontier.) These are some of the people who are risking their lives to bring to light some of the many cases of slavery in the distant reaches of Amazônia. My job was simply to go there and document them.

I traveled for part of the time with Father Ricardo Rezende, an expert in the field who involved me in many thought-provoking discussions as we braved the potholed roads. On my travels I was warmly welcomed and cared for by parochial staff in Porto Alegre do Norte and Vila Rica in Mato Grosso as well as by the nuns in Rio Maria and São Félix do Xingu in Pará. Many people offered me help and hospitality: My thanks go to Xavier and Pascale in Conceição do Araguaia, to the staff of the parish and the Human Rights Center in Acailandia, Maranhão, and, as always, to Sara and James in Brasília. Also to Claudia and her colleagues of the flying squad who generously permitted me to accompany them on a inspection mission, freely sharing with me their knowledge and experiences. That trip was kindly facilitated by Claudio Secchin of the Labor Ministry in Brasília.

Kevin Bales, renowned authority in the field of modern slavery, helped me acquire a global view of the problem, as did Mike Dottridge of Anti-Slavery International in London. My publisher Krishna Sondhi led me gently through the process of production, and Guy Bentham, coeditor, was good humored and helpful throughout. Back in Brazil, Maysa Monte Assis, valued friend and colleague, undertook the translation into Portuguese, supported by her husband and daughter. I am eternally grateful to those people who permitted me to share their stories, even when they were sometimes painful, among them Albertino of São Félix, Fátima of Porto Alegre, and Roque Quagliato of Fazenda Brasil Verde, who received me most graciously. Each of these and many more helped me understand their respective points of view.

My hope is that I have been able, to some extent, to give a voice to those who have no voice, and that their stories may inspire the reader to get up and get involved in the fight against slavery.

Finally, a big thank-you to my husband, Robin, who read the manuscript several times and was never too busy to discuss the finer points of jurisprudence, sociology, and ethics. Who gave me moral support and good advice during a series of long telephone calls when I was in the field, and who discreetly made sure that I had the time, space, and energy to complete the job.

Introduction

Slavery Alive and Well Around the World

The Brazilian Amazon: June 2000

The heat weighs so heavy that my slightest movement provokes a river of sweat, and although I fill my lungs to capacity I still feel starved for oxygen. Everyone in the stark little hospital room seems stupefied by the heat and by their pain. Even the flies are listless. I am crouching on the cement floor talking to Albertino. He has an ageless face, like polished black marble. He is sitting on a plastic mattress, inadequately covered by a small yellow towel. His right arm and chest are heavily bandaged. Within a week he will lose his arm, but he is lucky to be alive. Two days ago Albertino arrived with his friend Batista from a remote jungle camp where they had been held as slaves.

Batista speaks in a low voice, never once looking at me. Memories are raw and the words come with difficulty. "We just couldn't get work back home," he begins, "and then we started hearing stories that there was good money to be made up in Pará. This man Jair came to town looking for workers. Offered us eight *reais* a day plus our food, and a nice little advance. Told us we'd be home in a couple of months, with plenty of money in our pockets. Stood us a couple of rounds to celebrate, and said we'd be leaving next day. Off to seek our fortunes. We climbed onto the truck happy as anything.

"It's a long way to Pará, and it took us several days to get there. We finally came to the Xingu River and crossed on the ferry. It was thick forest, and there wasn't a road, just a muddy logging trail. The truck kept getting stuck and they made us push, until finally we had to abandon it and haul the stuff in on our backs. First thing we did was cut a clearing and make a shelter out of saplings and plastic sheeting. And then it started to rain. It rained and rained and the whole place turned into a sea of mud, with mosquitoes everywhere. They made us get up before dawn and work till dark, and the food was terrible, just rice and beans. But we couldn't argue with them, because they all had guns. We never got paid, and they told us we'd better not think about leaving. Not until the job was done.

"There was this one guy called Tim and he was always picking fights with everyone. Monday night he got drunk and started arguing with Albertino. Next thing we knew he'd whipped out his gun and pointed it straight at him."

"I remember his smile as he fired," says Albertino softly. "I thought I was going to die."

"Tim ran outside laughing," Batista continues, "and our first thought was: We've got to get Albertino away from here before they come back to finish him off. So we carried his hammock out into the forest to hide him. I wanted to take him a blanket later on, but I didn't have the nerve. Tim's hammock was right next to mine, and I was afraid that if I moved he'd kill me too."

"I'll remember that night as long as I live," adds Albertino. "It was raining hard, I was shaking with cold and fever, and there were swarms of mosquitoes. I was so weak that I couldn't move a muscle, so I just lay quiet in my hammock, and prayed. I could hear them crashing around the forest looking for me, but thank God they never found me, and before dawn Batista came back and carried me out of there."

"We knew they'd come after us"—Batista shivers—"so we didn't dare walk along the trail. We weren't even sure of the way, but by some miracle we found the trading post. The man there

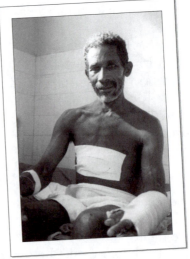

Albertino

radioed for a pilot, and they sent a plane in the next day. Well, the doctor never thought Albertino would make it. But he's a tough one, and you can't kill him off that easily!"

Despite the clammy heat, I feel a cold shiver down my back as I sense something of Albertino's pain and terror. Lured into the jungle by false promises, treated with casual brutality, he was worked to the limits of endurance, forcibly held prisoner, and discarded as one might stomp on a cockroach.

Cruelty? Savagery? Barbarity? All these, and more. The word for this is *slavery,* and if you and I are to call ourselves human beings we must recognize it for what it is, and pledge ourselves to wipe it from the face of the earth.

You probably didn't know that slavery still exists. I certainly didn't. Illegal migrants, yes. Migrant workers in appalling conditions reminiscent of *The Grapes of Wrath,* yes. But slaves, as in the old days down on the plantations in the Deep South, or the Nazi concentration camps, or the gulags of the Soviet Union? Surely not.

Yet Anti-Slavery International[1] estimates there are millions and millions of men, women, and children across the world caught in the chains of slavery, forced to work at the most degrading of jobs in the most degrading of conditions, subjected to every sort of violence, and deprived of that most fundamental of rights: the right to come and go. A dirty, undercover business thriving on secrecy and brute force, its tentacles extend from the most primitive, isolated, and backward areas of the world to its great cities, from villages in India and cattle ranches in the Amazon to sweatshops in New York and the kitchens of smart London houses. According to Kevin Bales,[2] international trafficking in people generates profits on the order of thirteen billion dollars annually. Ever and universally present are the demand for cheap, compliant labor on the one hand, and the supply of desperate, hungry people on the other. Mechanisms for trapping the unwary are innumerable.

From time to time we catch a glimpse of the people trade. A truckload of Chinese illegal immigrants suffocates to death in the Channel Tunnel, a cleaning woman reveals that she has worked for twenty years without pay in the home of a diplomat in Washington, a gang of pedophiles is smashed in Germany and we learn that young children have been kept as sex slaves. Yet by the very nature of the business the world hears only a tiny fraction of what goes on.

I came across the trail of modern-day slavery when I was in the Brazilian Amazon, learning first about the land, then about the land wars, and finally about the army of migrant laborers used to fuel the headlong development of the agricultural frontier, transforming the world's last mighty forests into a wilderness of unproductive cattle pasture.

Come with me on a journey to the heart of darkness, to see and hear what is happening on the last great frontier, where nameless men disappear into the deep forest, where the sleek white cattle live better than those who tend them, and where there is no law except the law of the gun. There will be many stories to hear, stories of unimaginable cruelty, of extraordinary courage, of humiliation and endurance, stories to make one ashamed and proud to be human. The small-town politician, the keeper of the rooming house, the gunman, the landless worker, the prostitute, all will have their tales to tell—tales that make up the mysterious patchwork story of slavery in the Amazon today.

Sitting on the bus as it bounces along the endless potholed roads of Amazônia, I reflect on the situation of slavery today in Brazil. Rubber tappers in the state of Acre still live in perpetual debt to the traders who buy their rubber in exchange for the bare necessities of life. Child prostitution flourishes in the remote gold mines of the interior, as well as in the big cities. Across the central and northern states of Brazil there are charcoal burners working twenty-four hours a day under the most inhumane conditions, burning the soles of their feet and coughing their lungs out, while deep in the Amazon men labor away cutting and burning the forest in a new version of the ancient evil of debt slavery.

I look through the window at the flat lands of Tocantins, the transition zone between savanna and forest. Patches of scrub are interspersed with huge fields littered with the sad carcasses of burned trees where the forest has disappeared forever—in one of the most reckless acts of devastation in the history of humankind.

This devastation was initiated in the 1970s when Brazil's military government decided to solve two of its most pressing problems simultaneously. One was the question of surplus rural populations displaced from the newly mechanized south and the drought-stricken northeast. The other was the populating of Brazil's vast Amazonian territories, which military minds saw as providing an open invitation to covetous neighbors from the north. Migrants would be encouraged to people the empty spaces, bringing the "men without land" to the "land without men."

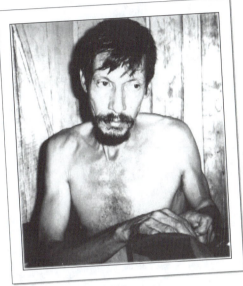

Sick peon

Amazônia needed labor and needs it still. The neighboring states in the northeast contain large numbers of desperate, hungry men looking for work. Distances are immense, violence is commonplace, and the only law is the law of the jungle. Enterprising contractors find no difficulty in recruiting truckloads of eager men, promising them good work and plenty of it, together with a decent wage at the end of the job. Buoyed up by extravagant promises of money and excited at the prospect of visiting far-flung places, they happily accept an advance on their salary and embark upon their great adventure. It is an adventure from which some of them will never return.

The Slave Trade

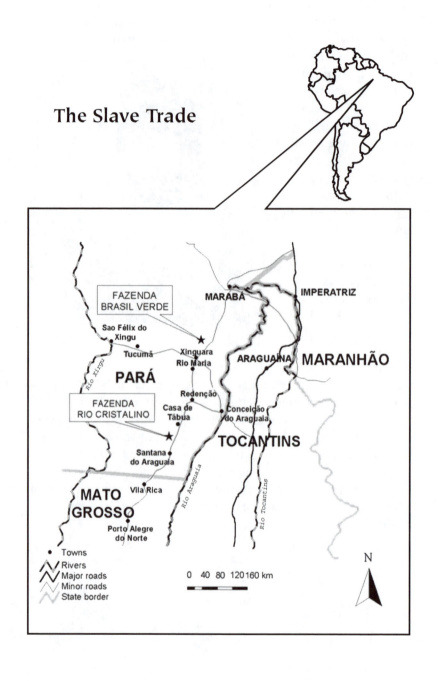

The Chain of Slavery

The Nuts, Bolts, and History of Modern-day Debt Bondage

It's been a long journey, and it doesn't look like we've gotten anywhere special. For more than twenty hours the bus has pounded up the road from Brasília, through grassy savanna and the scrappy vegetation of the transition zone, to the scattered palms that announce the beginning of the forest proper. Settlements are sparse. Occasionally we pass a small town, a row of low whitewashed houses, or a thatched palm-leaf shelter. We're in the state of Tocantins, and our destination is Araguaína, a town that looks ordinary enough but happens to be one of the chief points for the recruitment of slave labor.

I confess to being relieved at our safe arrival. The old man across the aisle has been regaling me with horror stories about bus hijackings. "Happened again last week," he says, sucking his teeth and looking slyly up under his bushy brows to gauge my reaction. "They forced the bus off the road and took everything. Everything." Unconsciously I feel for my money belt and wonder if I can devise a better hiding place for my valuables. The old man gives me a satisfied smile and settles back to doze, snoring gently, while I toss and turn and rehearse what I will do when the gunmen board the bus.

The bus station is swarming with activity: dark Amazon beauties in bright Lycra outfits, young men in jeans and cowboy hats, children everywhere, bundles, backpacks, boxes, bedding, battered suitcases, plastic bags, piles of coconuts, urchins selling snacks and little cups of dark sweet coffee, sellers of stolen watches and contraband cigarettes, and smartly uniformed bus drivers walking importantly around through the milling crowd. I scan the unfamiliar faces and suddenly there is Xavier. He enfolds me in a big hug, seizes my pack, and steers me through the mob to his motorbike. Dressed, like everyone else, in jeans and a T-shirt, Xavier is a Dominican brother from France who works in the Pastoral Lands Commission, locally known as the CPT.

Set up twenty-five years ago by the Catholic Church, the mission of the CPT is to support the rural population in gaining access to land, documentation, and technical assistance, as well as an understanding of labor relations and legal advice. This agenda inevitably leads them straight into the thorny arena of human rights and the most basic questions of survival and human dignity. Their clients? Squatters,[1] settlers, and slaves.

Xavier's house is directly opposite Nazza's bar—one of Araguaína's more lively and noisy establishments, which opens at sunset and builds up a sustained crescendo of noise and activity that culminates in the small hours. Shortly after Nazza closes, the charismatic Catholic church next door opens up for business. I cannot decide which makes more noise, and even with earplugs, thoughtfully provided by Xavier, it is hard to sleep. Since it is electioneering time, huge loudspeaker trucks ply the streets at regular intervals, bringing all conversation to an abrupt halt for minutes on end. I wonder how it will be possible to think coherently.

We settle down in the hot little kitchen over a breakfast of milky coffee, yogurt, and fresh rolls. No, we haven't come across any cases of slavery round here, he tells me. The ranches in this area aren't sufficiently isolated. You couldn't hide a bunch of workers without somebody finding out. Well, there was one case last year, about 120 kilometers south, on Fazenda Pantera. But most of it takes place across the river in the state of Pará. Araguaína is the assembly point for the workers.

"This isn't the kind of slavery where you buy a man like he was an ox," he begins, pouring me another cup of coffee. "These days it's a bit more subtle than that. You don't own the man, you just use him for as long as you need him. It's debt slavery. Here's how it works. The guy gets offered a job, given an advance, and put to work. When it's payday he discovers that he's in debt. He owes for his advance, he owes for his transport, he owes the canteen bill—food, tools, and medicines—and if he's been staying somewhere in town he owes for his accommodation. It ends up as an unpayable debt. But he doesn't realize that. Not yet.

"There's the question of his honor. That and his pride. He feels strongly that he can't leave while he is still owing, and he's often too proud to go home without any money. He won't admit that he's been had. He's terrified to point the finger at anyone in case they get after him. He prefers to forget it. Nine times out of ten if he does get away, he'll just go right back to work, often for the same contractor. So you can see that it's a hard thing to pin down, it's so elusive. What we see is only the tip of the iceberg. There's a whole chain of people involved, and everyone depends on everyone else.

"First, there's the rancher. What he wants is a cheap source of temporary labor to do a specific job, like cutting the forest, making pastures, keeping them clear, fencing, that sort of thing. The sort of job that requires a lot of manpower for a specific length of time. Say he has six hundred hectares² of virgin forest to clear for pasture. He'll look around for a contractor to get the job done. That's the next link in the chain. Round here the contractor is known as a *gato*—that means 'cat.' That's because he always lands on his feet! The *gato* makes sure that the work area is demarcated, figures out how much labor it's going to require—which depends on lots of things like the difficulty of the terrain and the length of time available—and then goes out hiring. He'll need so many men to go through the forest, cleaning out the vines and undergrowth so that the chain saw operators can go in. He's got to make sure they have all the right equipment: plastic sheeting for the tents, hoes, machetes, gasoline, and spares for the chain saws. Then there's the supplies: rice, beans, manioc flour, coffee, sugar, cornmeal, oil, dried meat. Lanterns, shot, first-aid stuff, medicines for malaria and stomach problems. Extras for the canteen: batteries, cigarettes, boots, hats, tools, whatever the men are going to need.

"Of course he has to have some overseers. Well, they call them overseers, but in practice they're just plain old gunmen. In the meantime he'll be looking for labor. There are two main categories: the local guys and the migrant workers. The local guys have got somewhere to live—even if it's only a shack on the outskirts of town—and they have some sort of family network. If they go missing, sooner or later someone will be out looking for them.

They'll make up a work gang consisting of their relations and friends, and often they'll do several jobs with the same *gato* because they know him."

"Just a minute," I interrupt. "I thought you said that half the time they never got paid?"

Xavier nods.

"And even so, they'll go back and work with the same *gato*?"

He smiles ruefully. "It's quite simple," he says. "They've got no choice; they need the money. And often they don't expect anything better. This kind of work is so hard and the conditions are so bad that nobody would do it if there wasn't the chance of making some good money. So if it didn't work out last time, well they'll just try again. Once in a while they do make a few bucks, and nine times out of ten they'll blow most of it in the bar. Stand everyone a couple of rounds, and suddenly they're the most popular man in town. The rest will go on the girls, and if there's any left it'll go to the families, and then it's time to head out and earn some more. Generally speaking the *gatos* like to work with the local guys because they're pretty reliable."

"And the other peons," I inquire, "the migrant workers? Their situation must be even more precarious."

Xavier agrees. "The migrant worker is virtually an outcast. He's on the very fringes of society. He's probably been on the road for a long time, and now he doesn't have anyplace to go. Many of them don't have identity documents, so as far as the state is concerned they don't exist. If they disappear, no one's going to miss them. Most likely they're illiterate, too, so they'd have trouble figuring out where their money went, if they ever saw any. They don't have too many friends. Sometimes they build up a relationship with the woman who keeps the lodging house where they stay in between jobs. And with the prostitutes. But most people, and that includes the local guys, would see them as unreliable and dangerous: womanizers, drunks, and quarrelsome. The migrant worker is pretty much at the bottom of the pile."

I think back to the time I lived with a bunch of street bums in a homeless shelter on the Durban waterfront. I was there because I wanted to find out about their lives, but they were there because they had no choice. Rejected by society, they indulged in antisocial and self-destructive behavior. It was often hard to see them as abandoned people thrown onto the garbage pile, and to realize that as a fellow human being I shared the blame for their plight.

"Tell me something," I say, raising my voice at the approach of a passing loudspeaker truck. "If this whole business is illegal and you're dealing with the underworld, how do you manage to get any reliable information?"

"Well, we've been tracking it for years," Xavier replies, "ever since the seventies."

"During the military dictatorship?"

"Exactly. And you need to remember that conditions were a lot worse in those days. This place was incredibly isolated. There weren't many roads and the ones they did have were terrible. There were hardly any phones, and information was tightly controlled. The press was censored. Politically the area was suspect, too. Lots of things were going on. Remember hearing about the guerrillas in the Araguaia?[3] This was considered a high-risk area from the point of view of national security. Then there were the land wars. The government was encouraging settlement schemes on the one hand and big ranches on the other, so all sorts of people were coming in. Of course they started clashing with the traditional populations, to say nothing of the indigenous tribes. People were falling over themselves to get into the ranching business because the government was handing out money right, left, and center. All part of their policy of letting big business develop the region. Those ranches needed a lot of labor in the early stages, and there just wasn't enough available. So they had to recruit labor wherever they could find it."

"That's not so different today, is it?" I murmur.

"No, it's not," Xavier affirms. "But these days there's nothing like the scramble to open up new ranches. There isn't the money available, and anyway this isn't really a good area for raising cattle. Not in my opinion, although the ranchers will tell you otherwise."

"So they were using slave labor to open up the ranches?"

"That's right. The first stories came out of Mato Grosso in 'seventy-two. It was the bishop, Pedro Casaldáliga,[4] who sounded the alarm. Published a report about it. He was based in the back of beyond, São Felix de Araguaia, and he's there still. Well, little things started to come up here and there, and he realized there was a pattern to it. Tales of men lured off into the jungle to work for good money, and never heard of again. Rumors of every sort of violence, physical and mental, of men dying of malaria, and others trying to escape and being hunted down like dogs."

I sigh deeply. This investigation is going to lead me into murky waters.

Xavier puts his head on one side and smiles at me. "I think before you go any further into that, you might want to catch a bit of sleep," he suggests gently. "These bus journeys aren't calculated to put you in tiptop shape, and anyway I'd better get over to the office. I'll leave some documents for you to study when you wake up. And later on I'll show you where the market is. That's the main pickup point, and you can get anything you want down there!"

"Thanks, Xavier," I nod. "I think I'll take up your suggestion."

I awake in the listless heat of the afternoon, covered with a film of sweat. Groggily I make my way to the shower, accompanied by the blaring of another loudspeaker truck coming slowly and inexorably down the street. Xavier left a pile of folders on the table, and as I flip through them my eye is caught by the following stark little paragraph from an interview with a peon[5] who escaped from Fazenda Sapucaia in the south of Pará a couple of hundred kilometers from where I'm sitting. Just across the Araguaia River. The article describes him as sick, starving, and mentally disturbed.

Q: How were things on the *fazenda*?
A: "I can't begin to tell you. It was a nightmare. There was one day I was so hungry I ate a dead rat."
Q: Didn't you get any food?
A: "Oh yes. But not if we were naughty."
Q: What do you mean by naughty?
A: "If we didn't pay the canteen bill. Anyway I'd rather eat dead rat than that rotten stuff out of a can."
Q: Did they beat you up?
A: "Only once. They thrashed me with a whip; I can still remember the pain of it. I treated the cuts with oil from the andiroba tree. But when the overseer saw that they

were healing he threw gasoline over them and then I saw
stars . . . "

Q: Didn't any of you ever think of escaping?

A: "Sure we did, but no one was stupid enough to try it on.
The gunmen were always on the lookout. Watching us like
hawks. Scared the hell out of us."

Q: How much money did they give you?

A: "I honestly don't remember. I once got 120 *reais*.[6] But my
canteen bill was R$150. I'd hardly even got the money in
my hands before the overseer snatched it away, accusing
me of trying to be smart with him."

Q: And what are you going to do with your life now?

A: "What do you expect me to do? I've got no schooling, I
can't read, and just about the only thing I can do is work
in the fields. My dream is a proper job with a salary."

In the five hundred years since the conquest of Brazil,
Amazônia has proved itself a fertile field for slavery. Distance
and isolation play their part, together with ingrained violence
and the lawless carefree culture of the frontier. The shadow of
slavery extends back to precolonial days and the repeated clashes
among rival indigenous groups, with the object not of acquiring
more land or seizing women but of capturing men for ritual cannibalism in order to inspire terror among their enemies. Cannibalism was the supreme horror that demanded vengeance,
leading to an endless cycle of vendettas. More aggressive tribes
like the Tupinambá would keep their captives for several months
before eating them. But not all tribes practiced cannibalism, and
those who did not would slaughter their enemies, having no reason to keep them alive.[7]

The first Europeans to arrive in the Amazon were able to persuade the indigenous people to work for them in exchange for
trade goods: machetes, axes, and cloth. But the Natives soon tired
of that. They were warriors and considered anything that wasn't
hunting to be women's work.

Accustomed to the notion of slavery that had become established on the Iberian Peninsula during the fifteenth century,[8]
the Europeans then hit upon the idea of seizing captives from
the tribes, justifying their actions by maintaining that they were
"ransoming" them from a worse fate (being eaten) and saving

their souls for eternity. The captives, however, often thought otherwise. One of them, quoted by sixteenth-century traveler Yves d'Evreux,[9] declared that he cared little about being eaten, "for when you are dead you no longer feel anything. . . . But I should be angry to die in bed and not to die in the manner of great men, surrounded by dances and drinking and swearing vengeance on those who would eat me before I died."

Meanwhile the Jesuit missionaries, who were vehemently opposed to slavery, were encouraging free Natives to join their settlements, where they would be set to work for God and for the brotherhood. Both the colonizers and the men of God felt perfectly free to decide the fate of the Native people, in a perverse pattern of colonialism that was to be copied wherever Europeans set foot on new lands. Overenthusiastic recruiting of the Native population soon led to a drastic decline in their numbers, thereby opening the way for the African slave trade.

After much scrapping among rival national groups, it was the Portuguese who emerged as the masters of Brazil, and over the centuries they presided over the creation of a distinctively Brazilian racial type that incorporated traits from Europe, Africa, and the indigenous people of South America. Amazônia's population was small, and most people lived along the rivers, adopting the Native lifestyle: hunting, fishing, growing a few staples on the floodplains, and taking what they needed from the forest.

One of the forest products that they harvested occasionally was latex from the rubber trees. The indigenous tribes had discovered how to use latex to make waterproof bags, bottles, and torches. This primitive rubber was waterproof but not weatherproof: In the heat it went sticky, and in the cold it turned hard and brittle. By the end of the nineteenth century scientists had discovered how to process it, and the invention of the pneumatic tire, first for the bicycle and later for the motorcar, led to a rush for the wonderful new commodity. By 1875 there were an estimated twenty-five thousand rubber tappers working in the region of Belém, and demand was growing steadily. They harvested the sticky white substance from the wild rubber trees, processed it in a rudimentary fashion, and traded the rubber to passing merchants in exchange for supplies. Unfortunately for them, isolation and illiteracy made them easy prey for the traders, who paid what they pleased and charged what they could. The rubber tappers frequently found themselves forced into the toughest of sharecropping arrangements[10] with those who claimed to own the forests where they worked. They were encouraged to pay "rent" in kind, they were often expressly forbidden from planting any crops or even from keeping any hunting dogs, and their compliance was assured by the presence of armed "supervisors." They were living, in fact, in slavery.

With increased world demand for rubber, the traders started looking for other areas to exploit. One of the richest of these proved to be in the far western Amazon, in what is now the state of Acre. It was a remote and isolated spot, and there wasn't enough labor to harvest the rubber. But luck was on the side of the traders. Clear across the country, the northeastern states were suffering from another of their periodic devastating droughts. Thousands of people had to leave the countryside in search of work, so the traders went in and signed up men as fast as they could. They offered to pay their fares and give them all the equipment they would need: guns, knives, machetes, food, and clothes. Acre was a highly malarial area and many of the new arrivals got sick and died, leaving the rubber bosses short of labor once again. This time they turned their attention to the indigenous tribes, hunting them down to provide extra labor. But the Natives proved to have no resistance to white men's diseases, dying in even larger numbers. So the traders returned to the dry lands in search of more recruits. What the new hands didn't realize was that they would have to pay off their debt in rubber—and that they'd never clear it as long as they lived. Neither would they ever be able to go home. They couldn't afford to send for their families, so they took local women instead. They paid rent to the bosses and traded on the most unfavorable of terms. They did a bit of hunting and a bit of fishing but never quite paid off their debts. They were trapped in the forest. Meanwhile, in the river ports of Manaus and Belém, the bosses were drinking champagne, going to the opera, and sending their laundry, so the story goes, to Paris.

Suddenly the bubble burst. In a shattering coup of industrial skulduggery, a British botanist succeeded in smuggling out the seeds of the precious rubber tree,[11] and within the space of a few decades the British had set up thriving rubber plantations in

Malaya. Meanwhile, back in the Amazon, the bosses went bust, and the rubber tappers were left to their own devices.

But the story of Amazon rubber wasn't quite over. During the Second World War the Japanese took over the Malayan plantations, and suddenly the Allies found themselves desperately short of rubber. America did a deal with the Brazilian government to buy as much rubber as the Amazon could produce, and the government sent recruiters to the northeast once again. This time the trade was set up on a patriotic footing. Recruits to the Rubber Army were promised all sorts of perks: uniforms, medical care, free passages, repatriation, military pensions, the lot. Once the rubber soldiers got into the forest they found themselves in exactly the same situation as their predecessors, and when the war finally ended they saw neither hide nor hair of their pensions.

You can still find rubber tappers eking out some sort of an existence on the rivers in Acre and Amazonas. Conditions have changed very little in the last hundred years, although there are signs of hope. Communications have improved, malaria is better controlled, and some of the children even get a rudimentary education. In the wake of the murder of Chico Mendes,[12] international attention was drawn to their plight; more importantly, the rubber tappers started taking steps to help themselves. They lobbied for the setting up of extractive reserves. They joined the unions, they formed cooperatives to handle sales and trading, and when the ranchers came in and started clearing the forest they got involved in peaceful protests, placing themselves in the path of the bulldozers and standing up for their rights and their forests. But the price for their rubber is very low, and unless they can diversify production their future is bleak. Many of them live in virtual slavery, and on the more isolated stretches of river they still call themselves *cativos*.

The rubber tappers may be among the most traditional of Amazônia's slaves, but they are far from the only ones. Outsiders often look at the Amazon and see an idyllic land of virgin forest with immense, priceless, and virtually untapped biological resources. Many of Amazônia's true riches, however, lie buried under the ground, and nobody knows their full extent. Preliminary estimates based on known deposits value them in the region of seven trillion dollars.[13] There are known to be very substantial reserves of petroleum, natural gas, copper, tin, tungsten, manganese, uranium, diamonds, nickel, aluminum, potassium, carbon, and lime. Who knows what other treasures have yet to be found? Yet of all Amazônia's resources there is one that has more power over humankind than any other: gold.

Gold mining is the stuff of legend, and it is easy for us to picture the miner as a hero of the frontier, wild, brave, and free. But the facts tell a different story. Some of Amazônia's wildcat miners strike it rich; most do not. All of them live dangerously on the fringes of the law, subject to frequent and crippling bouts of malaria, poisoning themselves with their carefree use of mercury, and getting themselves killed in drunken brawls.

Mines are dangerous places; stakes are high and notions of human rights count for little. The twin mechanisms of isolation and debt, reinforced by a few old-fashioned scare tactics, prove all too effective in immobilizing the labor force. Armed guards discourage anyone sufficiently unwise to contemplate fleeing, and rumors abound of beatings, torture, and the existence of clandestine cemeteries. A 1992 report on the Bom Futuro cassiterite mine near Ariquemes, Rondônia, estimated the population of miners as somewhere between three and four thousand, with an average of fifteen bodies removed weekly from the mine—in addition to the four to five *reported* deaths. While some of the miners were operating tractors and diggers, others were scrabbling at the soil with their bare hands. In the same year, and as a consequence of this report, the mine was expropriated.

Miners with a little gold dust to spare can easily be persuaded to part with it in exchange for a night of passion. A series of reports published in the *Folha de São Paulo* in 1992[14] revealed the existence of a chain of slavery involving thousands of young women and girls who were enticed with promises of high wages, transported to distant mines, and forced into prostitution. One of the mines investigated was called Cuiú-cuiú. Located in the state of Pará, it was four hours from the Xingu River and a five- to six-day boat journey from the town of Itaituba. Girls in Cuiú-cuiú were treated like chattel and forced to pay off their debt by working as prostitutes. Like the miners, they owed for their airfare, medicines, cigarettes, and sometimes drugs. Unlike the men, they also owed for clothes and perfume, to say nothing of repaying the price for which they had been sold—sometimes by their own families. If they refused to cooperate they were often denied food, or beaten up. One girl reported, "If we flee they go after us, and if they find us they kill us. If they don't kill us, they beat us all the way home to the brothel." A seventeen-year-old girl rescued by the Federal Police said, "I lived like a real slave and was beaten every time I refused to sleep with a worker." Another girl said, poignantly, "I used to be somebody, now I'm nothing." Shame too plays its part in immobilizing the girls. Not infrequently, if they are rescued and returned home their families refuse to take them in.

Another of Amazônia's mineral riches is iron ore, and its reserves at Carajás are among the largest in the world. To process the iron ore you need fuel, and the nearest and most convenient available fuel is charcoal. Charcoal production is dirty, dangerous, and hazardous to your health. Many charcoal makers also live in conditions approaching slavery. In March 1992 the Ministry of Labor sent a team of inspectors to the forests in the state of Mato Grosso do Sul to investigate conditions among the charcoal burners. They discovered somewhere between five and eight thousand people living in conditions that they described as "real human servitude." Many of them were in "an advanced state of malnutrition and a mournful state of drunkenness." Entire families worked a twelve-hour day collecting wood, and small children were used to stack the wood and fill the ovens. They lived in tents made of plastic sheeting, they had no access to clean water or any kind of sanitation, and they suffered from all sorts of health problems, including burns, lung disease, and circulatory problems associated with working at high temperatures.

Charcoal production requires many different types of workers: people who operate the chain saws, people who collect and stack the wood, people who transport it, and people who make the charcoal. This involves loading the oven—a skilled task that has to be done evenly—regulating the heat, cooling the oven, and unloading and packing the charcoal. The whole operation can take as much as nine days, depending on the design of the oven. Entire families are involved in charcoal production, and during the period of burning the ovens need to be watched twenty-four hours a day. Under these circumstances it is hard to get any time off, and those who think of leaving may well be deterred by the presence of armed guards.

While some may argue as to whether the truly appalling conditions under which many charcoal burners live do, indeed, constitute slavery—as opposed to enforced and degrading work—in 1992 the then–state secretary for agriculture in Mato Grosso do Sul didn't hesitate for a moment. When asked whether the charcoal industry had brought employment to the region of Ribas do Rio Pardo in his state, he replied unequivocally, "There's nothing left. Just the charcoal and the slaves."

Nazza's bar has just turned its sound system to maximum as I sit and reflect on slavery. At once primitive and highly sophisticated, it flourishes in the ideal conditions of Amazônia where immense distances and difficult communications provide innumerable places for it to lurk undiscovered. Large territories are hard to administer, and cash-strapped local governments simply cannot afford the infrastructure and policing necessary to establish and maintain law and order. Potentially large pickings encourage adventurers, while sheer human greed stimulates corruption. The culture of the frontier is the law of the jungle. I remember the public boast of a local policeman-turned-gunman, "What matters round here ain't what the sheriff says, ain't what the judge says, what matters round here is who's first on the draw." And since the man who is first on the draw is the man who makes the most money and acquires the most possessions, he is the man who runs the show. Mr. Big Rules. Just as the Portuguese colonialists turned non-Europeans into property to be bought, sold, and bartered, many of today's new colonists treat their labor as disposable commodities.

From across the road I can hear the voice of Chico Buarque, one of Brazil's favorite singers. One of his protest songs,[15] heard long ago, comes back to me with new urgency:

> Today you're the boss
> whatever you say goes
> there's no arguing with it, oh no.
> Today my people go round
> speaking in riddles
> with heads bowed.

It's you who dreamed all this up
whose idea was to dream up all this darkness,
you who dreamed up sin
but forgot to dream up forgiveness.

2

Links in the Chain

Boss, Contractor, Gunman;
Peon, Prostitute, Lodging Keeper

If you sit in Maria's bar you can get a clear view of the old bus station in Araguaína, and better still you'll be out of the direct heat of the sun. Maria's place serves iced coconut water and all sorts of delicious fruit juices, as well as single cigarettes and fried snacks, and if you want something more substantial you can go next door to Aparecida's. For one *real* she'll give you a plate heaped with rice and beans and spaghetti, together with gristly oxtail and gritty manioc flour. For two *reais* you can have fried chicken instead of oxtail. Maria's place is on the corner of one of the main market streets, where the stalls stretch along the sidewalk as far as you can see. They sell flyblown carcasses of meat, rice, beans, flour, corn flour, sugar, spices, and cans of oil. They also have plastic buckets and basins, cheap clothes, belts, bags, watches, hammocks, mosquito nets, pirated CDs, jewelry, combs, mirrors, alarm clocks, batteries, tool kits, sandals, old magazines, and more besides. It's hard to pick your way along the sidewalk, and if you step into the road you are likely to tread in something unpleasant. A variety of smells will assail your nostrils, chief of which is the smell of garlic cooking, mingled with drains and rotting garbage.

If you do wander along here you should keep a tight hold on your wallet, for this area abounds in thieves and dubious characters of every kind. It's a part of town known as the *feirinha*—the little market—and you can get anything you want, from women to liquor to drugs. It's also the main pickup point for slaves.

Here's how it works. Do you see the gas station on the corner? It's a major truck stop, but it's more than that. It's also the jumping-off point for truckloads of men hired as casual laborers to work in the ranches of the interior, locally known as *fazendas.*

Despite the unsavory reputation of its approach road as a stake-out spot for robbery, Araguaína is a convenient stopping-off point on the main highway north to the Amazon, and you'll see plenty of tough old Amazon trucks around the town. Battered and indomitable, these are the trucks that face mile upon mile of bone-shaking potholed roads that lead from nowhere to nowhere, varied only by the viciously corrugated secondary roads, covered with a thick layer of suffocating dust in the dry season and bottomless, glutinous mud in the wet. Their elaborately painted wooden bodies sport such inscriptions as I LEAVE YOU BECAUSE I MUST. I COME BACK BECAUSE MY HEART IS CALLING, or pious thoughts such as I AM THE DRIVER. GOD IS THE NAVIGATOR. Dangerously overloaded,

Araguaína: Street in the feirinha where peons stay

they carry huge tree trunks (almost certainly the products of illegal logging), boxes and bundles of every sort, cartons of fruit and vegetables, sacks of rice and beans, mattresses, boxes of supplies bound for far-flung settlements, shipments of livestock, and sometimes a load of men heading for Pará.

If the men are from out of town, they'll probably sleep on the little street behind Maria's bar, in an unmarked shed that belongs to Dona Helena. It may look like a shed, but it's really a rooming house for migrant workers. Those who can't afford the few *reais* a night that she charges will sleep where they drop, usually on the sidewalk. A weathered forty year old, Helena also owns a bar and eating place about two hundred yards up from where we are sitting. She gives the men a place to hang their hammocks and makes sure they get fed. She'll supply them with liquor, tell them where to find girls, and put them in the way of their next job. Most of the peons who sleep at her place hail from the neighboring state of Maranhão. Some come from yet farther afield: dirt-poor Piauí, drought-ridden Ceará, or the far reaches of Bahia. Many of them are known only by the name of their state; it's a rare group of peons that doesn't number at least one Ceará, Piauí, Mineiro, or Baiano. If you see them in town, they'll either be all dressed up and swaggering around gloriously with a little money in their pockets, or else they'll be lying drunk on the ground, money spent and pride abased. And these are the lucky ones, the ones who didn't get a bullet in their backs on some distant *fazenda*.

These are the migrant workers: peons who have been around a bit. Once they had a home and a family, but those ties have been long since lost. At some point they answered the siren call to seek adventure and make some money. So they left their homes and set off, perhaps in a painted truck like that one over there. It's called *pau de arara:* the parrot's perch. That's because of the steel arches that support the heavy tarpaulins covering the load. When the trucks are carrying men they don't bother with tarpaulins; they use the arches for stringing their hammocks. The truck will be piled high with supplies and the men will squeeze themselves on top, exhilarated at the prospect of making a few bucks. The journey may take several days, allowing for the occasional long detour over secondary roads to avoid highway checkpoints. They'll stop by the side of the road and cook their meals. Occasionally someone will smuggle a bottle of liquor aboard, and sooner or later there'll be a scuffle. Somewhere along the way one of the men may have second thoughts and attempt to leave. When he sees that the overseer carries a gun he will probably think better of it.

Not all the peons come from distant parts. Some of them have houses on the outskirts of town: windblown, garbage-strewn areas where the town council has donated a piece of land for low-cost housing or maybe a collection of homeless families has invaded the land and erected their shacks. Unlike the *favelas* of the big cities, these settlements are sparsely populated, far from any kind of infrastructure or transport. It is easier for the men to take a resident job on the ranches than to attempt to find work as day laborers where they may have to walk for an hour or two at either end of the working day.

By the time a peon lands at Helena's place he will be a veteran. He will have had at least one experience working on a ranch somewhere in the backlands. He may have come out with nothing, or he may have been comparatively well treated and finished up with a bit of money. A new pair of boots, a few rounds in the bar, a night or two with the girls, and he will need to start thinking about his next job. Word will get round that So-and-So is looking to get a team of workers together, and he will sign up for the next adventure.

The fundamental link in the chain is the *gato,* and there's one right there. That tough-looking customer sitting outside Helena's bar is her partner in both bed and business. Dressed in a blue-and-white-checked shirt, neatly pressed blue jeans, and cowboy boots, he's the one who finds the jobs and hires the men who end up sleeping at Helena's place. His name is João, but he's known as Doutorzinho, and most of the peons I talk to later say that he is a good *gato* and treats them well. Since Araguaína is known as a center for recruiting, peons will come there from far and wide, and Doutorzinho and Helena get themselves a good slice of the action.

In the mean little street where Helena has her rooming house there are any number of small bars. One afternoon while I'm walking along here, I notice three women sitting around a plastic-sheeted table drinking coffee and smoking. Instinct tells me they're connected with the night trade, and I feel sure they will have stories to tell. It's the lazy time of mid-afternoon, the time for idle conversation. *"Olá,"* I begin. "May I ask you for a glass of water?"

There is a silence as three pairs of eyes survey me. One of them nods and, muttering excuses, I climb up into the hot little room and sit down at the table. The woman on my left wears shiny stretch shorts in shocking pink. Her blond hair is piled on top of her head, her fingers are covered with gold rings; she weighs two hundred pounds if she weighs an ounce. She narrows her startlingly green eyes and inspects me closely. I have the distinct impression that she doesn't like what she sees. Next to her sits what I take to be one of her girls: a classic dark-skinned Amazon type with abundant black curly hair, already running to fat. It's the third of the trio who comes straight to the point. She has the face of one who has seen a lot in her time and can handle most things. She fills my glass with iced water, looks me shrewdly up and down, and asks me straight out if I'm looking to hire some peons.

I indicate, rather lamely, that I might be.

"Let me tell you, my dear," she says kindly, "peons are nothing but trouble. Nothing but trouble. I'm just back from the Xingu myself. I was there for three months. And the things that went on, you wouldn't believe. They're a rough lot, those peons. They'll kill each other if they get half a chance. Get them in town and they can be reasonably well behaved. Well of course they'll drink too much, but that's no problem if you know how to handle them. If you can make them respect you, they're fine. But over in the Xingu, let me tell you. It's not easy.

"We've had peons cheating at cards, smuggling in liquor and getting smashed, fighting, assaulting one another sexually; they're always running off and leaving us with their debt. I tell you, it's a nightmare. You simply can't trust them; I sometimes think they're no better than animals. They'll stab you in the back soon as look at you. Squabbling, fighting, always complaining. They'll lie through their teeth. And the worst of it is they're an idle bunch. Loafing about in their hammocks half the time, if you let them. Pretending to be sick. Won't do the work properly in the first place. I tell you, those guys just aren't worth the trouble. I'm through with it. Finished." She drains her glass and rolls her eyes.

"Are you a contractor?" I ask in surprise, tinged with respect. I haven't thought of it as a woman's role.

"Now and again I'll take on the odd job," she says comfortably. "But that's all over now. This trip was the last straw. You won't find me working my fingers to the bone for a bunch of ungrateful peons."

"Are they really that bad?"

"They're all right if you treat them tough," says Blondie. "You've got to get them to respect you. Mind you, overall they're an untrustworthy breed. They used to stay in my place, eating their heads off, drinking all they wanted, smoking, and sometimes even asking me for a loan, can you believe it? And you can't trust the *gatos* either. Sometimes they'd take a truckload of peons on credit and never even settle their bills. I tell you, I've been landed with bills for fifty, a hundred, even two hundred *reais*."

Her colleagues nod sympathetically, but Blondie is not to be deflected from her theme. "They're not all bad, mind you," she continues, "but one has to think of oneself first. One has to eat."

Well, yes.

A momentary silence is interrupted by the voice of Amazonian Beauty. "So where's your land then?" she asks with alarming directness.

"Over in the Xingu," I lie.

"And what's the job?" Blondie leans indifferently forward and swats a fly.

"Clearing the forest"—I am beginning to get into my new role— "six hundred hectares."

"How many men are you looking for?" asks the labor contractor.

"Fifty," I guess.

She nods, "That'll be about right. Got your own transport?"

I shake my head.

"That's not a problem, we can get you fixed up. I don't mind pointing you in the right direction, but like I said, I'm not wasting my time with the likes of them anymore. But Helena'll have some. You should talk to her. Did you meet her?"

"Not yet," I say, "but I can find her."

"If you have a problem," says the labor contractor, "you just come back to us."

"Thanks." I scrape my chair back from the table and say my good-byes.

Over at Helena's there are several peons sitting at the table drinking coffee. Two of them are extremely drunk, but they're all neat and tidy and very polite. Helena runs a tight ship.

"I can only let you have five or six at the moment," she tells me after listening to my story. "But we can round up some more for you, easy. If you come back tomorrow we'll see what we can do. I can't go with you right now."

I retrace my steps to Maria's place and start jotting down a few notes. I draw a line down the middle of the page. I order an iced coconut and chew the end of my pen, and then I write:

peon	boss
rooming house	contractor *(gato)*
prostitute	gunman

It's a chain of people, and each one is dependent on the other. The boss needs the job done so he hires the *gato*. The *gato* will have plenty of other players on his team: supervisors, gunmen, the canteen manager, the cook, the nurse, the trucker, the policeman who turns a blind eye as the load of peons goes through his checkpoint. He needs to be on good terms with the owner of the rooming house who will supply him with workers, and she needs him to take them off her hands and settle their bills. The peon finds solace in the arms of the prostitute—in exchange for a small fee. He needs the *gato* just as much as the *gato* needs him. After all, he has to eat.

It looks like the cards are pretty much stacked in favor of the boss and his team. But each member of the chain has something to sell and something to get. The boss needs the job done, but he leaves the execution of it to the *gato*. The *gato* needs the job done but can't manage without his supporting team. The boss may cheat the *gato* by changing the price halfway through the job. He may not pay at all, leaving the *gato* with large bills for supplies as well as payment for the workers. Equally, the *gato* may take the boss's money and disappear without doing the work. He may get it done and refuse to pay the peons. He may take the peons on credit from the owner of the rooming house and fail to settle her bill. She, in turn, may overcharge the peons who frequent her establishment.

Even the peon is not entirely powerless. He may take the advance and run away. He may do the job badly and leave the *gato* in the air. He may run out on the owner of the rooming house, leaving an unpaid bill. He may cheat the prostitute, or she may cheat him. She may steal his money while he is drunk. The opportunities for betrayal at each and every level are innumerable. But the bottom line is that everyone needs someone else, and everyone has to take some form of risk.

It's an intriguing circle of relationships, and I need to take a closer look. I decide to ask Xavier if he can take me to the outskirts of town to talk to some of the peons who have worked as slaves and survived.

We schedule our preliminary sortie for lunchtime, on the principle that we want to see the place by daylight. Xavier zips through the crowded streets and turns abruptly onto an atrocious dirt track, skidding over the bumps while I cling on like a limpet. Happily, I can see practically nothing through the scratched plastic of my helmet. We enter an area called Nova Araguaína, a place of broad dusty streets and garbage-covered plots. For the hundredth time I marvel at how such fastidious people can turn a blind eye to the filth. Inside, the houses are almost always immaculate. The area immediately outside the house is bare earth, meticulously swept once or twice a day. Beyond that there is a high-tide mark of rotting garbage, torn plastic bags, and broken bottles. It marks the point at which a person's property becomes no-man's-land. Xavier tells me you can buy a plot of land here for three hundred *reais.* A hundred and something dollars.

Some of the houses are built of crude bricks, while others are made of rough-sawn boards or mud and wattle. Roofs are made of tin, or asbestos sheeting, or palm thatch patched with black plastic that flaps in the wind. An untidy cat's cradle of wires connects the houses—illegally—to the electricity supply. Some of the houses sport television antennae, but none of them has either piped water or any form of sanitation. There are few people about; the children are in school at this hour, and the men at work. But behind one of the houses we find a young woman slapping her washing rhythmically in a large tin basin. She pushes back her blond hair with a soapy hand and gives us a big smile. "Of course you can have a word with me," she says, "I'm only too happy to take a break. You want to talk to some of the peons? You're not from the police are you?" She scrutinizes Xavier and then gives him an infectious grin. "I know you," she ex-

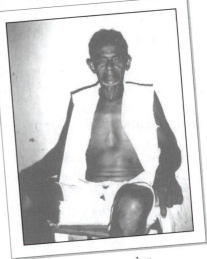

Migrant worker

claims. "You're a *padre,* aren't you?"

Xavier smiles and shakes his head. "I'm Brother Xavier," he explains. "I'm working with the Pastoral Lands Commission, and this is Binka. Yes, we would like to talk to some of the peons, if there's anyone around."

"You won't find anyone at this time of day," she says, laughing. "But here's what you can do. Come back this evening and ask for Félix. I know for a fact that he's around. I saw him only last night. His house is easy to find; he lives over by the chapel. Anyone can tell you."

We return in the evening to find the whole place is humming with activity. Children are playing in the dust, adults are lounging on plastic chairs or on wooden benches outside the houses, babies are crying, while here and there a man is lying in a hammock smoking a cigarette and gazing at the stars. The darkness hides the worst signs of poverty and transforms the dusty streets into a bustling, cheerful community.

Félix is a large, strong man in his late thirties. He has an open face and a forthright manner; the sort who will give you a fair day's work for a fair day's wage. Not one to let himself be taken for a ride. Like his four sons, he is dressed in shorts and flip-flops. He wears no watch. We sit in the warm evening air outside his house, and later he invites us in. It is a simple structure made of boards with a tin roof, clean and bare. There are benches around the walls and a rough wooden table covered with a plastic cloth. A baked-clay water filter sits on a shelf, together with a collection of steel mugs, and a sheet divides the living area from the kitchen.

"You want to know about that *fazenda* over in Iriri where the Feds went in?" He hands us mugs of cool water and asks his wife to make coffee. "I was there, yes sir. But I never saw any sign of the Feds. By the time they arrived I'd finished my job, taken my money, and left. I never heard about it until later. Came out on my feet? Of course I did. There wasn't any other way to do it. I walked as far as the road. Took me all day, it must have been about thirty kilometers, and the trail was thick mud. But I was lucky, I got a bus pretty much the moment I got there. I had to pay my fare because the *gato* didn't have any cash on him. But I'm sure he'll pay me back.

"How did they treat us? Well, I have to say I have no complaints. I can't say anything against them; it wouldn't be right. Except for the business of the bus fare. After all if a man says something he has to keep his word, isn't that so? The deal was that transport would be provided, so it stands to reason he owes me for my fare. But that's the only complaint I have. They supplied the tools and the food. Oh yes, they charged us, but it was good food and a fair price and I'm not complaining. No, the prices were perfectly reasonable. Boots for example. Mine fell apart so I had to buy another pair. The price here in town is ten *reais* and they charged me eleven. You can't argue with that.

"Did I notice a lot of coming and going? Well people come and go all the time, but you don't necessarily see them. We were all in our work crews, you see, so we didn't mix much with the others. Of course there was talk. Always is. What else can you do in the evenings but sit in your hammock and talk? They used to joke that once you went in there to work you never got paid and you never got out." He laughs.

"Sure, I've worked a lot with *gatos*. Lots of times. Do you know something? I've never had any trouble with them, thank God. And I didn't have any trouble this last time. No, I wasn't hired by Brás, I was hired by Raimundo, and, like I said, I've got no complaints. Apart from the fact that he owes me my bus fare. A man has to keep his word.

"That area, Iriri, there's a lot of new *fazendas* opening up there. Hardwood? You bet your life! They're hauling it out by the truckload. There's trucks coming out of Iriri all the time. Stacked with wood. No, the roads aren't much. But any trucker worth his salt can get through. Gunmen, did you say?" He laughs again. "I'd like to see the *fazenda* in Pará that doesn't have gunmen!

"Slavery? Well you hear lots of stories. People stuck on the *fazendas,* and beaten up, and that sort of thing. You even hear stories of murder. But I have to say that I've never been involved in anything like that myself. I guess I've been lucky. I work hard and I get my pay. Well, maybe I don't make a whole lot, but my family has never gone hungry, and that's the main thing, isn't it?

"But one thing I can say: You'll never be short of work round here. There'll be *gatos* knocking at your door any day of the week. I'll go back when they ask me. I need the money! That's how it is if you work on *fazendas.* You get home in the morning and you have to head back out in the evening. I tell you, I've worked all my life. And what have I got for it? I don't even possess a hammock! Land? No, I've never owned any land. All the land I possess is the dirt under my fingernails. That's all I've got." He has the deep, satisfied laugh of a man who has come to terms with life.

Either Félix has never got into a situation of slavery or he isn't saying anything. My hunch is that he's been lucky, or smart, or both. There will be plenty of others who haven't done so well.

One of the people who might be able to tell us more is Cicero, the local *gato.* He proves harder to find, however. We've already visited his house three times, making a wide detour around the vicious-looking dogs that run up and down a lead wire in the yard. We've chatted to Carmelita, his friendly forty-something wife, and she told us that our best chance was to catch him either early in the morning or late in the evening. On our fourth visit luck is with us, and Carmelita tells us he called half an hour earlier to say he's coming home. She invites us in, and we settle down on a large purple plastic-covered sofa. It is hot and airless, and the mosquitoes are out in force.

I imagined that a *gato* makes enough money to have a better house, but this isn't so different from the house where Félix lives. Instead of boards the walls are made of mud, and instead of wooden benches there is a sofa. We see no signs of children. Carmelita sits placidly enough doing her crocheting while she chats. She tells us that her family came from the south, moving first to Minas, then to Goiás, and finally to Tocantins, always in search of a better life. Have they found it? Well, they're making out. Although things aren't as good as they used to be. These days there's a lot more interference from the government. The Department of the Environment won't give people permits to clear the land. The Department of Labor is always on the backs of the ranchers. So there aren't the jobs like there used to be. Leastways, not round here. These days the jobs are over in the Xingu, and that means a lot more hassle. It's hard to get to, and conditions are difficult. Often Cicero is gone for weeks on end, and she never knows when he's coming back.

The roar of a motorbike announces Cicero's return. I turn to look, and suddenly there he is in the doorway, studying us. He's a big guy, and well muscled. Looks like he'd tear you apart with his bare hands.

He is also rattled by something. Turns out he's heard there are some people looking for him, and he figures we must be Feds. He is not reassured with our categorical denials. It's a tough job, being a *gato,* he tells us. Not that he would consider himself a *gato.* (At this point his wife gives a snort of laughter.) He's a laborer just like the rest, he assures us. He likes to get the job done, and he works shoulder to shoulder with the peons. He's worked on the land all his life. Loves it. But it's a tough job. It's easy for a *gato* to burn his fingers. The peons run away, or they get sick. The rancher cheats you about the size of the job, or he changes the price halfway through. Sometimes he just doesn't pay up. All sorts of things can go wrong. To say nothing of the government. These days they're on your back all the time. Fine you for chopping down a tree, fine you for not looking after your workers. Of course you look after your workers. Just like you look after your cattle. If you don't look after them they don't produce.

Our last call for the day is at Nezinho's rooming house, across town. It's conveniently located just off the main highway, but Nezinho isn't there. In fact the whole place is shut up. But we do strike up a conversation with a couple of sixteen year olds who are hanging out in the street smoking. They tell us they are cousins, and one of them is Nezinho's son. He explains that his parents are away for a couple of days but coming back tomorrow because they are expecting a bunch of peons to arrive any day now. Probably around twenty or thirty. No, they don't get the numbers they used to. He remembers his mom cooking for a hundred at a time. And they were a handful, you can be sure! These days the most they'll get is about thirty. But they're more trouble than they're worth. They'll sit round eating and drinking their heads off and then it'll turn out they haven't got any money. Next thing is, a *gato* will come and take them off to work, and sometimes he'll settle their bills and sometimes he won't. Ingenuous, with a slight stammer, the boy explains that his dad recently had a stroke, so he can't deal with large numbers anymore. Too much of a hassle, and anyway, he can't fit them onto the truck.

"It's my dad who's the trucker," says the other boy importantly. "Just so soon as there's a load of peons ready why he'll load them up and off they go. He knows all the roads round here and how to avoid the police checkpoints. If worse comes to worst he can always give the policeman a little something for keeping his eyes shut."

"These guys have got the whole business sown up," I mutter in Xavier's ear as we turn to leave. Sitting perilously on the back of the motorbike with the night air streaming over me like a warm bath, I suddenly get the feeling of tentacles spreading across town. Everyone is involved somehow: the husband-and-wife team of *gato* and rooming house keeper, the brothers who provide accommodation and transport, the truck driver who bribes a policeman. The rancher who is illegally felling the forest—and using slave labor to do it.

Xavier swerves over a speed bump and jams on his brakes. "Do you see that high wall there?" he asks, pointing to a three-meter wall topped with razor wire. "That's where Luis Pires lives. He's one of the biggest businessmen in this town, and he's also one of the very few who have ever actually been convicted for slave labor. He's got seven or eight *fazendas,* and one of them is over in Tucumã, on the way to the Xingu. The Feds raided it back in 1997 and they found two hundred twenty people, including thirty kids. They were living in terrible conditions; real slavery. Fazenda Flor da Mata was the first estate ever to be expropriated.[1] But this Luis Pires is quite a power in the land, and he took a group of federal deputies and senators down to Brasília to argue the toss with the government. Unfortunately it's not a question of outright confiscation. The government pays the market price for the land, and uses it for settlement. It pays extra for the improvements: roads, bridges, buildings, fencing, that sort of thing. Well, Luis Pires managed to get his place valued at two and a half million *reais*! We were so outraged that we mounted an investigation, and do you know what we discovered? That he'd only had the place for two years and that he'd bought it for one hundred thousand *reais.* He stood to make twenty-five times the buying price! As for all the so-called improvements, well, they were grossly overvalued, too. The whole thing was nothing short of scandalous.

"The CPT made such a noise about it that the government was forced to reconsider its offer. But even so they came up with a valuation of over a million![2] The way it works is that they pay for the land in government bonds, but they pay for the improvements in cash. So Luis Pires did pretty well for himself. The government settled four hundred families on the land, and then they finally brought a lawsuit against him. For slave labor. I bet you can't guess what happened. The judge disqualified herself and the whole thing was shelved, can you believe it? That'll tell you something about justice in these parts!"

As we roar through the empty streets I reflect on all the people who have come to Amazônia to make a quick buck: rich adventurers, starving peasants, shrewd businessmen, gold miners and good-time girls, a kaleidoscope of humanity with all its faults, greed, violence, ruthlessness, and lawlessness. Everyone has come from somewhere else, and each one has constructed a new persona. Like all migrants, they can never send home bad news, as a point of pride. So they are forced to make a go of it. Yet however much they try to reinvent themselves, they bring with them patterns of behavior inherited from their previous lives, patterns which they incorporate into their new culture. For the migrants, Amazônia is the Promised Land. It is a land of limitless opportunity, peopled with a cast of highly colored characters constantly creating and re-creating their own lives in a world of which a medieval pope once remarked, "South of the Equator there is no sin."

3

The Occupation of Amazônia

Land Without Men for Men Without Land

Looking back from the beginning of a new century it seems hard to imagine that not so very long ago people thought of the Amazon region as a sort of eternal breadbasket. With hindsight, and taking into consideration the immense areas of virgin forest that have been transformed within the space of little over one generation from green jungle to red desert, we are now beginning to understand how fragile the tropical forest ecosystem actually is. But it is easy to be misled by the fantastic proliferation of its life, without fully understanding the extraordinary recycling system whereby its true riches exist not in the soil, but in the biomass. Tropical forests have developed a complex and delicate system of synergies, with waste matter being rapidly broken down into its constituent minerals by fungi and insects that recycle it in an endless chain of death and life.

When you walk into a tropical forest the first thing that strikes you is its astonishing exuberance; the sheer numbers of unfamiliar species. It is difficult to get your bearings because no two plants look alike. Within a small area you may find a wealth of different species, but only one or two examples of each, and many of these will be endemic. In temperate-zone forests you can easily identify many examples of the same species within a small area, but tropical forests are just the opposite. A large variety of species can exist only where they use different sets of resources, and rain forest species have reached a high level of sophistication in terms of specialization. Estimates of the numbers of species in the world vary wildly, falling somewhere between hundreds of thousands and tens of millions, and the tropical forest ecosystem is by far the world's greatest reserve of genetic diversity.[1]

Within the last decades we have learned that the immense fertility of the rain forest is in truth a phony fertility, but for generations scientists thought that rain forest soils could feed the world or supply it abundantly with commodities like rubber and cellulose. What they did not realize was that the soils themselves are too fragile to sustain monocultures. Huge projects have been set up to grow one crop or another, and all of them have failed to meet expectations. Tropical soils simply cannot cope with such demands being made upon them, and tropical biodiversity includes an interminable variety of bugs that chew their way through the best-planned agricultural schemes.[2]

For centuries the Amazon forests sustained their small human populations, providing them with food, fuel, shelter, and medicines. But over the last fifty years the forests have been subjected to a sustained onslaught whereby they have been stripped of their hardwoods, hacked and burned to provide space for roads, airstrips, settlements, and colonization projects, devastated for their mineral resources, and clear-felled to provide land for large-scale ranching projects.

Until relatively recently the Brazilian government paid little attention to the Amazon; it was too large, too distant, and too unmanageable. They were content to leave it to the adventurers who traveled its rivers in search of medicines, or rubber, or souls, or slaves. For a few heady years starting in the 1890s the Amazon supplied rubber to the world, and huge fortunes were made by the traders. Easy come, easy go, and after the collapse of the rubber boom the Amazon sank back into its centuries-old slumber; the legendary Mad Maria railroad, set up to carry rubber from Bolivia to the River Madeira, was left to rot; and the sounds of coloratura sopranos were heard no more in the opera house in Manaus. The Second World War brought another brief boom to the dying rubber trade, which soon relapsed into oblivion.

The rubber trade may have been all but forgotten, but the Amazon was not. For the first time the Brazilian government began to dream of what could be done with its vast empty spaces, bearing in mind that the Amazon region occupied more than

Venezuela
Guyana
Colombia
Roraima Suriname French Guiana
Amapá
Ecuador
Amazon River
Peru
Amazonas Pará Maranhão Ceará Rio Grande do Norte
Acre Paraíba
Rondônia Brazil Piauí Pernambuco
Tocantins Alagoas
Sergipe
Mato Grosso Bahia
Brasília
Goiás
Bolivia Minas Gerais
Mato Grosso Espírito Santo
do Sul
São Paulo Rio de Janerio
Chile Paraguay
Paraná
Santa Catarina
Rio Grande
do Sul
Argentina Uruguay

Brazilian Amazônia
in South America

Amazônia
● National capital

N

400   0   400   800   1200 1600 Km

half the entire country and contained four-fifths of all its forests, as well as two-thirds of its frontiers. In 1953 the government of Getúlio Vargas created a special agency for the economic development of Amazônia, the SPVEA (Agency for the Economic Valorization of Amazônia), which defined the boundaries for the region and laid down the guidelines for its economic development. Three years later they came up with an emergency development plan based on the confirmed existence in the region of manganese and petroleum, and the strong probability of finding other significant mineral deposits. (They were right on the mark, and today the Amazon is known to possess mineral deposits of incalculable value.) The emergency plan described the development of Amazônia as "an imperative part of our national destiny," and went on to speak of "enlarging our economic and cultural frontiers which, by their geographical position, constitute a limitation to the country's chances of development and a threat to national security and unity." The plan spoke of Amazônia's vocation as being the extraction of its biological, mineral, and natural resources. Had this extraction been carried out in any sort of rational manner, things might have been very different today.

Large territories require large thinking, and questions of national sovereignty and pride dictate that far-flung regions be incorporated into the state. The first step was to set up the Amazon Credit Bank, a regional bank to facilitate credit; the second to construct electricity plants in Belém and Manaus, and the third to embark on a massive program of road building, starting with a magnificent new highway to link Brazil's new capital to the Amazon River and following up with a road from the central western savannas to Porto Velho on the Rio Madeira.[3] Built with the eminently sane intention of bringing development to the area, the Amazon Penetration Roads, as they were called, were to be the forerunners of uncontrollable waves of migration, conflict, and destruction.

In 1964 Brazil followed the majority of its neighbors into military rule, and its first military government targeted Amazonian development as an urgent national priority. The strategy was to settle and develop the region before anyone else could gain economic influence over it, and the slogan was *"integrar para não entregar,"* which translates roughly but effectively as "use it or lose it." They were thinking particularly of their big neighbor to the north, the United States. It was becoming increasingly clear that the Amazon contained a veritable treasure trove of mineral wealth, and careless tongues in America were referring to the region as a heritage for humankind. The Hudson Institute in New York talked of damming the river in order to create an immense system of lakes that would allow access to much of the region and open it up to mineral prospecting. Their grand project[4] included connecting the Orinoco to the Rio Negro, constructing a canal between the Guaporé and Paraguay rivers, creating an alternative to the Panama Canal in Colombia, and building a highway along the frontier from Colombia to Bolivia. Uncle Sam wanted to make the world safe for democracy, and if that included massive interference in Latin America, what was good for America was surely good for the world.

The Brazilian government was equally determined to protect its national interests, and this determination was amply confirmed by the discovery first of manganese (1966) and later of immense iron ore (1967) deposits in the Carajás Mountains in southern Pará. As well as being a top priority, Amazon development now became an issue of national sovereignty. The vast empty spaces must be secured without further delay, and the quickest and most effective way to do so would be through the alliance of government and the private sector. In 1966 the government issued a challenge to business known as the Declaration of Amazônia, which began, "The Amazon must be occupied by Brazilians, and Brazilian businessmen must take the lead."[5] Former deputy Sérgio Cardoso de Almeida was thinking of profits first and patriotism second. His comment was, "Businessmen will need to know where to invest their money to get the highest returns, since this is the best way to respond to the patriotic summons for Brazilians to occupy the Amazon." After successful negotiations combining patriotism with profit making, a joint declaration was issued that opens: "Government and business united in Amazônia under the inspiration of God, determined to preserve national unity. . . . "

In keeping with its objective of facilitating Amazon settlement, in 1967 the government changed the name of the former credit bank to Amazon Bank (BASA), set up FIDAM, a private investment fund for the region, and transformed the old SPVEA into a new development agency known as SUDAM. Its brief was to stimulate investment, but it turned out to be a textbook model of how not to do development, handing out enormous sums of money for the most unsuitable projects, with a minimum of supervision and accountability. Thirty-four years later, in 2001, SUDAM was closed down amid a flurry of accusations of incompetence and gross corruption.

On the question of agriculture, and in order to implement the 1964 Land Statute, the government set up three agencies: the first for agricultural reform (IBRA), the second for agricultural development (INDA), and the third for agricultural policymaking (GERA). But it is debatable that they ever entertained any serious intentions regarding agricultural reform, in view of remarks allegedly made in Congress by then–minister of planning Roberto Campos: *"A lei era para ser aprovada, mas não para ser colocada em prática,"* (the law was to appear on the books, but not to be put into practice).

SUDAM's initial five-year plan, 1967–71, defined the government's agricultural strategy as combining security with settlement—citing the necessity to safeguard the area in the face of a possible local guerrilla movement, the chronic political insecurity in neighboring countries, and the ever-present threat of communism. Their motto was, "Land without men for men without land." Settlement was to be carried out through a series of colonization schemes whereby landless poor from the southern and northeastern states were to be encouraged to take up small-scale agriculture in specified settlement areas, for which the government would provide the necessary infrastructure and technical assistance. The theory was that the poor would get land and the wherewithal to live on it, that they would grow food for the new population centers that would spring up along the major highways, and that enough people would be attracted to the frontier to assure a plentiful supply of labor.

So did the Amazon settlement schemes work? Settlement schemes aren't easy to manage at the best of times, even given better soils and better communications. Most of the would-be settlers who rushed to the Amazon had little experience in managing credit, and some lacked even the basic skills required to make a living off the land. The southerners were used to a temperate climate and far better soils. The northeasterners knew only how to work with the harsh arid climate back home; none had any experience in the delicate business of managing fragile tropical soils, they were scared of the forest, scared of the Natives, and scared of getting malaria—which they did with depressing frequency. They struggled to produce crops in unfamiliar and hostile conditions, and when they succeeded, they couldn't get them to market. Distances were immense, roads atrocious, and instead of storing their production until the price went up, they had to sell as and how they could. Nor did the government make good on its promises to deliver credit and infrastructure. On some projects the failure rate was up to 40 percent—twice the national average. Yet if 40 percent of the new settlers gave up, 60 percent toughed it out, feeding their families and producing a surplus for sale.[6]

Despite the government's limited success on the social front by settling the landless, it was clear from the outset that the economic development of the frontier would require a massive inflow of capital and technology. The logical way to do this was to provide incentives for agribusiness, which in turn would stimulate the development of new settlements and, in due course, a series of service industries. They planned to start by establishing large-scale cattle ranching, on the model that had successfully developed the American West. The government dreamed of transforming the Amazon into a major exporter of beef, offering large sums of money on exceedingly favorable terms to those prepared to set up ranching projects.

Alas, the export of foodstuffs was hardly the first thing on the minds of the businessmen who lined up to receive unprecedented sums of public money for projects that seldom, if ever, came to anything, but had the advantage of providing their owners with substantial tax breaks, large loans at negative interest, and considerable areas of land. SUDAM-funded cattle ranches averaged 48,000 hectares each, and in the south of Pará alone they occupied 3.8 million hectares. By 1974 SUDAM had approved 321 projects with a total investment of $523 million U.S., making an average of $1.2 million U.S. disbursed per project. One of the most famous projects at the time was Fazenda Rio Cristalino, belonging to Volkswagen, about which we shall read more later in this book. Rio Cristalino was a model *fazenda* in its day—as well it might have been, considering its own investment of $38.8 million in addition to the SUDAM contribution of $116.4 million. It was also one of the first *fazendas* to be accused of employing slave labor.

Despite its monumental investment, SUDAM's projects showed a lamentable success rate—producing barely 15 percent of what they promised. All projects, without exception, overran their original budgets, and a joint evaluation carried out by IPES (Institute of Economic and Social Planning), BASA, and SUDAM in 1985, in which a total of thirty-three projects was inspected, discovered that only four were functional. Many of the ranches were operating with phantom herds, which were sometimes moved from one ranch to the next just ahead of SUDAM inspectors. One project that predicted an annual production of 2,779 head of cattle (in normal conditions annual production would be on the order of 40 percent of the herd, implying a herd size in excess of 7,000) was found to possess a grand total of 683 head.[7]

Among the 85 percent of nonfunctional projects, the ranchers indulged in a veritable fiesta of money laundering. The money they received was applied to one project, which then acted as collateral for the next, or was used for speculation, or (most frequently) was applied directly to other projects outside the region. At a time of high inflation, the SUDAM subsidies were a gold mine, and the agency itself was so mired in corruption that projects were seldom canceled, despite wholesale flouting of the rules. Projects were exempt from income tax for ten years, but the money thus saved was used for speculation instead of being applied to the project; moreover, any mechanism for proving that the projects were under way was largely ignored—and SUDAM did nothing about it. It wasn't until after the 1985 report that the agency canceled the first projects, but even so no serious steps were taken to repossess the money, and in one case it took the agency seventeen years to file a suit against a bankrupt project. Even when they did go after the money, they had little chance of getting repayment at current values, and ranchers and businessmen knew perfectly well that the Brazilian justice system was so clogged that lawsuits were unlikely to come to trial. If they did, the state was unlikely to convict them.

The ranching projects were designed to add six million head to the national herd as well as generating thirty-six thousand jobs and transforming São Luis and Belém into the world's largest ports for the export of beef. Each ranch was supposed to have its own system of schools and health posts as well as a workforce with signed work contracts, but in fact six of ten *fazendas* had no infrastructure of any sort, and almost all of them paid their workers by the day, using the canteen system of charging for their food—which often meant in practice that living expenses consumed almost all their salary. The old system of debt bondage was alive and well once more.

Not surprisingly, the arrival of the ranching schemes provoked considerable conflict between the new landowners and the people who were already there. For there was one great flaw in the concept of men without land for land without men: It wasn't quite true. The Amazon had never been empty, always sustaining small, scattered populations of indigenous peoples, wildcat miners, rubber tappers, and river people. Those who practiced subsistence agriculture had long since discovered how to work with forest soils. They raised their crops on the flooded valley bottoms or in forest clearings, which were abandoned after a few years to recover their fertility. These people regarded land not as a capital asset but rather as a gift from God; to be lived on and worked, but not owned. Under the law of *usucapio*[8] they did acquire some rights over the land, but they never knew it. So when the businessmen and adventurers came swarming up the new roads in answer to the government's call, the stage was set for conflict. The new arrivals bought the land from under the squatters, or simply grabbed it. They knew how to manage the system, they knew where to get credit, and they knew where to hire the gunmen. Thousands of squatters were evicted from their lands, and those who resisted provoked violent reprisals from police and gunmen.

The area around the Araguaia and Tocantins rivers, strategically located on the intersection of two major highways, Belém-Brasília and the TransAmazon, and close to the Carajás mining concessions, needed to be pacified at all costs. It had acquired a reputation for violence, which resulted in the arrival of a large military force, first to conduct ostensive maneuvers, and later to install themselves as the Jungle Battalion.[9] In response to the tightening of military control throughout the country a small number of urban guerrillas had relocated to remote rural areas, including, in 1972, the banks of the Araguaia River. The government's reaction was to mount three separate military campaigns, but even so it took them two years to wipe out the guerrillas—who enjoyed a large measure of support among the local population but proved to number no more than sixty or seventy. Not that the military had everything their own way; the losses were on both sides, and the guerrillas and their supporters inflicted their own summary justice on gunmen and police alike. There can be no doubt that the resentments aroused by this state of undeclared war exacerbated the tensions that persist to this day.

With the defeat of the guerrillas, Amazon development acquired a fresh impetus, and President Geisel joined his predecessors Medici and Castello Branco in dreaming up further pharaonic schemes.[10] He designated fifteen centers for development, including Araguaia/Tocantins and Greater Carajás, site of the recent mineral prospecting. The region around Marabá, which was located on the confluence of the Araguaia and Tocantins rivers and within striking distance of Carajás, was designated both for colonization projects (65,000 hectares set aside) and for large-scale ranching (561,000 hectares). Further colonization schemes were set up by government and private sector alike, and even, in Conceição do Araguaia, by the Catholic Church. But they continued to suffer from inexperience and lack of even the most elementary inputs, and were often plagued by contradictory and confusing land titling, which led to a chronic state of violent conflict.

The Figueiredo government (1979–85) presided over the end of the economic miracle, and also the end of the military dictatorship. The situation of landownership was increasingly unclear, and violence was becoming commonplace, so in 1980 the government created a special agency to deal with the Araguaia/Tocantins area, called the Executive Group for the Lands in Araguaia/Tocantins: GETAT. This agency had all-embracing powers and was answerable directly to the National Security Council. The Greater Carajás Project was set up in 1981 in order to initiate the mammoth task of extracting and processing the enormous mineral wealth of Carajás. The project area covered 450,000 square kilometers, half the size of eastern Amazonia,[11] and the project included the construction of a railroad, the upgrading of the port in São Luis, the generation of electricity through the huge new dam at Tucurui, and the setting up of medium-sized agricultural projects to service the new industrial corridor.

This development model was created to generate exports, pay off the national debt, and stimulate the regional economy. All this required labor, and the available supply was sadly small. But migration is an integral part of the history of Amazônia, and people streamed in from all sides, looking for land, looking for gold, looking for work. Seasonal work was available in construction, in the mines, and also on the cattle ranches, where large numbers of peons were required to cut down the forest, mark the boundaries, build the fences, clear the land for pastures, dig the dams, make roads and airstrips, and build houses and barns.

With hindsight it is easy to assess the remarkable amount of damage that took place during this period. Indigenous tribes and squatters were expelled from their lands, huge sums were fraudulently spent from the national coffers—provoking decades of inflation and economic chaos—corruption was rife and predictable. Everyone was out for himself, and the Devil take the hindmost. Thousands of kilometers of incalculably valuable forest were wantonly destroyed, uncontrolled fires polluted the air, uncontrolled use of mercury polluted the rivers, uncontrolled migration provoked violent conflicts, and casual and cruel treatment of the workers often amounted to slave labor. The old Amazonian evils of intertribal fighting and slavery had been replaced by more subtle and effective evils, which provoked widespread destruction at a rate that far exceeded the capacity of the environment to restore itself. After centuries of exploitation violence had become endemic. The difference was in the scale. The combination of the rich and ruthless on one hand and the poor and desperate on the other was, and continues to be, highly explosive. Motivated by greed, the rich and ruthless were prepared to go to any lengths to secure their property, while the poor and desperate had nothing to lose and might as well resolve their disputes at the end of a shotgun. Rapid migration, the prospect of free money, land for the taking, gold for the digging, the reservation of what most people considered to be disproportionately large areas of land for the indigenous, the massive presence of the military, and the existence of a small band of squatters who were increasingly determined to stay on their lands—all these factors combined to make conflict inevitable.

Conflicts between squatters and the indigenous tribes, conflicts between squatters and ranchers, conflicts between miners and everyone else sprang up like a series of forest fires. The indigenous tribes were, as ever, the losers. So, in many cases, were the squatters. They were beaten up, burned out, thrown off their lands, and murdered, and not surprisingly the situation in the rural areas was one of high tension. Paulo Fontelles, a lawyer and former state deputy who worked on behalf of the dispossessed peasants, noted that the "silent war in the countryside is marked by murders that are both selective and unpunished." Shortly after this comment he in turn fell victim to the silent war, gunned down at the behest of the local landowners.[12]

For the truth is that, despite various attempts at militarization, the state has never been able to exert an effective hold over Amazônia's enormous and intractable spaces. The place has never been tamed, and the business of the state is conducted variously by the military, the landowners, and the church, while law and order is precarious at best and at worst left in the hands of whoever is fastest on the draw. For centuries the Brazilian rich—which usually means the landowners—have settled any disputes with the use of hired guns. But not until the threat of land reform loomed over their heads did they take to using private armies.

It was 1985, and the military government had been replaced by a civilian government ineffectually led by José Sarney, when the often discussed and much delayed question of land reform raised its head once again. Brazil had then and has still one of the most unequal systems of land distribution in the world, whereby less than 12 percent of the landowners hold more than two-thirds of the land,[13] leaving the rest in the hands of the small farmers. The very mention of the words *land reform* was enough to upset the large landowners, who reacted by promptly forming their own union, the Rural Democratic Union (UDR). Officially its brief was to advise the government on the question of land reform, but its secret agenda was to make sure that such a thing never came to pass. In this it was brilliantly successful, and to forestall rural discontent it set up a network of private security firms that oversaw the elimination of troublesome rural leaders, unionists, and activist members of the church and the legal profession. The UDR's corps of security-guards-*cum*-gunmen were sometimes joined by off-duty members of the police.

At the dawn of the twenty-first century little has changed. The tentacles of organized crime stretch throughout Amazônia, whether it be arms peddling, drug smuggling, land grabbing, or good old-fashioned murder. And you don't have to restrict your thinking to the classic figure of the gunman, or *pistoleiro*. Crime involves public prosecutors, judges, police chiefs, mayors, federal deputies, senators, landowners, and businessmen of all kinds. The UDR has changed its style but is still active. Large isolated *fazendas* provide airstrips for unregistered planes to carry arms to Colombia or cocaine to Suriname.

If we could run the gauntlet of the guards and gunmen, it would be on these distant *fazendas,* deep in the forest and effectively beyond the reach of the law, that we would find the Brazilian gulags. Held fast by isolation, threatened night and day by *pistoleiros,* trapped by their debt, thousands of men labor away for their keep, to be discarded like empty beer bottles when their usefulness is past. In the country that bills itself the land of tomorrow, this is the legacy of Cain and Abel: These are Brazil's twenty-first-century slaves.

4

Debt Slavery: The Bosses

Connivance and Impunity from the Ruthless Rich

The rains are late in Benin, West Africa, and there is nothing to eat in the village. A passing trader swings through, offering an advance on next season's crops. He has another business proposal to make: For thirty dollars U.S. he will take the family's eight-year-old daughter and apprentice her to a market worker in Gabon. She will be well cared for, he says, and able to send money home. After an anxious discussion, the family decides to let her go—little knowing that they are sending her on a one-way journey into slavery.

Leelu Bai, a tribal woman in India, became a slave when she married. "My husband's family had been bonded for three generations to the same landlord," she said. "They took out loans for marriage, for illness, for education, and so on. I used to work from six A.M. in the landlord's house, cleaning, fetching water, and then I would go to work on the farm, harvesting and threshing until seven P.M. or later. Sometimes I would have to go back to the landlord's house to clean and wash everything. Only after I had finished could I go back to feed my family."

In a small village in Ukraine a young woman, desperate to escape to the city, is offered the chance of a lifetime. She can get a job in Prague as a waitress, earning all the money she wants. Finally she will be able to buy all the pretty things she deserves. She embarks on her clandestine journey, but along the way she loses her papers. Unfortunately for her, there is someone prepared to "sponsor" her, and she too vanishes into the underworld of slavery.

A young man in the dry lands of northeastern Brazil has quarreled violently with his father. Determined to prove his mettle, he storms out of the house to seek his fortune, and signs up with the friendly labor contractor who has just come to the area looking for real men who aren't afraid of hard work. They'll be working in the distant state of Pará, the pay is good, and when they finish this contract they'll find it easy to get another one. They don't need to take a thing; everything will be supplied. Two of his friends decide to join him, and before leaving they are each given an advance of twenty *reais*. Off they go arm in arm to the nearest bar to have a good time. The next morning the *gato* finds them sleeping in the gutter and loads them aboard his truck, bound for adventure. None of them will ever come back.

Four examples of debt slavery, taken from a world total of perhaps twenty-seven million.[1] Twenty-seven million disposable people who have followed the same path into bondage. All of them are desperately poor. All of them need to eat. Some are born into debt slavery; others are enticed into it through accepting a loan. It can be as little as ten dollars—the price of medicine for a child, a loan to tide the family through until the harvest, the payment of an outstanding bill, a small advance on a job. It could be the fare to the new workplace. It could be the cost of a pretty dress. But once the debt is contracted it may never be repaid.

In addition to the loan, they have been ensnared by false promises. They have been offered good work at good rates, but neither the work nor the money will turn out to be good, and many of them will never break free. The tribal woman from India, although freed physically, will carry her psychological scars for life. The young men from the interior of Brazil will never make their fortunes and never go home. The little girl from Benin will find herself working as a factotum for a market woman, while the young woman from Ukraine will end up as a prostitute. All of them will be terrorized. Most will be physically isolated and separated from their network of family and friends. Some will be beaten, humiliated, or sexually abused, and all will be threatened by physical or psychological violence. Worst of all, they will be deprived of their liberty; they will no longer be able to come and go as they choose. They will, in effect, be reduced to the condition of marketable commodities, no longer human beings but things.

"It is difficult to believe that as this great and tragic century draws to a close the problems of slavery and slave labor remain unresolved," said Mary Robinson, UN High Commissioner for Human Rights, in 1998. "All of us have a critical role to play in ensuring that the issues of slave labor and debt bondage are returned to the top of the human rights agenda."[2]

Slavery is as old as humankind itself. It took root in ancient Egypt, flourished under the caste system of South Asia, became institutionalized under the Greeks and Romans, was used as a method of colonial labor recruitment for the plantations in the Caribbean, South America, and later in the Belgian Congo,[3] and, to our shame, it exists to this day. And it will continue to exist as long as there is a supply of desperate poor people on one hand and people ready to exploit their misery on the other. Unless we do something to stop it.

It's hard to get any sort of accurate figures on the numbers of people involved in debt slavery in the Amazon. It's an undercover business, and those who do escape from it with their lives are often reluctant to do anything more than go home—if they have a home to go to—and try to forget. The Pastoral Lands Commission states that in the south of Pará and the neighboring areas of Mato Grosso—an area of 153,000 square kilometers—annual figures of *cases that have been detected* are probably in the region of a few thousand and rising. Subjective evidence points to a considerably higher figure, and it's important to remember that most migrant workers in the region move into and out of debt slavery in a continuous cycle. Whatever the figure, it is only the tip of the iceberg, since 90 percent or more of cases never see the light of day.[4]

While the traditional image of the slave master wielding a whip may still exist with very little updating, we will need to look farther to see where the chain of slavery begins. We will surely not expect to find any connection between the young men lying drunk in the gutter and the carpeted offices of state governors, judges, politicians, doctors, and businessmen. And they, in turn, will insist, most likely with great vehemence, that they have no connections with such an inhumane business—if indeed it truly

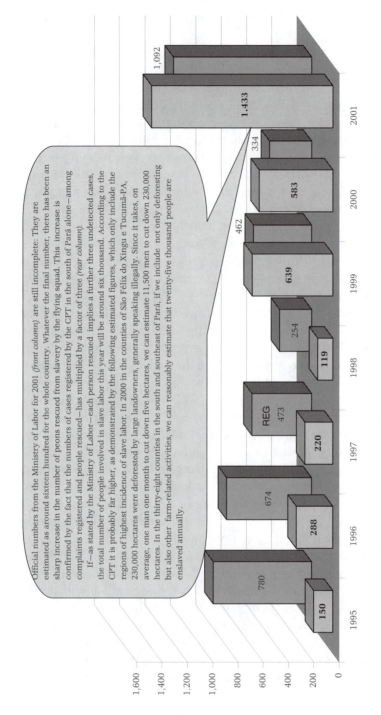

Official numbers from the Ministry of Labor for 2001 *(front column)* are still incomplete: They are estimated as around sixteen hundred for the whole country. Whatever the final number, there has been an sharp increase in the number of peons rescued from slavery by the flying squad. This increase is confirmed by the fact that the numbers of cases registered by the CPT in the south of Pará alone—among complaints registered and people rescued—has multiplied by a factor of three *(rear column)*.

If—as stated by the Ministry of Labor—each person rescued implies a further three undetected cases, the total number of people involved in slave labor this year will be around six thousand. According to the CPT it is probably far higher, as demonstrated by the following estimated figures, which only include the regions of highest incidence of slave labor. In 2000 in the counties of São Félix do Xingu e Tucumã-PA, 230,000 hectares were deforested by large landowners, generally speaking illegally. Since it takes, on average, one man one month to cut down five hectares, we can estimate 11,500 men to cut down 230,000 hectares. In the thirty-eight counties in the south and southeast of Pará, if we include not only deforesting but also other farm-related activities, we can reasonably estimate that twenty-five thousand people are enslaved annually.

SLAVE LABOR CASES REGISTERED BY THE YEAR
Brazil (source, Ministry of Labor) and south of Pará, (source, CPT)

exists and is not just fevered liberal fantasies. When questioned about alleged slave labor on his *fazenda* in Pará in August 2001 the secretary of agriculture for the state of Piauí, Francisco Donato Filho, maintained that his family always treated its workers well, and blamed everything on the *gato*.[5] We shall look at this case more closely later in the book, but at this point we need to take note of the fact that in the modern-day slave trade no one is responsible, everyone hides behind everyone else, no one knows, and no one's telling.

Despite their protestations of innocence, many from the carpeted offices are involved, directly or indirectly, with the slave trade. Their involvement may take several forms. While not everyone in the rural areas is a rancher, everyone knows someone who is. The shopkeeper depends on the ranchers for his business. The lawyer handles their legal affairs, the doctor looks after their health. The schoolteacher and nurse depend upon the mayor for their jobs, and the mayor himself is almost certainly a landowner, as is the state deputy. Everyday conversation is likely to center largely on the vexing question of getting labor, focusing on the latest scandal or fight or murder. The judge may well share the ranchers' views, and his natural inclination will be to give them a favorable hearing in cases of dispute. The lawyer and accountant will be involved in the complex and time-consuming process of balancing the ranchers' books, and the police chief will be called in when trouble strikes. He will have plenty of troubles of his own. He will be in charge of a large and probably violent area with too few men, too little equipment, and a pitifully small budget. He may well have developed a dislike for the troublesome underclass of society: the squatters, the peons, and the prostitutes, with their quarreling, rowdy ways. They give him a lot more work than the landowners, and he will probably sense their latent hostility toward him. The landowners, on the other hand, are more willing to help him out in the course of his duties—especially when resources are short. They are in a position to lend him a vehicle, supply him with a tankful of diesel, invite him to a barbecue, and treat him as a friend. Some of the police may resort to hiring themselves out in their spare time to supplement the ranks of overseers and to keep the peace on the *fazendas*. Everyone has his price.

But there will frequently be more subtle forces in play. The power system in Brazilian society is based on a complex web of favors and loyalties, starting with the extended family, stretching to include business associates, godparents and their families, members of the same club or association, fellow Freemasons, Spiritualists, Evangelicals, Roman Catholics, or members of the same political faction—while everyone owes ultimate loyalty to the local patriarch.

The rancher hires the contractor to take care of large-scale seasonal jobs such as cutting more forests, cleaning the pastures, or fixing the fences. He wants to get the job done in the quickest and most cost-effective way. He may or may not be aware of abusive labor practices, but most probably he will not be interested in the details. Few, however, will be as explicit as Eujácio Ferreira de Almeida[6] of Fazenda Moça Bonita, Eldorado dos Carajás, who stated flatly, "My contract is with the *gato*. I don't care if he killed somebody's father, or somebody's mother, or some peon. The only thing I care about is that he gets the job done."

The hiring of large numbers of temporary workers in strict accordance with the labor laws is something that ranchers will do everything in their power to avoid. The reasons for this are all too obvious: Brazilian labor laws are inflexible, fearsomely complex, and governed by a code of 922 articles that is constantly being amended by supplementary laws and decrees. Hiring a worker on a signed work contract is not unlike entering upon a forced marriage without the option of divorce. If the boss wishes to terminate the contract, he has two options. First, he can attempt to show *justa causa*, which, apart from being hard to prove, will severely prejudice his employee's future job prospects, leaving him resentful and very possibly vindictive. In the lawless backlands it is all too easy to set a fire, steal a bunch of cattle, or ambush an enemy. Second, if the boss settles for termination without *justa causa*, he must pay his employee a fine amounting to 40 percent of the fund he would receive on retirement, as well as getting the transaction registered in the local labor office—which may be located miles away. And terminating a contract is but one of the long list of hurdles to be overcome in keeping the contract updated. Every sickness must be marked in, every day off accounted for, every change of duty noted in two different registries, one of which is in the possession of the employee. In the study of jurisprudence a law that is generally obeyed is considered to be a good law, and by this remarkably sensible criterion the labor laws must be considered as bad law. As a result of their complexity, they are largely ignored, especially in the rural areas. Well-intentioned interference on the part of the state pushes landowners farther into their corner, reinforcing their conviction that they are their own masters and can do as they please.[7]

Brazilian labor laws may exist to support the weaker parties (the workers) in the labor contract but, setting aside the question of whether or not inherent inequalities are best dealt with through the mechanism of the law, they are generally unworkable because there is no adequate mechanism for enforcing them. This raises the whole issue of the presence—or absence—of the state. At the federal level it is limited to policing the highways and dealing with matters such as immigration, interstate smuggling, interstate slavery, crimes with national implications, and matters about which the local police force is manifestly incompetent—this last one a veritable recipe for interpolice conflict. The state government enjoys a wide level of autonomy and is exempt from interference by the federal government except where this is judged necessary by Congress. Police officers are appointed by the state government, as are some members of the judiciary, after competitive examinations. Since areas are vast and resources are minimal, much of the business of government is carried out de facto by the local Big Men; in the more remote reaches of the interior powerful local families run large areas as their private domains.

The power of the landowners is based on their personal estates, which often include a network of commercial, service, and agricultural interests. As we have seen, until fifty years ago land in the Amazon wasn't regarded as a capital asset, and therefore land ownership wasn't particularly desirable. Amazon fortunes were made, instead, by trading. After the collapse of the rubber trade, the next profitable business to emerge was dealing in Brazil nuts. Long leases were granted for government lands rich in Brazil nut trees; the rents charged were low and often went unpaid. By the 1980s the question of Amazon lands was beginning to acquire greater significance, and the lucky holders of the leases were granted land titles by the then–minister of agrarian reform, Jáder Barbalho.[8] Huge tracts of government land were effectively transferred into private hands, and the new landowners were in the fortunate position of being able to sell out to the business-men and speculators who were streaming into the region. As the newcomers arrived, two things happened. First, they began to transform the largely unused lands into ranches, using available government money; second, they started using large numbers of laborers for short periods of time. Many of these were work-ing under conditions of slavery.

One of the families who made their fortune from nut trading is the Mutrans. Their sizable empire is based on trade, agricul-ture, and the media, which happy combination puts them in a strong position with regard to politics, at both local and state levels. For many years the Mutran family ran the district of Marabá as their private fiefdom. At one point in the late 1980s Vavá Mutran, doyen of the family, was state deputy, his brother Guido was town councilor, his son Nagib was mayor, and an-other son, Oswaldo, was the common-law husband of the judge. It didn't do to cross the Mutrans. Vavá was known for making death threats against people he disliked, and had a formidable reputation for making sure that his threats were duly carried out. Nor did he tolerate criticism. When a nasty little scandal blew up about alleged abuse against the child laborers who were hired to clean the city streets, Vavá shouted that the whole story was a bunch of lies from start to finish.[9]

But the stories wouldn't go away. A clandestine cemetery was uncovered on Fazenda Cabaceiras, property of the Mutran fam-ily. The gravedigger in Marabá was indiscreet enough to give an interview to some journalists[10] regarding the large numbers of unmarked graves in his cemetery. He stated that, over the pre-vious six years, he had buried the bodies of more than one thou-sand people—of whom four hundred had been shot. When asked about the provenance of these bodies, he added ingenuously that they had been sent by the Mutrans.

Benedito Mutran followed Vavá's footsteps into politics, and was several times elected state deputy. Benedito was one of Brazil's largest nut exporters and also owned a stud farm near Belém, but his reputation was no purer than the rest of the family. He was accused variously of abusive labor practices, sexual abuse, and murder. One of his properties was Fazenda Espírito Santo, and it was on account of an incident that took place there that Brazil found itself being denounced to the Organization of American States—for slavery.[11]

It happened in 1989. A youth aged seventeen whom I shall call Antonio had gone with his friend Paraná to work on Fazenda Espírito Santo, but they didn't like anything about the place, and decided to run away. It wasn't long before they were recaptured by a bunch of *pistoleiros* under the leadership of Chico Gato, and told to start walking. Paraná was shot in the back of the head and died instantly, but Antonio had the presence of mind to clasp his hands behind his neck, thereby saving his life. The shot caught his finger, entered through the back of his head, and came out just below his eye. The bodies were slung into a pickup truck underneath an old tarpaulin, and as they drove along Antonio could hear the *pistoleiros* discussing whether to throw them into the river. They were dumped, instead, outside neighboring Fazenda Brasil Verde—of which we shall hear more later—and miraculously for Antonio he was picked up by the manager and taken into town. His eyesight was damaged, but he lived to tell the tale. Four weeks passed before the local police went in search of Paraná's body, which had been left by the roadside for many days but mysteriously disappeared before they arrived. Although Antonio identified the *pistoleiros,* no arrests were made, and when Benedito Mutran was questioned about the case he stated that he had never heard of Antonio and that no such person had ever worked for him. He issued a cordial invitation to the police to inspect his property at any time, but they alleged that they had no funds to buy fuel.

Don't imagine that the Mutrans are unique in the area. The majority of large landowners treat their workers with the same combination of sternness and paternalism, seeing themselves and being seen in turn as the strict and generous father who rewards his children and punishes them where necessary.

They have no patience with accusations of wrongdoing toward their workers. They regard themselves as patriots and pioneers, providing employment, producing food, and paying taxes, and then being unjustly accused by a bunch of bleeding-heart

NGOs, priests, and nuns who have no understanding of the realities of life in the Amazon. You can't apply labor laws to these people, they maintain; they are unqualified, unreliable, illiterate, lazy, promiscuous, and addicted to liquor. In fact, say the ranchers, it's the bosses who are victimized, forced to provide employment and care for the peons while being treated by the Federal Police as if they were terrorists. "We're the ones who are the slaves," announced Gilberto Andrade in an interview with *Veja* magazine on 24 July 1991. Gilberto was a big rancher who was known for recruiting his workers personally. He used to make the rounds of the local brothels paying off debts and handing out advances. When the peons were sufficiently drunk he would throw them into the back of his truck (known as the Slave Ship) and haul them off to work. "Unfortunately," he once said, "it's impossible to obey all the labor laws, since the peons have no papers." Ten years later Gilberto hadn't changed his views. When caught out in abusive labor practices by federal inspectors, he flatly refused to pay up.

Gilberto's brother, Jairo Andrade, has one of the most formidable reputations in the area. Jairo is a very rich man; in fact, he likes to be thought of as the king of Zebu cattle. He was the first national treasurer of the ranchers' union, UDR, and mingles easily with ministers and former presidents. In addition to his cattle—one hundred thousand head—he owns a gas distribution company, a construction business, and a printing press. And a lot of land. Jairo prides himself as being a hands-on rancher, and this makes it difficult for him to allege ignorance in the face of repeated accusations of slave labor on his property Fazenda Forkilha (dating from 1978, 1983, 1984, 1990, 1997, 1999 and 2001). He is also an extremely dangerous man who is quite prepared to take the law into his own hands.

Jairo's third son, Tarleyzinho, president of the local branch of the UDR and former manager of Fazenda Forkilha, was the apple of his father's eye. When in 1994 the neighboring ranch, Fazenda Agropecus, was invaded by the landless, there was a lot of conflict and tensions were high. Like his father, Tarleyzinho was known to be quick tempered, and when he challenged a truckload of timber that was coming off his ranch, things turned very ugly. Harsh words were exchanged, guns were drawn, and the incident ended in murder. Tarley's body took fifty-six bullets.

Jairo swore to take his revenge personally. "It took me nine-teen months and cost me seven thousand head of cattle," he later told reporters,[12] adding that all those who had participated in the murder of his son had been eliminated, either by him personally or by hired hands. Jairo's especial rage was reserved for squatter Errol Flynn Barbosa, who had admitted to firing two shots into Tarley's face at point blank range and had later threat-ened to kill Jairo, too. Errol Flynn escaped from jail and fled to a remote border area, but Jairo had him hunted down. Bound and gagged, he was thrown into a truck and driven back to face his doom. "I took him back to the place where he had murdered Tarley," said Jairo. "I told him to raise his arms in the form of a cross. I had him tied and then I started to cut off his fingers. No, he didn't cry for mercy, he was too much of a man for that. He did ask for water, but I didn't give him any. I cut off his fingers one by one, and then I shot him fifty-six times. The same num-ber of bullets that Tarley got."

Jairo was allegedly involved in the murder of Paulo Fonteles, the former state deputy and lawyer who worked to support the squatters in the area. "No, it wasn't me," he told a reporter, mat-ter-of-factly. "But I know who did it. And if he hadn't died, there would have been even more trouble with land invasions." He also stated that since he believed in the values of hard work and the concept of private property, he wouldn't hesitate to kill any-one who threatened his lands.

Jairo didn't hold with outsiders meddling in his affairs. He had a particular dislike of the local church authorities; he couldn't understand why they were always supporting the peons and squatters, and accusing people like him of using slave labor. He even claimed to have poisoned the bishop[13]—although this was never proven. When the Labor Department and the Federal Po-lice carried out a blitz on his fazenda and accused him of slave labor he treated them as unwarranted interference, refused to show them the books, and stated that he wasn't going to pay his workers.

It was an old habit of his. One of the peons who had worked on Fazenda Forkilha later testified that Jairo's *gatos* used to tell the workers to collect their pay in town. Amerivaldo Borges Leal stated that he waited twenty-two days in town, was never paid, and finally returned to the *fazenda* at the suggestion of the *gato* and worked another four months—after which the *gato* ran away and left the peons stranded. With no transport except their feet they journeyed into town and went to the ranch office, but Jairo refused to see them, and they were afraid to insist, because of his reputation for violence.

Twenty-five years ago, in the good old days of SUDAM credits, many of the ranches were in corporate hands: Volkswagen, Supergasbras, the fertilizer firm Manah, edible oil manufacturer Pacaembu, or large banks such as Mercantil, Bamerindus, or Bradesco. Large industrialists also jumped on the bandwagon, and while today most of the corporate ranches are long since gone, you will still see the names of Bannach, Barbosa de Melo, Quagliato, Mutran, and Murad. But things have changed over the years. Not only did the subsidies dry up, but people also discovered that setting up and maintaining pastures in those hot, humid Amazon climates was a lot of hard work for very little reward. Pasture maintenance required a big workforce, which was difficult to come by and increasingly fractious. Poor roads made it difficult to get to market, and anyway productivity was lamentably low. Some of the more alert ranchers had noted this from the start. Robert Milne, who was running the Santa Fé ranch on behalf of the Caterpillar dealership, commented in 1980, "What you've got to realize is that no one is really making any money here. And if it weren't for the government and their give-away programs, everyone would be in deep trouble. Like I said, nobody's making any money. It's just a way to keep from paying taxes and hope that something big happens here. I'm one of those who thinks it isn't going to happen." His views on the SUDAM program were succinct. "Those who bribe the most get the most, that's God's honest truth. Nothing is done honestly, on merit. The whole program is corrupt." Neither did he think that ranching was sustainable. "The bloody jungle creeps back too fast. I can't keep it back. In the end the jungle will win."[14]

By the mid-1990s when inflation was finally controlled, land prices dropped disastrously, and the ranchers were beginning to feel the pinch. Everyone was agreed that the Amazon needed to be developed, but no one had yet been able to come up with an economically and environmentally sound way to do it. If you want a textbook example of environmental destruction hand in hand with rampant economic speculation, head west to São Félix do Xingu. This is the new frontier and it is the burning season. A thick pall of smoke hangs over the town, but the streets are bustling with activity, and business is brisk. People from across the country are swarming into the area, all set to make a quick buck. What is it that attracts them? Is this another feverish round of land grabbing? Is there gold out there? Are they dealing drugs? Or arms? To what extent are local authorities ignorant? Or powerless? Or conniving? Given that large numbers of peons are heading almost daily to work in the jungle, what is to be the end product?

5

The *Gatos*

Men in the Middle: Overseers and Gunmen

It is a stiflingly hot afternoon in the *feirinha,* and Maria beckons me over to join her in the bar for a cold drink. The heat is rising in waves off the tarmac road; I have to screw up my eyes against the shimmering heat haze. I stagger in out of the heat and fling myself down on a wooden bench in the shade.

The old man in the corner gives me a toothless grin. "I remember you," he announces. "You're the one that keeps asking questions."

"That's right," I say, "and now I'm going to ask some more—if you don't mind."

"Ask away," says the old man, delightedly. "I can tell you a thing or two."

"That's right," adds Maria, "Zé here, he's been around a lot."

"I'm sure he has."

The three of us settle comfortably around the table, Maria and I sharing a freshly blended passion fruit shake while the old man happily accepts an ice-cold beer.

"You must have worked on a lot of the *fazendas* in your time, haven't you?" I inquire as the old man takes a deep and satisfying draught of his beer.

"Yes ma'am, I certainly have." He wipes his mouth and gives a happy sigh. "Of course I'm too old for that sort of thing now. These arms haven't got the strength." He rolls up his sleeves and bares his skinny arms for my inspection. "But in my day I used to work up and down the state of Pará, down in Mato Grosso, over in Amazonas, Roraima, Rondônia, just about everywhere.

When it comes to clearing that undergrowth, why, they don't come much better than me. Off we'd go with our team into the forest. We'd stay there a month or two and then we'd come back into town, and we'd have ourselves a party. Have us a drink or two, find a pretty girl, and we'd be on top of the world. Yes, ma'am." He closes his eyes and smiles, the years dropping away. I can see him standing there in a clean shirt and a new pair of boots with money in his pocket and the good times rolling.

"Tell me about it," I coax.

"Well," he says, still smiling, "I'm not from these parts, you see. I was raised in Barras, Piauí, in a family of twelve. Must have been around fourteen years old the first time I went off with a *gato*. I can remember it as if it was yesterday. They sent a loudspeaker truck around the villages and they were promising the moon. They put it out on the radio, too. They said there was plenty of work and plenty of money. You just couldn't get work in Piauí, so when I got to hear it I was desperate to go, of course I was. I wanted to see the world and make some money. My mother didn't want me to leave, but I was determined to have my own way. So I jumped into the back of the truck, and that was the last I saw of Piauí. Never went home again. But I had me a good life; worked hard, played hard. Plenty of liquor, plenty of women."

"Was it hard to get work?" I inquire.

"No ma'am," the old man says. "Word gets round that there's a job on one of the *fazendas,* and pretty soon they're lining up to go. Me, I worked a lot with the same *gato,* Raimundo his name was. Over in Pará. He'd take us off to do the job, and bring us back to town. There we'd stay living the high life and pretty soon he'd be back. And off we'd go again."

"I've had *gatos* coming in here, looking for peons," Maria adds, "but this isn't the sort of place where they hang out. I don't let them run up a tab, that's why. Strictly cash, that's how I work. It saves a lot of bother. Anyway, as I was saying, there's lots of places where they can hang out and drink, but not here. I'll send them all up to Helena's, peons and *gatos.*"

"Yes ma'am," affirms the old man, dragging deeply on a villainous-smelling cigarette. "The *gato* comes into the bar, stands everyone a round, and offers to pay off the tabs of anyone who'll sign up to work. Course they're all falling over each other to join his team."

"What he's really doing is buying them," Maria says. "But they don't see it that way; they just think he's helping them out. And there are two things you can be sure of. When the peons get onto the *fazenda* they'll find themselves with twice the work and half the money they were expecting."

The old man sucks his teeth and nods sagely.

"If the *gatos* are short of hands they'll go over to the jail," adds Maria. "Spring bail for a few peons. It suits everyone, gets them off the hands of the police. Put them to work and make honest men out of them, say I."

The old man laughs so hard that it provokes a fit of graveyard coughing, followed by some violent throat clearing. He catches Maria's warning glance and carefully aims a gob of spittle onto the sidewalk.

There is a short pause, and then we all begin talking at once.

"How did they treat you, those *gatos*?" I ask the old man.

"Well," he says sententiously, "there's good ones and bad ones. Sometimes you get treated well, other times you don't. That's life, isn't it? I mean you can be out there in the forest shivering with the fever, feet rotting in the mud, but you've got a good team and the food is tasty and there's plenty of it, and things don't seem so bad. Then again you can be out there with nothing but rice and beans, and *pistoleiros* ready to beat you up, and it's a different story, isn't it? Thank you kindly, yes, I will have another beer."

Later that evening I walk over to call on Brás, one of the local *gatos*. Brás lives near the bus station, behind high walls with a prominent sign saying VICIOUS DOG. I arm myself with a stone before ringing the bell. The gate swings open, I tell my story to a small girl and am hospitably invited in. Brás is sitting in a plastic chair on the front veranda, fanning himself and eating sweet rolls. Although a young man, he is immensely overweight and sweating freely. Business isn't what it used to be, he tells me. It's all this government interference.

"These days you just can't get people to work for less than eight *reais*, he complains, "and they don't like to stay for more than thirty days. Sixty maximum. Of course I try to work with peons I know. Fellows from Araguaína. If they want to bring a friend along and they'll vouch for him, why then I'll usually take him on. But two things I won't allow. I don't allow drink and I don't allow women. No. I take a man to do the cooking. If the worst comes to the worst, I'll cook myself. I'm a pretty fair cook." He laughs and helps himself to another sweet roll.

"Troubles? You bet, particularly back in the early days. Even ten years ago. There was no law, you see. So you had peons getting into fights and killing each other, or killing the *gato.* Running out on you and leaving the job unfinished. Sometimes the ranchers wouldn't pay up and then you'd be stuck with all those peons and no money. But things are different now. There's a lot more control. More police, more interference from the environmental department. They've started saying you're supposed to have a document from the government before you can cut the forest, can you believe it? Trying to put us all out of work.

"The last job I did, for instance. I had to do a runner. I heard that the rancher didn't have the paperwork straight and the Feds were nosing around, so I pulled my team out just like that. I wasn't about to get into trouble with the law. I have enough to worry about already. We had to come out on our feet. Thirty kilometers. But what else could I do? The cops would have been on to me otherwise."

Brás's young wife brings out the baby and five-year-old Luciana to join us. She is carrying a tray of coffee and more sweet rolls, and Brás helps himself lavishly. He is setting himself up for a heart attack and diabetes at the very least, but it isn't for me to tell him so.

"But the money isn't as good as it used to be," he says sadly, licking the sugar off his lips. "I've only had two jobs this year, believe it or not. And I had to abandon the last one halfway through. You see, with all these inspections it works out cheaper for the rancher to nip in with a tractor and chain and just knock the forest down. He's less likely to get caught and he'll get the job done in a quarter of the time. No comparison.

"Not that labor is a problem. This town is full of people looking for work. It's the economic situation. But what to do? I have to look out for myself. I've been thinking of setting up a small business. But there again there's the question of work contracts.

I'm not about to sign a contract for some peon to work maybe thirty days and then run out on me. I mean, if you look at it logically, I'd do a lot better to be running a bar or something. It would save me a lot of hassle. Because you have to look after them, you see? No, I don't give them money if they're out of work, but I'll go and get them some medicine from the pharmacy. Or I'll give them a plate of food. No one gets turned away from my door. I'm not having them go hungry." He helps himself to another sweet roll, and settles himself comfortably back into his chair.

To judge by the size of his house, Brás isn't doing so badly. And the peons who work for him confirm that he is a decent guy and treats them right. But he's a relatively small-time *gato*. He tells me he'd never hired more than 120 men. Whereas *gato* Luis Bang from Mato Grosso—whose résumé also includes periods of employment as *pistoleiro,* mayor, and gold miner—has told me he had handled as many as a thousand men in one contract. Of course he wouldn't be able to do this without a team of *subgatos,* backed by a contingent of overseers, *pistoleiros,* and other toughs. Their job is to supervise the day-to-day work, measure up at the end of the contract, and keep a sharp eye out for trouble.

You can tell who is who by their dress. Peons wear jeans and a T-shirt, with boots if they have them, otherwise flip-flops. Trusty peons can progress to an intermediate state known as *bate paus—* those who wave sticks about—and their job will be to keep the team under control. The *subgatos* will wear short boots and a baseball cap. The chief *gatos* will dress in cowboy boots and belt, with gold chains and a big hat. Successful *gatos* get lots of work, and you will hear the same names cropping up over and over again: Adão Franco, Raimundo Fogoió, Abilão, Chicô.

Chicô is fifty-eight and has been active in the business for more than twenty-five years. He has worked the length and breadth of southern Pará, and has managed to get himself elected town councilor in his home town of Santana do Araguaia. Chicô has a reputation for violence; he has been busted for using slave labor on twenty different *fazendas.* But he's only once been in jail, and he didn't stay there long. He doesn't allow scruples to get in his way. He even had the nerve to turn up at the funeral of

Gato

a peon whom he had helped into an early grave, telling his mother, "There's people round here who say that I'm responsible, but you'd better not tangle with me. I'm a rich man and I can pay to rub out anyone I want."

Abilão, who has frequently worked together with Chicô, is a big man who likes to wear checked shirts and sports a gold chain with a crucifix. Chicô and Abilão worked together on Rio Cristalino, the famous model ranch belonging to the Volkswagen company, about which we shall hear more later.

When the conversation turns to *gatos,* one of the stories that keeps coming up is the story of the peons who were burned to death in a fire set by a *gato.* By now the story has acquired legendary status, and you will hear it both from Mato Grosso and across the border from Pará. Dates and locations vary, but the facts are consistent. And the name that is most often mentioned is that of Zezinho. Zezinho de Codespar.

Zezinho himself is dead. Murdered on a gold mine, long since. But his wife, Alice, lives in Rio Maria, Pará, not far from the gold mine where Zezinho was gunned down. She lives in a beaten-up old wooden house with several children and grandchildren, and these days she makes her living selling snacks.

Alice is in her late forties, attractive and outgoing. She welcomes me with a smile and invites me to sit with her in her little backyard. Loud singing from church on the corner comes clearly across the night air, but it doesn't faze Alice. She simply raises her voice.

"You're not bothering me in the least," she insists, "I love to talk about the old times. It brings them back to life, somehow. Makes me feel young again. Now what was it you wanted to know? How long I've been here? Well, you could call me an old-timer." She smiles. "Twenty-five years I've been in Rio Maria. And let me tell you something, there was nothing here when I arrived. A few shops, a small restaurant, a gas station, and an infirmary. There was no telephone, no bank, and no electricity. We had to use lamps. This town was founded on lumber, and everyone worked in the sawmills. And it was a violent place. Full of *pistoleiros.* People used to get killed all the time.

"My husband's name was José Gomes Pereira but they called him Zezé de Codespar. That was because he worked on the Codespar ranch. It belonged to the Lunardelli family from Riberão Preto. Old man Lunardelli is still alive. Do you know Codespar? To get there you go to Redenção, and turn off at the Casa de Tábua. Codespar is in there, behind Cristalino. A long way from here.

"But Zezinho didn't care about distances. What he enjoyed most was opening up new ranches. He was a born adventurer. He'd knock down the forest and have the place under pasture in no time. He used to work clear over on the River Xingu, and the only way in was by boat. From here he had to go up to Marabá, over to Altamira, and down the river. It used to take weeks.

"That ranch over on the Xingu, let me see, he must have opened it around seventy-eight or seventy-nine. Yes, that would have been about it, because our son was just a year old. They made the airstrip by hand, and it always was a dangerous place to land. There was a high hill there, Monte Belo, and the pilot had to be careful not to hit it. I remember going in there several times to visit Zezinho, and I always had my heart in my mouth when the plane was landing. And there was another thing. That place was terrible for malaria. The men used to get such terrible fevers that the whole tent used to shake, can you imagine? I never saw anything like it. Zezinho used to get malaria all the time. But it didn't bother him.

"He loved challenges, did Zezinho. Tough jobs. Places with problems. Like squatters, for example. Any kind of conflict, and Zezinho was your man. He was very brave, I've never seen anyone like him. He didn't care how far away the job was, or how many people he needed, or how dangerous it was. The tougher the job the more he liked it. All he cared about was the money.

"That's why he went off and became a miner. Around the time that the Goiaba mine opened up. We went in there and we did fine. Until they came after him. It was a bunch of ranchers from Redenção, Dr. Rubens, Dr. Gervase, and another lawyer who had him gunned down. Twenty-three bullets he took.

"He left me with six kids, the youngest scarcely weaned. I stayed on that mine for eight years, and let me tell you it was no life for a woman. What with all the machinery breaking down, and I didn't know how to fix it, did I? But I stuck it out. I paid off all my debts, and I raised my kids.

"But I do miss Zezinho. Those were such good days! This place used to be bursting with life. You see this backyard?" She points to the neatly swept sandy space. "There used to be a big tree here, and it was all lovely and shady. And it was always crammed with stuff. Boxes and bundles and sacks and rolls of plastic for the tents. And peons all over the place. They used to hang their hammocks in the shed, and they'd stick around here until everything was ready, and then off they'd go.

"Even when Zezinho was off in the bush there'd always be peons hanging around my door. Wanting news of the next job, or asking for medicine or a plate of food. Zezinho always told me to give it to them, he used to say they'd pay him back when it came to working.

"Everyone liked him. They respected him. They knew he was tough. But then you've got to be, with peons. They aren't easy to manage, oh no! Always bugging him for money, they were. They needed to buy hammocks, boots, tools, that sort of thing. Sometimes they'd take the money, sign a note, and then do a runner. But Zezinho always went after them. He'd catch them and then he'd shout: Sonofabitch, you're gonna pay me what you owe. I'm not going to sweat my guts out on your behalf and have you walk off with my money. Stealing the money from the mouths of my children. You sons of bitches, you'll work until you've paid me every last penny!

"They'd get up to all sorts of tricks. But he'd go after them. Once he had to chase a bunch of peons across a river. Well, Zezinho never did learn how to swim, but he got himself across and then he caught them and knocked the shit out of them. Made them carry him back across the river and when they got to the other side he belted them again."

There is a brief silence, broken suddenly by the voice of the priest starting on the homily.

Alice stirs in her chair and, turning to me, she says vehemently, "You can't imagine how I miss those times! There was so much going on. We had such fun. I used to send Zezinho out with all the supplies he needed, and off he'd go and stay several weeks. Sometimes he'd come to town for more supplies and medicines and then he'd go right back in. I used to go with him for a few days to visit. If we were getting on well, that is! I went to Belém, and Marabá and Altamira. And he'd buy me a new dress, or take me dancing. We were never short of money. You see that old shed? I've still got a great big trunk over there. It's full of cock-roaches now but it used to be full of money! Zezinho used to leave money all over the place for me to find. Inside the pots and pans, in boxes, on the top shelf. Everywhere! Once I found that the mice had made a nest and eaten a lot of banknotes! I never told Zezinho, though.

"Kill? Oh yes, he killed people. But it was always in self-defense. Those were dangerous times. It was kill or be killed. One evening we were sitting here and I was grinding the corn. He was sitting in his hammock chatting and all of a sudden there was a noise outside the door and I went to look and there was a bunch of *pistoleiros*. They had some cock-and-bull story about having killed someone and asking for shelter, but I didn't like the look of them. I know a killer when I see one. So I shouted for Zezinho and he told them they'd better start walking and not look back.

"Zezinho was never afraid. But sometimes he'd tell me there was someone after him and he'd go off to a friend's house for the night. If ever he did that I'd know that things were serious. Once they came after him but they killed the wrong man. It was a friend of ours from Belém and he was lying in Zezinho's hammock when they shot him dead. We rushed him to the hospital but there was nothing they could do. Our neighbor alerted the police, but they never picked up the gunmen. But we knew who they were. Two nights later Zezinho saw them drive past, and he was so mad he yelled: You bastards! You killed my best friend. You didn't even have the balls to face me.

"Mind you, he had his faults. He ate too much and drank too much and he was a dreadful womanizer. He used to come home all covered with lipstick. But I loved him. He was a real man. And when we went to bed it was all worth it."

She bustles up to get a drink of water, smiling nostalgically, and then continues. "His bosses loved him. He worked so well. He always hung in there until he had finished the job. Do you know why he was called Zezinho de Codespar? When they were inaugurating the *fazenda* the owners went there and they had a ceremony but they couldn't agree on the name. They invited Zezinho up onto the platform to speak and he said right out 'This is Fazenda Codespar. . . .' And it was because of Codespar that he died.

"They say he killed a hundred people in a fire, but it's not true. Of course they were always setting fires. It was the quickest way to clear the forest. You clear around the section to be burned and then the fire burns its way into the middle. Well the story was that the peons' camp was in the middle and they all got burned alive. But Zezinho always denied it.

"One day I asked him straight out. We were in bed and Zezinho was in a good mood. I said to him: Zezinho, I want to ask you something. I don't want to offend you; I only want to know the truth. This story, is it true? He turned to me and said: Alice, if I'd done a thing like that do you think I'd ever be able to look my children in the face? And there's another thing, he said: Those peons, they've all got families. If it isn't a wife it's their parents. If it had been true, they'd have come after me, wouldn't they? No one ever came after me.

"There was this forest, you see, with 120 men in there. The story was that he set the fire and they all got burned. All except one who escaped and told the police. It was nothing but a wicked lie, but the story went around like wildfire. And Zezinho was arrested. But I tell you, a real man like Zezinho would never have done a thing like that. Zezinho told the police that if they couldn't carry out a proper investigation he'd do it out of his own pocket. Lunardelli swore that such a thing had never happened on his *fazenda*. He testified that he had known Zezinho for twenty years, and he would never do such a wicked thing.

"They sent Zezinho down for twenty years but he got out after three months, thanks to Lunardelli. I was seven months pregnant at the time, but I ran around, I can tell you. I was determined to get him out of there. Mr. Zezinho was lucky to get out of jail, and it was all due to me. I may be black, and I may be poor, but I'm smart. I know a thing or two, and I went after it.

"I'm a good wife, a good mother, I try to do my best for my kids, and at least I have plenty of love to give them. I do what I can; I own my own house. Nobody comes after me for the rent. And I make out. My dream is to build a new house. Right here, over this well. I love this well, the water is marvelous, and clear. I love this place. It's old and ugly but one day I'll make me a new house. That's my dream."

Airton is short, dark, serious looking. In his late thirties, he wears glasses and tends to look preoccupied—until his face is transformed by the biggest and warmest of smiles. These days he works in the CPT office in Xinguara, but when he was a kid he lived in Rio Maria and earned a little money working in a watchmaker's shop. His boss used to buy gold from the local miners, and one of their most regular customers was Zezinho de Codespar. Airton remembers him well. "To see him, you'd never think he was such a dangerous man," he tells me. "He was a striking man, tall, dark skinned, he had a mustache. He always wore a black hat, and the one thing I remember about him was his smile.

"The peons used to reckon he had a charmed life. Because no one could ever kill him. They said he was a shape-shifter; he could turn himself into a tree trunk and hide in the forest, and the only way he would ever lose his powers was if his daughter gave away her virginity. Well, he had a very violent temper and he used to beat up his kids. One day he hit his daughter so hard that she decided to take her revenge on him. She ran out of the house and she went with a man—just to spite her father. And sure enough he lost his protection and soon after that he was murdered. Hundreds of people turned up to his wake to see if he was really dead."

I walk back through the streets of Rio Maria pondering Zezinho and the peons. The story has come up so often that there must be some truth in it. As I draw level with the church the doors open and dozens of people spill out into the road.

"Binka, I'm so glad to catch you." Sister Sueli comes running up and thrusts a key into my hands. "We'll be a little late this evening, there's a pastoral meeting we have to attend. But please make yourself at home; there's food in the refrigerator."

Gratefully I take the proffered key and walk back through the dark streets to the sisters' house. Settling down at the kitchen table with a glass of milky coffee and a slice of cake, I take out a bunch of papers from my backpack and settle down to read an interview with a well-known *pistoleiro*.[1] I feel I need to be able to get inside the heads of people like Zezinho de Codespar.

The *pistoleiro* gave his name as "Alan" and his base of operations as the state of Goiás. But he was quick to point out that the *pistoleiros* could be hired wherever and whenever they were required.

Thirty-four years old, Alan was married and had one child. A former officer in the military police, he had been fired for "murder aggravated by cruelty." Since then he had worked as a hired gun. But he didn't consider himself a rich man. "A gunman's money is like a gold miner's: easy come, easy go," he laughed.

"There's two classes of people I can't abide," he continued. "One's traffickers and the other is rapists. It's on account of a rapist that I was thrown out of the police."

The story was this: After hearing of the rape of a twenty-month-old girl, Alan had galloped after the rapist, tied a rope around his body, attached it to the saddle of his horse, and dragged him for miles cross-country. When he finally reined in his horse, the man was dead.

I stir uneasily. I am beginning to find such levels of violence almost routine. I pour some more coffee, stronger this time, and read on.

Q: How many people have you killed?

A: "Fifteen. Five of them were policemen. They knew too much."

Q: How do you feel when you kill someone?

A: "Nothing." [laughs]

I wonder what Zezinho felt when he saw the flames licking up around the tall trees. I wonder if the peons had been in there, and if he had heard their screams. I wonder whether the story is true, and whether Alice thinks it's true. I wonder how you can feel nothing when you kill someone. I turn the page.

Q: What's your technique?

A: "I like to make sure they get plenty of bullets, so they don't get up and walk away."

Q: Who are the biggest pistoleiros in Goiás?

A: "Well there's a mafia in the military police. From the colonel all the way to the new recruit. But the ones who kill for money are the civil police."

Q: How much do you charge to kill someone?

A: "150 head of cattle."

Seventy thousand *reais.* That's a lot. I've heard stories of people being wiped out for less than a hundred. I hope, briefly and passionately, that I will never get used to these atrocities. My thoughts turn to the dark night and the gunmen at the door and I start violently when I hear the key in the lock and see the sweet shiny face of Sister Sueli hurrying in.

"I'm so sorry to keep you, Binka," she says breathlessly. "The meeting is still in progress but I decided we couldn't leave you here all by yourself, so I came back to keep you company."

"How kind!" I say fervently, putting my documents away. "And how was your day?"

6

The Peons

Held Fast by Their Debt, Their Isolation, and Their Ignorance

The road south from Rio Maria leads you to Redenção. Twenty years ago it was known as the most violent town in the Amazon. There'd been a series of gold strikes and the place was buzzing with wildcat miners, prostitutes, traders, squatters, Kayapó Indians, ranchers, *pistoleiros*, mechanics, and pilots. There were seventy planes working out of the town, and since they didn't have an airstrip they landed on the main street. The police reported an average of one murder a day, and when *pistoleiros* put a bullet through the head of one of the local landowners who wouldn't allow prospectors onto his ranch, they emphasized their point by leaving his body to decompose behind the wheel of his pickup truck on Main Street. These days the gold and the timber are gone, and the center of town is brightly painted up and filled with large four-by-fours driven by cowboys in oversized Stetsons. The mayor has put up little signs everywhere announcing that Redenção is the Town of Happy People, and the sidewalks are paved with octagonal cement blocks with smiley faces. I don't see any decomposing corpses either, but maybe I'm not looking in the right place. I do notice that the police wear flak jackets and carry some impressive-looking weapons.

After Redenção you travel through a lot of land, as they say in these parts. The paved road runs straight as an arrow through mile upon mile of fenced pastures, dotted with large rocks, termite hills, and long-eared white cattle. Crossing the bridges requires constant vigilance to avoid dropping a wheel into the gaping void in the middle. You pass the shabby little settlement of Casa de Tábua by the entrance to the Codespar ranch, you pass the small unassuming sign to Fazenda Rio Cristalino, once the pride of the ranching industry, and finally you come to the town of Santana do Araguaia where they built the finest slaughterhouse in the region—despite the lack of roads to link it with the ranches, or power to run the machinery.

The paving runs out at the state line, landing you on one of those hideous Amazonian roads where the traffic weaves across the road to avoid the giant holes, and rusted iron bridges stand like gigantic skeletons because they've never been connected. In a haze of heat and dust the road stretches to the horizon and hundreds of miles beyond, through scrappy pastures and scrappy forests, past decrepit wooden shacks selling cold beers and gritty rutted roads leading off to the ranches of the interior. Eventually you come to Vila Rica, an untidy little town that was formerly the headquarters of a settlement scheme bringing in migrants from the south: blond, blue-eyed people who found it difficult to adjust to their new home. "They didn't like us and we didn't like them," an old man told me later. "They worked from sunup to sunset, never stopped to enjoy themselves, produced surpluses and couldn't sell them. . . . They just couldn't understand how Amazônia works." Next down the road is Porto Alegre do Norte, a classic run-down Amazon settlement of tatty wooden houses and shops lining the impossibly broad main street—originally the airstrip—and dirty side streets where the garbage blows in the hot wind and the skinny dogs lie limply by the open drains. The houses have no piped water, the hospital is the place where you go to die, and the mayor has been thrown out for corruption.

There are other settlements dotted around, one of which is called Confresa. It's not up to much, but it's not as bad as Porto Alegre. The main street was built as a street instead of an airstrip, so you can see across the other side and even walk across to the other side if you are quick enough to avoid the murderous and deafening motorbikes that roar up and down looking for action. I'm traveling with Ricardo Rezende, a charismatic figure who was formerly the parish priest in Rio Maria. He became so deeply involved in the land struggles and in denouncing the ranchers for using slave labor that he narrowly escaped at least one assassination attempt and finally pulled out. Ricardo is currently pursuing his doctorate on slave labor and has come back to do research. He has the advantage of being known and loved in many of the communities but some people don't feel comfortable talking to a priest, so we have joined forces and make a good team.

Feliciano

It is often hard to find people to tell you about their experiences, particularly if they have been painful. But we do find one man who is willing to talk. Feliciano is in his late thirties and has worked all his life as a peon on the *fazendas*. For many years he was a migrant laborer but now he has settled down; he just started a job in the local sawmill. He invites us into his neat bare house, where we sit at a wooden table in the front room, furnished with a shelf of shiny pots and pans, a water filter, and a gas stove. (But no money to fill the cylinder.)

"I come from Santa Inês in Maranhão," he tells us. "I left there when I was thirteen, and I haven't seen my family since. Adrift in the world, that's what I was. Like so many of them. Mind you, I've been about a bit. Amazonas, Roraima, Pará. I came to Mato Grosso sixteen years ago. No, I came alone. I had a wife once. And two kids. But she left me, and now I've married again."

Right on cue, his second wife appears. A passionate woman, dark, strong, used to fighting tooth and nail. She looks at Feliciano with a mixture of exasperation and affection. "Let me tell you something, Feliciano," she says pointedly. "If you hadn't married again you'd have been dead by now, you'd better believe it." She looks at us challengingly. "I don't suppose he's told you about his accident?"

We shake our heads.

"Well, he nearly died, that's what. And I had to make the rounds in Porto Alegre before I could find anyone prepared to help me. I ended up selling my little house to pay the medical bills. A nice little house I had, half paid up, and I sold it. What could I do? But I won't let him go back to the *fazendas*. Why, he's never been the same, not since the accident."

"I've worked on *fazendas* all my life," says Feliciano defensively. "What else can I do? I'm a peon. And a good one too. I've worked on dozens of *fazendas*, with dozens of *gatos*. They're all alike. Don't do a stroke of work. They steal from the peons, cheat them over payment, cheat them over the prices in the canteen. No, it's not the ranchers who steal. But they should see that the peons are treated right. There's nowhere for the peons to go, don't you see? Even the unions are useless."

Feliciano's wife breaks into the conversation. "When Feliciano went this last time, I said to the *gato:* I want to know the name of this *fazenda*. And the address and the name of the rancher. Well, the *gato* told me not to worry my head. He said I didn't need to know all that. But he'd write it down and leave it at the peons' hotel, anyway. And do you suppose he did? Several times I went there and they didn't know a thing. Feliciano just plain disappeared.

"I'd started buying a little house, and I'd been taking in washing to keep up the payments. When Feliciano left I quarreled with him. I said to him: Feliciano, you ought to take a few *reais*. You're so stupid. But he never would accept an advance. He didn't like to be in debt. Like I said, I fought with Feliciano before he left. I just felt in my bones that it wasn't going to work. The moment I set eyes on that *gato*, Antonio Avelino his name was, I knew he wasn't to be trusted."

"It was over in Pará," says Feliciano. "In Tucumã. The *fazenda* was called Maciel Two, although I only found that out later, after the police went in. There was a big bunch of peons from all over. They went from Confresa, and Porto Alegre and Vila Rica and some of them went from Pará. I went in on the eighteenth of January in 'ninety-nine and left on the second of March. The work was hard but it wasn't so bad. We used to sit round at night in our hammocks, chatting, singing songs, or telling stories. Sometimes we'd pray, other times we'd go fishing. One day I was clearing the forest and there was a tree stump I didn't see. I was using the chain saw, and it must have kicked back in my face. I don't remember anything. We were working about four kilometers from the canteen, and my friends carried me there in a hammock. There was a nurse there, but I don't think she was a proper nurse. She gave me some medicine but no stitches. I remember that it hurt like hell. And the medicine didn't do me any good, because three days later it was hurting even worse. So they decided to get me out of there. It was a hundred ninety kilometers to town and the road was terrible. They carried me in a hammock; six kilometers through the mud, and then they put me in the Toyota. When I finally got to the hospital they took an X-ray and gave me a shot. After a while they moved me to a hotel, but I knew I'd never get better in a hotel. The doctor told me I mustn't do anything at all for five months. Five months I spent, just sitting around and feeling terrible, and they never paid me a penny. Later on I heard that the Feds had gone in to the *fazenda* [this occurred in March and April of 1999] but that was too late for me. If I'd been still there I'd have got a work contract and some medical expenses. But since I wasn't there I missed out. I did call the lady from the Department of Labor and she said they were going to try to take the rancher to court to get me some money. Of course nothing has happened."

"Were you badly treated, Feliciano?" I ask.

"No I can't say that," he answers thoughtfully. "Well, the *subgato* used to try to provoke us. He used to say bad things and try to humiliate us. But we didn't react and he never actually beat us up. Oh, yes, the *gato* was armed. But I never saw him use a gun. Avelino was okay. But he shouldn't have treated us that way, not paying properly."

"Did you ever think of running away?" asks Ricardo.

"Never in my life. Not once," Feliciano answers roundly. "If I owed you a hundred *reais* I'd work till I died. That's the way I see it; if I'm owing, I have to pay."

"Did you run up a big debt?"

"Yes, I did. The deal was we were hired *cativo*,[1] you see. You don't have to take a thing with you. The *fazenda* provides it all. All the stuff we got from the canteen was written down and they told us what the prices were. I knew it was *cativo* when I went there. I didn't complain. But then I had my accident. . . . "

His wife chips in, "And he couldn't work for five months. We had to buy everything on credit. We're still owing. I don't like to show my face in the shops anymore. If Feliciano hadn't got himself a proper job with a proper salary starting today, I don't know what we would have done. Thank the Lord he's still able to work, that's what I say."

Feliciano damaged his health, his wife lost her savings, but he didn't lose his life and they didn't stop him from leaving the *fazenda*. Feliciano was a lucky man.

That night I sit in my hot little room and leaf through my notes. I close my eyes and think of Elizeu, who had worked on Fazenda Estrela de Maceió, down in Santana do Araguaia. He wasn't injured, like Feliciano, but he wasn't allowed to leave, and was lucky enough to have been rescued by the Federal Police.

Elizeu comes from Guarai, Tocantins. It's the town that lies on the intersection of the main Belém-Brasília highway with the road to Pará, and it's a convenient point for rounding up peons to work on the *fazendas*. Elizeu lives in a small wooden house with no number, on a street with no name. I am traveling with Xavier; it takes us some considerable time to locate the house, and when we finally find it there doesn't seem to be anyone home. But the neighbors tell us that Elizeu was there, and so we persist. Finally the door is answered by a skinny young man with a big smile. "That's right, I'm Elizeu," he says. "Yes, I was on Estrela de Maceió. I've been off work for a few days with malaria, but I'm getting better now. Yes, I'll tell you about it. Come on in." He motions us inside and we settle ourselves on a dark red woolly sofa.

Elizeu tells us he is twenty-three, but he looks younger. "It was back in 'ninety-eight," he says. "I heard they were looking for people to work over in Pará, so I decided to go. The pay was good; six *reais* a day, and they gave us an advance. They paid my bus fare, although I didn't realize I'd have to pay it back. We took the bus to Redenção and then they stuffed us into a cattle truck. There were a lot of peons on the *fazenda;* a hundred twenty, or so we heard. Forty went from Guarai. There were six in my gang, and we were put on to clean the pastures. We lived in plastic

"We lived in plastic tents."

tents and to start with it was fun. It was only later that we heard they wouldn't let us leave. Not until the job was done.

"They'd agreed in advance that we could go home for Christmas, but then the *gato* changed his mind. There were three overseers—Zé Maria, Índio, and Antonio Luis—and they used to go around armed. They told us we'd better shut up and get on with the job, otherwise we'd be sorry. We thought it was just talk, but then we found out it wasn't. Two of the guys tried to run away, but they got picked up and one of them had a gun stuck in his mouth. That was when we really started getting scared.

"We had to buy everything from the canteen, food and tools and stuff, and they charged us double the going price. I'd been there over two months, and I remember that I was beginning to wonder whether I'd ever be able to pay my debt, when all of a sudden the Feds arrived. It was like a miracle. They arrived on a Sunday, in two Toyotas, and they stayed almost a week. We heard that one of the peons had got away and he had alerted the police. He had to come in with them to show them how to get there, but he wore a mask, just like on the television. The owner arrived the next day, and they issued our work contracts and paid us our money. The police asked if anyone would like to stay on, but we all said no; we wanted to go home. So they put us in a bus and sent us home."

It wasn't the first time that Fazenda Estrela de Maceió had been accused of slave labor, and it happened again after Elizeu and his team were rescued. Which must prove something about the type of punishment handed down. It's not effective. After a blitz in 1994 the local rural workers' union sent a note to the state prosecutor complaining that they had neither judge nor prosecutor in the county, and emphasizing that they needed honest men who wouldn't be intimidated by the ranchers. Had the state had some sort of presence, it is possible that the *fazenda* would not have reverted so quickly to its old ways.

Elizeu didn't see the half of it. According to José Martins dos Santos,[2] six men tried to run away, and only three were ever seen again. "Fazenda Estrela de Maceió, I can't abide to hear the name," said José. "The *gato* was Batista from Redenção. He used to go about with a machete and a revolver in his belt. I worked one month and twenty days and do you know how much they gave me? Forty-eight *reais!* Just enough to pay off my debt. I left that place without a red cent in my pocket."

Wanderley Araujo dos Santos worked fifty days on the *fazenda* and left as penniless as he'd arrived. After he left there was a police raid, which freed fifty peons but didn't help him. Two months later Wanderley reported almost ninety peons living once again in conditions of slavery on the same *fazenda.* Meanwhile he was back in the rooming house waiting for another job.

Antonio Pereira da Silva worked there, too, and he was determined to escape. The *fazenda* was a long way off the road, and after spending two nights in the forest he was caught, beaten up, punched on the jaw, and sent back to work. His second attempt was more successful, until he was picked up by the local police, put in jail for three days, and sent back once again. "I wouldn't do that to a dog" was his comment.

José Orlando de Barros was equally determined. His first attempt to escape was frustrated when he was caught on Fazenda Rio Cristalino and returned to work. But he did manage to make it out, and he was the one who alerted the Feds, leading to the release of the peons, among them Elizeu. "My mother warned me not to go," Elizeu tells us with a smile. "And she was right. Next time I'll listen to her."

One of the strategies for keeping the peons down on the farm is knocking them to pulp. In a statement issued in 1996 referring to

Fazenda Lucy near Xinguara,[3] José Carlos Gonçalves Trajano and Carlinho said that they had been recruited in the state of Goiás by *gatos* Boca Rica and Russo and offered a good deal to work in Pará. On arrival they discovered that the goalposts had been moved, and that instead of working with cattle as had been agreed, they were going to be clearing the dense scrubby under-growth. Three months later, without receiving any money, they plucked up their courage and tackled the foreman about the question of pay. Carlinho was violently beaten and pistol whipped and they were told to get back to work. They crawled to the tent and decided to run away.

Carlinho could hardly walk, but Zé Carlos supported him and they staggered out into the night, heading into the forest. Covered with scratches and vomiting blood, they finally made their way to the nearest settlement, a hundred kilometers away. From there a bus driver took pity on them and gave them a ride to Marabá, where they went straight to the police. The police chief said he could do nothing for them, since he was busy and besides, he was just leaving on a business trip. So they went to the nuns, who sent Carlinho to the hospital. Zé Carlos hitched a ride to the town nearest his home, and went to the town hall to beg for the bus fare. The town hall told the CPT,[4] but José said he wasn't making any statement because he wanted to go home. The CPT sent a note to the Human Rights Division in the House of Representatives in Brasília. No further action was taken.

More drastic methods of securing the peons include physical restraint, just like the old days of black slavery. In 1990 José Pereira dos Santos, known as Baiano, was hired by *gato* Raimundo to work on his farm. Baiano and his wife worked there for a while but received no money, so they left and found another job. Raimundo sent his henchmen after him, and, on the pretext that he owed money, they beat him up and dragged him off to work on Fazenda do Silva.[5]

The amount of the debt was grossly exaggerated, but Baiano had little choice. One of his fellow peons, Ceará, demanded to leave, whereupon Raimundo declared that the two of them were nothing more than a "pair of rebels" and must be taught a lesson. Both of them were repeatedly and savagely beaten up and put in irons. Raimundo threatened to give Baiano a flogging, and swore to kill his wife and unborn child. Henchman Moreno confirmed the beatings, saying that he himself had been ordered to participate, and his statement was confirmed by Ceará. Tractor driver José Donizete de Castro overheard Raimundo telling Moreno to kill Baiano, saying that there was nothing else to be done with him.

Peon Francisco Xavier da Silva stated that Raimundo had forced him to sleep with another man's wife—and then forced her husband to beat her. He also confirmed that Ceará had been repeatedly beaten for three days, both on the head and also on the body, and had finally been chained in a sitting position.

Despite his chains and padlocks Baiano managed to escape, and six days later the police carried out a raid. The rancher was called in; he declared he knew nothing but was perfectly willing to settle up with the peons. *Gato* Raimundo disappeared and the police were unable to locate him, since no one was prepared to say where he lived.

Nor was this an isolated case. When the Feds raided Fazenda São Judas Tadeu in Paragominas in 1988 they found whips, chains, vicious dogs, and a clandestine cemetery. Edval Pinto, who was working on Fazenda Alto Rio Capim, was tied in a hollow tree[6] together with the remains of some food, and left for three days at the mercy of the ants. On Fazenda Taina Rekan, *gatos* had perfected a form of torture known as the Death Flight.[7] Offenders were beaten with a wet rope, revived with cold water, and forced to balance on a plank in the back of a pickup, which then drove full speed down a hill, often causing the victim to lose his balance and fly out of the truck to his death.

It's hardly surprising in view of this treatment that the peon suffers from low self-esteem. If you don't have a name, and you don't have any documents, and you don't belong anywhere, who in the world cares about you?

There are two categories of peon, although as in most things connected with the slave trade, boundaries are fluid. There are those with families, like Félix or Elizeu, and those like Ceará and Baiano who are migrant laborers. The first have some sort of support network; they may live with their parents or may have a house of their own, and they won't be adrift in the world, as Feliciano used to be. But they may go adrift. They may travel to distant states and never return, or they may move from one partner to another, fathering children as they go. They may alternate periods of work on the *fazendas* with stints on a building site, or working as street traders, and in between jobs they may return to their families.

The migrant worker may dream of a triumphant homecoming, but he will never go home. He has cut his ties and gone off to seek adventure. He may set up a family or two along the way, but he is more likely to remain a bachelor all his life. The typical migrant worker is young, unattached, unskilled, illiterate, a drifter. He has few friends, nowhere to live, and he is much given to drinking and womanizing. His code of honor—which is pretty well all he has to remind him that he is a man—means that he won't run out on a debt, and he'll work as long as he owes. If he does manage to accumulate some money he'll probably spend it all on a grand splurge and get gloriously drunk, thus perpetuating the myth that migrant workers are no use to anyone. His relationships are with other peons—although he can never fully trust them—with the women who own the bars and rooming houses, and with the prostitutes. Sometimes he develops a relationship with the *gato,* who pays his debts, finds him work, and occasionally bails him out of prison.

What does he think of himself? One of the links that binds everyone in the chain of slavery is fear. Fear for his life, fear of betrayal, fear of sickness, fear of failure. He leaves home to make money, promising himself that he won't go home until he succeeds. All his life he'll be a loner, although he may develop some sense of comradeship with his team. He can't trust anyone and he can't be trusted. Yet he does not allow himself to be entirely reduced to the state of a victim, developing several mechanisms of self-defense. He may cheat the *gato* by doing less than agreed, he may walk out leaving the job half done, or he may take his money and run. He has a reputation for being quarrelsome, and his fondness for liquor will lead him into many a fight. Sometimes he will kill.

Here's how he describes his life: "We lived in a pigsty; we were transported like cattle; if we weren't tough we'd go crazy." One peon who escaped from Fazenda Itamarati in Mato Grosso said, "We lived like dogs," and Luis Barbosa, who fled from

Fazenda Big Valey, said,[8] "I escaped this time. But I don't have enough money to get out. I'll have to go and work on another ranch. If I'm lucky I'll get paid, if not I'll move on to the next job. There's no point in trying to seek justice. It's risky. You get death threats, you don't get paid, but you've just got to keep on working."

Society sees the peon as a threat; a lazy, good-for-nothing, argumentative drunk. Although the brothel and hotel keepers depend on him for their living, often they too see him as worthless. *Peão do trecho não vale nada:* Migrant workers are no use to anybody. Even those who work to help release them from the chains of slavery acknowledge the problems. Valderez, coordinator of one government flying squad of labor inspectors, remarks sadly, "They are held fast by their debt, by their isolation, and by their ignorance." Her colleague Claudia notes wryly, "If you talk to the landowners they don't think there's anything wrong with what they're doing. The sad thing," she adds, "is that most of the workers don't either."

7

The Women

*Those Who Wait, Those Who Comfort,
Those Who Profit*

The first area to profit big time from the SUDAM financial incentives was southern Pará—between Marabá and Santana—and, to a lesser extent, northern Mato Grosso. A more recent agricultural frontier has been in the direction of the Xingu River, and across the other side.

São Félix do Xingu, on the confluence of the Xingu and Fresco rivers, is a settlement that dates back more than a hundred years although you wouldn't think so to look at it. Formerly accessible only by river, the town first gained road access in 1985 when a private colonization company, Andrade Gutierrez, founded the settlement of Tucumã. They were given four hundred thousand hectares of land in exchange for putting in a road and developing it. Tucumã was to be a scheme with a difference, and the land was carefully zoned. First they would build the town, and then they would zone the land in concentric circles around. The area nearest to town would be devoted to producing truck crops, with an inner ring of medium-sized farms that would grow rice, beans, and corn, then an outer ring of cattle ranches. They planned to restrict the settlement to migrants from the south, reckoning that they were better farmers than the locals, and toward this end the guard post was instructed to allow only the blue eyed to enter. The brown eyed were detained at the guard post, but they had the last laugh: The guard post was sited on top of a gold strike. Overnight a new settlement sprang up: Ourilândia, the land of gold, and the frantic influx of settlers rapidly became uncontrollable. The colonization company gave up in despair and sold the land back to the government.

There's an outpost of the CPT in Tucumã, manned by a French Dominican called Jean and his colleague Amarildo. Tall, gaunt, chain-smoking, Jean is obsessed with the fate of the settlers and squatters who are abandoned in areas so distant and so inaccessible that often they can only be reached by tractor. A former Carmelite, anarchist, and mystic, Jean is a man with a mission who exposes himself to the dangers and discomforts of travel without a second thought. Amarildo too is a people person, a born investigator, courageously confronting the isolation and hostility of the local ranchers.

I am interested in finding out what becomes of the women when their sons and husbands disappear to the ranches, sometimes never to return. Amarildo offers to take me to meet them, and together we set off in his elderly Volkswagen Beetle to the outskirts of Ourilândia, along a gravel road to nowhere. An untidy jumble of houses is scattered raggedly along the road. Some are made of uneven lengths of planking with thatch and plastic sheeting for the roof; others are better finished, and some have flowers planted around. One even sports a TV aerial, although I don't see electrical lines anywhere.

We park the Beetle in front of a small bar and set off in search of Antônia, whose husband has been away for many weeks. We find her sitting under a tree pounding rice in a mortar. An attractive woman of forty-something, she has a pleasant, open face. "Come, sit in the shade."

Antônia

She beckons us to come behind the house. "It's like a furnace inside."

She has only recently gotten together with Raimundo, she tells us, as we settle onto the bench beside her while a tangle of small naked children and puppies plays in the dust.

"No, I don't know exactly where he is, but I do know it's far away. One and a half hours by air. He left, let me see, nearly six weeks ago, and I don't know when he'll be back.

"Oh yes, I know the name of the *gato* all right. Paraíba. He's notorious round here. A thief, that's what he is. Raimundo sent me a letter with sixty *reais,* but when it arrived it only had a fifty-*real* note, and I never found the rest. I asked Paraíba straight out what had happened to the other ten *reais* and he said he knew nothing about it. And I haven't had another cent since then.

"Not that I'm alone in the world. I have two grown sons and they send me money when they can. And I work in the school as a cleaner, so that brings in a little something. But I've been sick recently and I had to pay for the medicines, and now I'm owing in all the stores round here and don't dare show my face."

Antônia's neighbor comes softly around the corner, eyes wide with curiosity. In her early twenties, she is a typical Amazon beauty, dark and sexy. She is carrying a small child whom she sets down on the ground to join the children and the puppies.

"Know the name of the *fazenda?*" She favors Amarildo with a smoldering smile. "Not me! I haven't the least idea. No, I don't know when they'll be back, but it won't be soon. They have to take the ferry and it only goes every second week. And don't talk to me about Paraíba! He's a liar as well as a thief. He told us we could go and buy food on credit in the supermarket but every time we go there they refuse us. We went three times to his wife after our money, me and Antônia. But he never sent any, and finally she gave us something out of her own pocket. She knows what it's like to be stuck with kids to feed and nothing in the house.

"Slave labor? Well, we do sometimes hear rumors of bad things, but you can't believe everything you hear, can you?" She tosses her hair and looks under her lashes at Amarildo.

Antônia invites us in for a glass of water. The house is almost completely bare. I glance through into the bedroom; a mattress on the cement floor, and a few bits of clothing hung on string suspended across the room. The kitchen has an earth floor, a shelf with a water filter, a few glasses, and a bunch of green bananas in the corner.

There's a cheerful camaraderie among the women. The young pretty one is on her second husband. Antônia has just traded hers in for Raimundo. The children are treated as communal property, being hugged or admonished by the nearest adult. There's a lot of laughter. In this world of changing alliances and changing fortunes you have to be resilient to survive.

One of these abandoned women ended up winning the Anti-Slavery Award in London. Dona Pureza lives in the state of Maranhão, and she is no stranger to tragedy. Several members of her family had already gone missing, and when her son Abel went off to Pará early in 1993 and did not return, Pureza determined to do something about it. A Bible-believing Christian, Pureza knew that God was on her side, and that wherever she traveled she could always find a bed or a meal among her fellow believers. She sold her house, sold her plot of land, and went off to battle. Pureza went to talk to the government in Brasília but didn't get much joy out of them. So she traveled hundreds of kilometers on foot, through the *fazendas* in Pará, Bible in one hand, notebook in another, tape recorder hidden in her voluminous clothing. But she couldn't find her son, and *gato* Bala of Fazenda Agronunes told her that the peons were known by numbers, not by names.[1] Pureza's odyssey lasted two years, and she accumulated enough information to reinforce her conviction that these men were indeed slipping into the jaws of hell.

She never found Abel in Pará, but four years later he showed up at home, sick and sorry. He had indeed been a victim of slavery. Dona Pureza made so much fuss about it that she ended up attracting international attention to the problem, and was given a prestigious international award. She arrived in London to tell her story on the same day as a Brazilian minister who had gone there to testify to Brazil's excellent record on human rights.

Pureza is a notable exception, because she was old enough and tough enough to get on the road and go look. But who knows how many of the women in waiting are secretly nursing a broken heart? Padre Ricardo told me the story of a woman he'd met in the distant state of Piauí in June 2001. In 1995 her husband and brother-in-law had gone off to work on Fazenda Primavera in Pará. One day her brother-in-law appeared at her house, in a state of high agitation. Life on the *fazenda* had been a living hell, he reported. His brother had been tossed out of the back of a truck and broken his neck, he had heard rumors that no one who succeeded in making any money would get out alive, and he had found a pile of human bones when he was bathing in the dam.

The distraught widow determined to go to the *fazenda* to get her husband's documents, which would allow her to register his death and become eligible for a state pension. She took with her a little cross to put on his grave, but the ranch manager wouldn't allow her to erect it—in case it attracted undesirable attention from any passing policeman. When she begged for his documents, they gave her a work contract with the vital pages torn out. With no proof of her husband's death, she was unable to draw her pension.

Another woman told him of the night four years before when she came back from the fields and found her seventeen-year-old son sitting in the back of a pickup truck en route for Pará. She tried in vain to persuade him not to go, but he refused to pay any attention. The *gato* had already supplied them liberally with liquor, they were off on a great adventure, and nothing that she could say or do would stop him. The truck drove off into the night, leaving her alone with her fears. She never saw or heard of him again.

No one in her family could read or write. They lived in a house without a number, in a street without a name. They'd not thought of contacting the local priest, nor the police, nor even the radio station. Their son had disappeared without a trace and they had no idea what to do about it.

There was a strong current of fear and hopelessness among the women in waiting. So many of them seemed to have no information about their men; they didn't know where they were, they didn't know whom they had gone with, they didn't know when they would come back or even if they would come back. They suffered from ignorance and fear and fatalism. But not all of them were passive in the face of disaster. Some of them went in search of their lost men, and Pureza traveled to England to be a spokeswoman for her sisters.

There's another group of women who act as friend, confidante, mother, or mistress to the peons, supplying them with stability and human warmth while at the same time taking their money and sometimes delivering them into the hands of the slavers. These are the owners of the lodging houses and brothels, as well as the prostitutes. Padre Ricardo and I are in the unprepossessing town of Porto Alegre do Norte in Mato Grosso when we talk to Dona Maria Cecé, owner of a bar and rooming house.

Maria Cecé is small, dark, in her forties. She wears shiny white pedal pushers and curly shoulder-length hair. We chat with her on the front veranda of her bar, just off the main street. Our conversation is constantly interrupted by loudspeaker trucks plying the streets, selling pineapples or coconuts or extolling the virtues of one or another candidate for the upcoming elections.

"I used to run a rooming house up until a year or so ago," she tells us. "But I found it was too much of a hassle, so now I run a bar instead. It's almost the same thing, except you don't have all the trouble of having the peons hanging around all day. Well, once in a while I'll give hammock space to an old customer, but I prefer not to.

"I've worked with all the local *gatos* in my time. Donizete was the big number round here, but there were plenty more: Abel Borges, Raimundo, Domingo Parente—he's dead now—and Antonio Avelino. He was probably the most famous.

"The peons would stay three or four days, sometimes longer. They'd run up a bill of a hundred or a hundred fifty *reais,* and then I'd pack them off to work with the *gato.* I wouldn't accept them if they didn't agree to go. I'd have made a loss otherwise, wouldn't I? After all I had to pay the bills at the store, and sometimes at the pharmacy, too.

"They come from all over, Pará, Maranhão, Tocantins, even Piauí. All ages, from the youngest to the oldest. But no one underage, because it's against the law, and the *gatos* don't want trouble. They come all year round. Well, almost. They work from October to January, and from January to April. Not so much in

May because it's the dry season, although there are always little jobs to be done like fencing and clearing firebreaks.

"Problems? Well, every job has its risks, doesn't it? I've had peons run out on me without settling their bills. Once in a while the *gato* doesn't pay and I'll make a loss. But I never bother to go after them. The police wouldn't do anything anyway. And half the peons haven't any documents. They're nothing but rolling stones.

"But these days you don't see the numbers of peons around that you did. See, they're not chopping down the forest like they used to. The government won't allow it. So there isn't the call for these large labor forces. There are still jobs, but only small stuff, and I find it's not worth my while to stay open.

"Of course you can't help feeling sorry for them. I mean, it's not an easy life; we hear all sorts of stories. About *gatos* pushing their bills up higher and higher, about beatings and fights, and peons who vanish off the face of the earth. I can think of many a peon who used to come here regularly and who has just disappeared. But there again, they're free spirits, these peons. Not answerable to anyone. They may be on the run, they may have set up a new family, they may be dead. We've got no way of telling."

A loudspeaker truck comes barreling down the street, and I wonder for the hundredth time how anyone can preserve their hearing, much less their sanity, in the face of such a violent noise.

Ricardo leans forward confidentially. "Tell me, Dona Maria," he says, giving her the full benefit of his hundred-watt smile, "dozens and dozens of peons must have passed through your hands. Some of them must have come back to you again and again, isn't that so?"

"That's right," she acknowledges. "Although, like I said, there's a lot that just disappear."

"But the ones that come back. They go off to the *fazenda,* make some money, come back and blow it all, and off they go again, is that it?"

She nods. "But you can't exactly blame them for that," she says. "After all, there they are stuck in the jungle for weeks on end, all work and no play, and it's only to be expected that when they come out they're going to want to enjoy themselves. It's grinding work in there, and they get treated worse than animals sometimes. Accidents, fevers, rotting feet, insects everywhere. And I reckon they're scared half the time. You'd be scared if you had those *pistoleiros* hanging round, and you couldn't see how you were ever going to get out of there alive. And if you did get out, you'd probably go a bit wild yourself."

I try to imagine myself under those conditions; sick, scared, broke, with no choice and no hope. I think of the women, of their fear and ignorance and helplessness in the face of the un-known. I think of the ones who got away, like young Elizeu. And I think of the piles of bones and the nameless corpses on distant *fazendas* and of those women who are waiting for a son or hus-band who will never come home.

Maria Cecé sends us to see Fatima, the manager of the brothel. "She's an old professional," she tells us. Fatima worked as a *gata* in her time, so she can tell us both sides of the story. "I reckon she can tell you as much about peons as anyone round here," says Maria Cecé.

The *cabaré* is discreetly located down a little sandy track on the edge of a marsh, and we get there in midafternoon. There are no customers, but the girls are preparing themselves for their evening's "program," showering, fixing their hair, and painting their nails. A couple of small children are rolling around in the dust, and the atmosphere is that of a large family.

A well-built woman in her fifties, Fatima comes out hospita-bly to greet us and presses ice-cold Coca-Colas into our hands. We sit on plastic chairs in the shade of a mango tree, and she fans herself vigorously as she talks. She doesn't own the *cabaré*, she explains; she is the manager. But she is no novice to the business. Worked all over, she has, from the gold mines to the ranches and almost all the towns round about. She's owned land, she's owned cattle, she's had four children and once upon a time she was the wife of Raimundo Fogoió who was one of the best-known *gatos* in the business.

"That's life isn't it?" She fixes us with a warm smile. "Here today, gone tomorrow. And here I am washed up in a border town in Mato Grosso. Well, I guess it's like all border towns. Full of outlaws. You must have heard about that murder yester-day. Rancher Japonês beaten up and burned to death in his car."

She shuddered. "That sort of thing never used to happen in Marabá."

I think of the Mutrans and their record of violence and shudder in turn.

"No," she says reflectively, "I won't deny that I prefer Marabá. But it's not so bad here. Business is pretty good. I've got nine girls working at the moment, and they're good girls, all of them."

"Do you get a lot of peons coming through?" I inquire.

"Oh yes." She nods. "Although not so many as we used to. There don't seem to be the large numbers there were just a few years ago. But we still get our regulars, and of course there's the town trade."

"Do the peons give you any trouble?" I ask. "I know they like to drink a lot."

"Nothing that I can't handle," says Fatima robustly. "And they don't come to the *cabaré* just to drink." She gave me a delicious smile. "Sometimes they argue about using condoms, and then we say to them: And if there's a baby? Are you going to take responsibility? That usually sorts them out.

"After all, they come here for a bit of fun. The peons lead a hard life, you know. They get sick, they get lonely, they get afraid. They tell us their troubles. How lonely they are, how they live in a tent, how they have to cook at night for the next day. How they get fevers and lie there shaking in their hammocks."

"Do any of them fall in love with your girls?" asks Ricardo. "I see you've got some good lookers."

"Well"—Fatima smiles—"five of the girls have left us over the last year. Maria de Jesus married a peon, and she's living in town. He's off on a *fazenda* at the moment. Mônica married a fellow called André. He's another peon, but he seems a steady type. Then there's Ana who married a driver, Bruna married a cowman, and Valdênia married someone who got himself a job in a shop. It's nice to see my girls getting settled. And of course others are always coming in. We get girls all the time looking for a job.

"I don't take the very young ones. Oh, I'll give them a bed until they get settled. But I prefer my girls over twenty; I find they're more sensible.

"My girls set their own rates. My cut is that I rent out the room, and I charge for the food. And the liquor, of course. It's five *reais* for a quickie and ten *reais* all night. I do food as well, but most of the fellows don't eat.

"Do the girls fight? Not usually. They might fight over little things like losing a lipstick or something like that. And they're very honest. I insist on that. If a fellow arrives and he's very drunk I'll get him to check his wallet with one of the girls before he goes to sleep. It saves a lot of trouble. They always remember how much money they had when they came, but they don't always remember exactly what they've spent.

"They'll arrive after two or three months in the bush with a bit of money. That's the lucky ones. Of course plenty of them never get to see any money at all. . . . Anyway, as I was saying, they arrive with a bit of money and it's fair burning a hole in their pockets. When they were stuck there out in the forest they were dreaming of things they were going to buy, but once they get here all that's forgotten. I get very cross with them, I can tell you. I mean some of my regulars, why, I consider them as members of my family. 'Have a little self-respect,' I tell them. 'Get yourself a haircut. Smarten up, buy some soap, get yourself a pair of boots or a hammock or whatever you need. Then you can have yourself a party!'"

"Do you think that the peons feel discriminated against?" I asked.

"Oh yes, I think so. Even here! They hang about on the fringes of the conversation. They won't come and join us even when we invite them. They think we don't really want them. They don't think they're good enough. For example, they won't go into town with the girls when they're all prettied up. 'Oh no, I can't go,' they'll say, 'I'm far too ugly.' It's a shame really. Because they're good boys, most of them. I'm like a mother to them, I can tell you."

We nod, and Fatima refills our glasses. I feel that if I drink any more Coca-Cola I'll explode, and I surreptitiously pass my glass to Ricardo when she isn't looking.

"Tell me something, Fatima," I say. "Do the *gatos* come to you looking for peons?"

"Sometimes they do," she says. "But it's more often the other way round. They'll bring a team of peons here for a day or two before they go off to work. They tell them not to drink too much or get into fights, tell them what time to be ready to leave, and then they come back and settle up."

"Did Raimundo used to do that?" asks Ricardo.

Fatima gives a deep belly laugh. "Sure he did!" she says roundly. "He used to bribe the fellows in the bar to keep the peons around. Give them some food and some girls and make sure they didn't get away. That way they'd be sleeping on the journey and wouldn't give any trouble."

"Did he carry a gun?"

"Of course! Everyone did."

"Did you?"

"Well now." Fatima smiles a trifle coyly. "Shall I say, I'm a good shot."

We nod.

A young man on a motorbike skids to a halt and salutes Fatima respectfully.

"Good afternoon, Antonio." She gives him a warm smile.

"Good afternoon, Dona Fatima," he replies.

"Were you looking for Maria José?" she asks teasingly.

He blushes scarlet.

"She's gone shopping," says Fatima. "But she should be back by six. Why don't you come back then?"

"Thank you, Dona Fatima, I will." He drives off in a cloud of fumes.

Ricardo and I realize that we are encroaching on working time and take our leave. "Thank you so much, Dona Fatima," says Ricardo as he shakes her hand. "It's been a pleasure talking to you."

"The pleasure was mine," says Fatima. "Come back anytime."

"Thank you," he says, "we will."

We decide to ask Fatima out for a pizza after Mass on Sunday evening and send around a note inviting her. When we drop by for our date she's all dressed up and asks us very politely if she can bring one of her girls, Marilene. Marilene is dressed in skin-tight white jeans that emphasize her generous curves, her hair is cut short and hangs in damp curls around her ears, and she wears a white sparkly top with a small gold cross around her neck. She looks the essence of propriety. We drive them to the best joint in town, the *pizzaria* on the main square, and our little party attracts some curious stares from the adjoining tables.

Fatima promptly downs two drinks and starts entertaining us with stories of her life with Raimundo.

"Everyone knew him," she tells us. "He was famous. He and I worked together, I'd buy the stores and keep the accounts. At the end of the job he'd go and collect the money from the bank and I'd set up a little table under a tree and make the payments. We'd pay off all the peons, and then we'd add up our expenses and settle our own bills. It was a lot of work but I enjoyed it."

"What sort of profit margin would you get?" inquires Ricardo. "Somewhere around fifty percent?"

Fatima inspects her long red nails while she reflects. "Yes," she says, "it must have been around that. Raimundo charged more than the others but he always kept his word. He did a good job, and the ranchers always used to ask for him by name. I've known cases where they'd delay the contract if he couldn't handle it. Better to wait a bit and get the job done properly, they'd say.

"All I can say is that his family never lacked for anything. Very generous, Raimundo was. He used to say that he worked hard and he wanted to enjoy the fruits of his labor. I had a couple of girls to work in the house, and we had a car. And a telephone. All my kids got an education. I've got one who's studying medicine in São Paulo."

I hope I don't look as surprised as I feel, hearing this bit of information. It seems a far cry from running a brothel in a down-at-the-heels border town.

Fatima continues unperturbed. "Oh yes," she says, draining her glass, "those were good times. Good times. We built up a nice little inheritance for our children. There was the *fazenda,* and our house in town, and then we bought a supermarket, and of course we had a lot of cattle. But life has its ups and downs, doesn't it?"

We nod sympathetically, waiting for the next revelation.

"He was a terrible womanizer, was Raimundo," she says, matter-of-factly. "Well, I wouldn't have minded so much if he'd been discreet about it. But when I discovered he had another woman and a child, and he used to take them off working with him, why then I decided to cut loose. I said to him, 'Raimundo,' I said, 'I'll work under the hot sun for you, I'll work in the rain, I'll bear your children. For the love I have for you I'd even stay with you. But I must have respect.' And I walked out. Left him flat. So I'm making my own way in life."

Ricardo orders another round and we wait for the next installment.

"I moved out of Marabá quicker than light," says Fatima. "I decided to move to the gold mines. There's always money to be made there. I bought a bar . . . "

"And that's where we met," says Marilene, suddenly breaking into the conversation. "I was looking for a job and then I went to Dona Fatima's *cabaré,* and I've been with her ever since. . . . "

"How did you get onto the mines?" I turn to her.

She blushes and looks down.

"Ran away from home, poor little mite," says Fatima. "Like so many of them."

"I went swimming in the river and someone stole my clothes," she says, hanging her head. "My mother was so cross that she beat me, and I decided to run away. I hitched a ride to the gold mines and started working . . . "

"How old were you?" I inquire.

"Nine," she says flatly. "But after a while the police picked me up and sent me home. So I ran away again, and this time they didn't find me."

"You have a child, don't you?" I ask her, thinking of the small boy I saw playing in the dust in front of the *cabaré.*

"I have three," she tells us. "And another one on the way."

"And the father?"

"No, she's not going to marry him!" Fatima says sternly. "He's a good-for-nothing and besides he's only seventeen."

Marilene smiles. "You know how it is." She turns to me. "You fall in love and then you think that maybe, just maybe, they'll marry you and take you away from all this . . . "

"But it's not going to be this time!" says Fatima, giving her an affectionate squeeze. "Now, what kind of pizza are we going to order?"

8

Violence

The Cycle of Rural Conflict

I suppose one of the things that I find scariest about this whole investigation into slave labor is the fact that violence is beginning to seem so trivial. Such a commonplace occurrence. There's Albertino telling me in a voice devoid of expression, "I remember his smile as he fired. I thought I was going to die." Or the girl prostitute, "I lived like a real slave and was beaten up every time I refused to sleep with a worker." The woman in the *feirinha* referring to the peons, "I sometimes think they're no better than animals." Jairo Andrade the rancher on avenging his son's murder, "I cut off his fingers one by one and then I shot him fifty-six times." Alan the policeman-turned-*pistoleiro,* when asked how he feels when he kills someone, "Nothing."

And what makes it even stranger is the fact that Brazilians are known to be such congenial people. Visitors to Brazil are delighted by their friendly welcome. Day-to-day life in Brazil, although marked by the frustrations inherent to a society that is overburdened with bureaucratic rules and regulations, is nonetheless more fun than in most other places. Yet it has its dark side: muggings, murder, massacres, rape, incest. Slave labor.

One of the roots of violence is colonization: the subjecting of one people to another. In Brazil there have been successive layers of subjection. The indigenous tribes fought among themselves and often subjected the losers to ritual cannibalism, while the Portuguese subjected first the Natives and then the Africans to slavery. Based on the notion of inequality, power goes to the stronger, the richer, those who know how to manage the system.

Pale skins dominate dark skins, men dominate women, the educated dominate the illiterate, the rich dominate the poor.

The white colonist built his dominion on the ownership of land, reinforced by the labor of the Native or the Negro, secured by hired guns, and backed by the church and the state. Since there was no one to challenge his appropriation of the land, he consolidated his kingdom in the form of the *latifúndio*—a tract of land that can be larger than entire European countries or North American states. The *latifúndio* was a world unto itself, and the *latifundiário* took upon himself the absolute rule of the people within his dominion.

From Southern Europe came the notion of *machismo* (male superiority), whereby the *latifundiário* or patriarch was the pioneer who conquered and subdued the land, defended his property tooth and nail, and treated his workers with a mixture of generosity and sternness that could easily turn into cruelty. Since he was the ultimate power in the family, he could dispose of his inferiors in the way that seemed best to him. Those who didn't belong to his family became his clients, dependent on him for favors. When they behaved he would reward them with bread and circuses in the best Roman fashion. If they offended him, he reserved the right to punish them as he saw fit, secure in the knowledge that even if he killed them he was unlikely to be called to account. Every bully needs a victim, and there is in the Brazilian character a streak of fatalism that bows to the authority of the patriarch, or the priest, or the state. It's a legacy of the old days of slavery and the more recent era of military dictatorship. Under those circumstances it's safer to keep your head down and your mouth shut. Hence the answer to any question requiring some sort of stand: *"O senhor é que sabe,"* which translates freely, "You're the boss, you tell me," but actually implies, "Have it your own way, I'm not going to risk an opinion." Hence too the belief that a child who dies will become a little angel in heaven—it must have been the will of God. Equally, politicians are widely considered to be corrupt but few people think of challenging them. It's just the way things are.

And while things are changing, in a country the size of Brazil change doesn't happen overnight. One of the main causes of violence in the rural areas is the grossly unequal system of land distribution, plus the fact that many of the large landowners don't even bother to cultivate the land. Add to that large numbers of small farmers with marginal holdings and even larger numbers of families with no land at all, and you have all the ingredients for conflict.

Modern-day land disputes first arose when the government started opening up the land for settlement—in the 1970s. Once the access roads were in, conflicts sprung up on all sides. Settlers, squatters, ranchers, and the indigenous tribes all wanted to secure their lands against all comers. Naturally it was the little guys who lost out. Entire tribes were evicted from their traditional lands, as were thousands of squatters—by people who declared themselves to be the lawful owners, backed by court orders, and reinforced by the presence of police and hired guns. Those who were unwilling to abandon their lands could be persuaded by terror tactics, such as beatings, fire, and even murder.

At that stage the country was still under military rule, the police were authoritarian in the extreme, the press was censored, and communications between Amazônia and the rest of the country were precarious. The small guerrilla movement based near the Araguaia River was held by many Brazilians to be a dangerous precedent for the spread of communism, and by extension they considered the population of Amazônia to be backward and possibly treacherous. Small wonder that little attention was paid to the burgeoning land wars, the violent repression, and the rumors of slave labor that occasionally emerged from those distant territories.

As the twenty-first century dawns, the situation of rural violence in the Amazon remains unresolved. Land conflicts continue in a cycle of increasing tension whereby the landless routinely occupy unused land, are routinely evicted, reoccupy (or invade), and are evicted once again. Police participation in evictions is often accompanied by levels of violence that are as unnecessary as they are unconstitutional. Small-town politicians indulge in a frenzy of fraud, diverting government funds destined for health, education, and roads into numbered bank accounts, accumulating fortunes that bear no relation to their declared salaries, and making sure that opposition is silenced. In the remote ranches of the interior anything goes: large-scale land grabbing, using slave workers to cut down the forest, dealing arms to neighboring Colombia, acting as a way station for the cocaine trade . . . You'd better not get involved with these people or you could end up floating upside down in the river with a bullet in the head.

Given that Brazilian Amazônia is a land without law, how did this state of affairs come about, and what can the government do about it? Part of the explanation lies in the fact that, after the withdrawal of the military, the federal government, in an attempt to simplify the business of government, very laudably decentralized its powers to a considerable extent and devolved them to the states. Unfortunately many of the larger and more remote states (including those located in the Amazon) do not possess sufficient infrastructure to be able to cope, with the result that the business of government is left, de facto, in the hands of the local politicians. Far from the prying eyes of federal inspectors and auditors, state and local governments can and do run their states as they see fit—and it's easy to see that happening right now in the states of Tocantins and Pará, to name but two.

There are lots of ways to dominate people, but the obvious ones will be omission and oppression. Omit to give them the resources they need—education, health services, markets for their produce, roads—and you have a captive population who won't be able to give you much trouble. Make sure they don't know what's going on, and if they find out, silence them. Identify all focal points of opposition—the schoolteachers, the union, the church—and do all you can to discredit them. Buy the chief of police. Buy the judge if you can. If you can't, make sure he is so swamped with work that he can't operate. Easy to do in Amazônia; it's so far away that who's to care?

So what can the state do? Since Brazil is no longer a military dictatorship, questions of law and order should be in the hands of the police. And Brazil has three police forces: federal, civil, and military. The Federal Police are based in Brasília, with small delegations located in major cities in each state. Their job is to look after issues that affect national security, as well as cases of interstate smuggling (including the smuggling of peons for slave labor) and questions that the state police are unable to handle. They are considerably better educated and better paid than the other police forces and are consequently held in higher esteem by the populace.

The Civil Police are in charge of criminal investigations, and while less well trained and far less well paid than the Feds, the local police chief is expected to be a law graduate. In practice this is often not the case, particularly in the rural areas, where chiefs can be sloppy, untrained, poorly paid and often corrupt. Generally speaking they will be unwilling or unable to prosecute the local elite, and such action as they do take can be classified as too little, too late. Crimes are incorrectly registered, registered too late, or not registered at all. Investigations are mounted with paralyzing slowness, witnesses are not interviewed, suspects are not arrested, forensic and ballistic exams are not done, postmortems are not conducted. Dossiers, files, and documents of every sort disappear, inquests are derailed for frivolous reasons, and cases of arrest are frequently followed by jailbreaks.

Day-to-day policing is left in the hands of the Military Police. They are under the authority of the state military commander, who is nominated by the state governor. Responsible for most police functions with the exception of criminal investigations, they are frequently criticized for indulging in excessive force, making unlawful arrests, and for torture, and while they too do not have a high level of education, they are smart enough to know that it's not worth their while to go after the rich. They are also able to get away, literally, with murder.

A dossier on police violence, compiled by the Pastoral Lands Commission in Xinguara, Pará, in 2000 and presented to the UN High Commissioner on Torture, quotes and documents cases of police brutality, incompetence, and corruption, pointing out that none of the officers or men mentioned has been subject to any form of sanction, whether administrative or criminal. One of the most striking cases cited is that of José, aged fifteen. José had hired a motorbike and was riding around town when he was pursued by policemen Raimundo Pacheco and Raimundo Monteiro Ribeiro, who caught him, handcuffed him, took him to a deserted place, roughed him up, kicked him, pistol whipped him over the head and on the genitals, and threatened him with death. The police had discovered that he was in possession of a small quantity of hash—which he said he had been given to try. Having finally got something on him, they kept him incommunicado for three days, without permitting visits from his mother or his lawyer. As a result of this vicious and totally illegal treatment he developed severe psychological problems and has been interned in a psychiatric hospital since July 1999. The police blame his condition on having taken drugs, but the hospital blames it on the police, stating that they think it highly unlikely that he will recover. José's case was cited by Amnesty International as one of the twenty most outrageous cases of torture worldwide in 2000.

The CPT dossier cites cases of beatings, electric shocks, suffocation, and sexual humiliation that not infrequently lead to death. Convicted gunmen escape from jail with laughable ease, often in exchange for a handsome bribe. Barrerito, who was serving a twenty-five-year sentence for the murder of union leader Expedito Ribeiro de Souza, was permitted to work in the kitchens of the Marabá jail without supervision. He found no difficulty in escaping, following in the footsteps of twelve of his colleagues who had broken out some days earlier. In the meantime no steps had been taken to avoid further jailbreaks. Similarly, Wanderley Borges Mendonça, accused of several murders, was released from the Xinguara jail by Detective Lucival Haroldo, who opened the cell and gave him a ride in the police vehicle. On this occasion there was a perfunctory inquiry, but Detective Lucival managed to get himself certified as mentally incompetent and claimed immunity from any form of punishment. "None of the police officers or men involved in these crimes has been convicted or suffered any type of administrative or penal sanction," states the report, adding that the men responsible "continue to exercise their professions, while some of them have even been promoted."

One of the most shocking cases of police brutality was the 1996 massacre at Eldorado dos Carajás. It happened like this.[1] The Landless Movement (MST) had recently occupied an unproductive *fazenda* in the hope of forcing the government to schedule it for compulsory purchase, in accordance with the law. Discussions had been held with the authorities concerned, but they were not progressing as fast as the MST would like. So they decided to send a delegation to the state capital to see if they could speed things up. In order to strengthen their case, they hit upon the strategy of blocking off the main road and demanding that the authorities supply them with fifty buses and ten tons of food. Major Oliveira of the Military Police undertook to deliver a list of their demands to the authorities, in exchange for which they agreed to unblock the road. On the following day he returned with a negative response, so they decided to blockade it again, erecting a barrier of sacks in the middle, with a human barricade on either side. In the middle were women and children; next to them was the sound truck from which the leaders were coordinating the action.

Colonel Pantoja from the Marabá Military Police was instructed to clear the road, so he arrived from the northern side with eighty-five men, while Major Oliveira took up his station on the southern side together with sixty-nine men. Numbers are hard to estimate, but there were probably around fifteen hundred men, women, and children trapped between the two forces.

Oliveira had been told to start action when he heard shots being fired into the air from Colonel Pantoja's contingent. Tensely the two groups faced off, and then the first shots rang out. One of the landless, Amâncio Rodrigues da Silva, was a deaf-mute and never heard the shots. He ran toward the police waving a stick, and the police responded by knocking him down. When he fell his body took three shots. Infuriated, the landless started advancing against the police with sticks and stones, and the police withdrew momentarily, only to return with guns blazing. In panic the landless scattered to the sides of the road, leaving the bodies of the dead and wounded where they fell.

Pantoja called Oliveira to ask how things were, and Oliveira replied the situation was serious. Pantoja inquired how many had been killed, and Oliveira replied that he had counted six dead and many wounded. Yet nineteen bodies were delivered to the mortuary, most of which had been savagely beaten as well as shot. In the opinion of the doctor who performed the autopsies, both the beatings and the shootings were sufficient to cause death.

In the police inquiry Pantoja stated that he never saw his men shooting at the landless, but that he had heard shots being fired and seen the landless scatter to the side of the road, leaving several bodies lying there. He had no way of telling whether they were alive or dead. Sergeant José Antonio Garcia testified that he had never fired his gun, but did admit to mislaying twelve of the twenty-five cartridges he had been issued. Sergeant Ronaldo

Nunes de Castro said he had been unable to fire since his machine gun had stuck, and stated that he too had mislaid his ammunition.

The Order of Advocates report on the massacre of Eldorado dos Carajás said the following: "The military police of this state is completely unprepared for the sort of operation that took place at Eldorado dos Carajás. There is no such thing as a specialized unit trained to deal with such a situation. We believe that the massacre began because the police were frightened when they found themselves the objects of attack by the landless. There was no negotiation and no attempt at peaceful crowd dispersal, nor were the police adequately protected with riot shields. Instead they were armed with heavy combat weapons as if they were in a battle situation—hence the large numbers of dead and wounded."[2]

But to the local ranchers it was all a storm in a teacup. "Massacre?" snorted Carivaldo Ribeiro, president of the local ranchers' union. "That was no massacre. Only a handful of people died. Do you southerners really believe that we pay a lot of attention to that sort of thing? Up here we don't think anything of it."

Vavá Mutran, of whom we have already heard, refused to comment. "I'm not saying a word to any goddamn journalist," he shouted. "Go fuck yourselves!"

9

Resistance

Liberation Theology and the Role of the Church

W hile it is the responsibility of the police to maintain law and order, the broader question of social justice is too important to be left solely in the hands of the government. This is where you and I and each member of society must play our part. Changes are brought about by people who are aware of the problems and willing to do something about them, and this requires good leaders and good followers. In a situation as fraught with peril as that in Amazônia, both leaders and followers will need generous quantities of personal courage—particularly in view of the numbers of deaths that have already taken place.

Back in the early 1970s at the height of the military repression, the Catholic Church was the only institution that had the clout to defy the military. Traditionally it had always allied itself with the government and the status quo, handing out food parcels and spiritual consolation to the downtrodden and never dreaming of preaching revolutionary concepts such as social justice. But faced with authoritarian regimes across the hemisphere, Catholics in Latin America began to think out new ways of living as Christians. As racial integration and the peace movement broke out across the United States, as the European powers relinquished their colonies and the old order changed forever, a new wind blew through the corridors of the Vatican and some members of the church took up a radical new option—to live and work in solidarity with the poor. The term *human rights* became common coinage, and idealists from across Brazil came to work in the backlands. They lived among the people, they talked the politics of freedom, and they walked the walk.

The revolutionaries were few in number but on fire to change the world, and they were going to do so by living and preaching Liberation Theology. The Second Vatican Council[1] had taken a long hard look at the role of the church, and had decided that Christians should follow Jesus in working to bring about social justice. This involved taking a stand against every sort of oppression: social, economic, political, historical, cultural, and moral. The Latin American bishops took this a step farther[2] by identifying poverty and oppression as systemic evils to be tackled both at institutional and personal levels. They were going to go out and do theology, rather than talk about it.

Liberation Theology preaches freedom and justice here and now. God's people are to live in community, with the Bible as their manual and their goal the search for justice, righteousness, and peace. A heady doctrine, and one too hard for many of the priests and laity. They preferred the old-style Mass with the priest in his pulpit, and no mixing of politics and religion.

Revolutionary or not, the church was held in considerable respect by the government, which, despite suspending the right of assembly, never went as far as forbidding religious gatherings. So it was under the mantle of the church that liberationists were able to meet together and to mingle their worship with discussions on social action. By forming the base communities— bringing the church to the people rather than the people to the church—they created a new awareness of day-to-day reality, and provided a safe space for planning and undertaking community actions.

Even in the darkest days of military repression prophetic voices in the church had never been entirely silenced, and a handful of courageous priests and bishops raised their voices to speak out on some of the more glaring forms of violence and injustice. This was perhaps the finest hour for the Brazilian bishops, and they displayed a courage and breadth of vision that is sadly lacking in these softer, gentler times. Paulo Arns of São Paulo was unyielding in defending the victims of injustice against the military rulers. From the northeast came the voice of Helder Câmara, speaking out on behalf of the downtrodden sugarcane cutters, and from the distant reaches of Mato Grosso came the voice of Pedro Casaldáliga on behalf of the slave laborers. In Conceição do Araguaia Joseph Hanrahan faced up to the Military Police when they came to close down the prelacy's radio station, and from Goiás Tomas Balduino presided over the setting up of the Indigenous Missionary Council and the Pastoral Lands Commission.

Pedro Casaldáliga identified so closely with the rural workers that he didn't even possess a pair of shoes, and on one occasion his parishioners were forced to have a quick collection so that their bishop wouldn't go to the Vatican in flip-flops. The bishop wasn't concerned about shoes; he was much more interested in people. His 1972 paper on the confrontation between church and *latifúndio* was a landmark document that drew attention for the first time to the plight of the peons being forced into slave labor. Led by the bishops, the liberation church took a stand on the issue of justice, and despite the hostility or indifference of many Catholics, it remains true to its mission.

The Bishops' Council was in a unique position to shelter emerging civil society groups, covering a broad spectrum of issues from human rights to Save the Whales. Consistently courageous, they exposed themselves to taking the flak over a whole range of issues, some of which they didn't necessarily support and some of which they never fully understood. But they did understand that without their protection these groups could not survive, and they deserve special recognition for their commitment to freedom.

At the height of the military repression in 1975 the bishops moved to found an organization devoted to supporting the rural population over the land question. They called it the Pastoral Lands Commission (CPT), and it became a highly skilled and extremely effective task force. Its mission was to support rural families who were facing eviction from their lands, to encourage and assist them to work together, to denounce injustice, to announce a new era of hope, and to press for peaceful and just solutions to land and labor conflicts. A few years later it extended its brief to include legal advocacy, using the mechanisms of the law to support the powerless rather than to oppress them. The bottom line was that the rural poor needed land and needed the means to survive on it so that they could lead lives worthy of being called human. More importantly, they needed hope for the future and the self-confidence to know that they could make it.

The sheer size of the task could have daunted less courageous souls. Distances were immense, populations sparse, and infrastructure primitive. The prelacy of Conceição do Araguaia at that time covered an area of 55,000 square kilometers—larger than Holland (35,540 square kilometers) or Belgium (30,514 square kilometers). It was divided into three counties: Conceição do Araguaia and Santana do Araguaia in the state of Pará, and Couto Magalhães in Goiás. The population of the prelacy was one hundred thousand, and there were thirty pastoral staff.

Meanwhile there had been repeated attempts at reviving the moribund trade unions, which had been virtually deactivated since the beginning of the military government. It was a long, hard apprenticeship, marked by fear and suspicion. Union officials (often government stooges) squabbled among themselves, spent their members' money, and collapsed in the face of threats from the ranchers. Again and again union members were encouraged to take responsibility for their own lives, and as they began to show signs of making some progress, they increased their nuisance value to those who were not interested in seeing power in the hands of the people. Elections were rigged, votes were bought and sold, and terror tactics were employed. Community leaders were targeted to die, and many of them did. In the town of Rio Maria alone five activists were murdered in the space of fifteen months, and a highly suspicious car accident very nearly took the life of Ricardo Rezende the parish priest.

Padre Ricardo may have been marked to die, but fifteen years later he is still very much alive, and still a thorn in the sides of the landowners. His mission is to tell the world about modern-day slavery. And to abolish it. He pulled out from the front line before he was shot and is now drawing on his experiences in those turbulent years to study, reflect, and write.

Fifty years old, Ricardo is a man of medium build, arresting brown eyes, and an easy smile. He could have made a career out of his looks and charm. Instead he left the comforts of his middle-class urban life and disappeared into the wilds of Amazônia. He spent ten years working with the CPT in Conceição do Araguaia, and it was the local people who encouraged him to go for ordination. Ordained a priest, he moved in 1988 to a small and insignificant settlement in southern Pará called Rio Maria. It was a logging town, with no amenities and only one telephone— a quiet little backwater where he could get on with his priestly business.

Ricardo's arrival heralded the eye of the storm, which had been brewing all along. A spate of murders took five lives, and there were several others besides Ricardo who had narrow escapes. As he lived out his vocation, bringing the teachings of Christ to the suffering people of Rio Maria, and telling with them the long litany of sorrows at each successive death, Ricardo kept a journal. *Rio Maria: Song of the Earth* is the story of the unquenchable courage of the people of Rio Maria in the face of violence, intimidation, and murder. It also reveals Ricardo's commitment to justice and his extraordinary personal bravery.

It was a terrible time, a time of unbridled violence. A time when huge stretches of land were gobbled up by large corporations, while small farmers and squatters were pushed to the edge of desperation and beyond. A time when men scrabbled in the mud for gold, and killed one another on the slightest of pretexts. A time when men were thrown, drunk, into the backs of cattle trucks and driven hundreds of miles into the jungle to work as slaves. A time when even priests were roughed up, jailed, and murdered. A time of brave new development projects that left a few people richer and a lot of people in grinding poverty. But hope was not altogether dead, and help was at hand. Pastoral agents, popular educators, lawyers, union leaders, priests, and laypeople were springing up even in the most remote corners of the Amazon, united in their desire to work for social justice.

Many of the heroes of the fight are anonymous and unsung, but some, through force of circumstance, find themselves in the public eye. One such is a French Dominican priest, Henri des Roziers. Henri is a man in a hurry. He doesn't tolerate fools. Or injustice. Or people who think too much of themselves. An intellectual with classic French face and mannerisms, who might, had things been otherwise, have happily enjoyed the finer things of life in Europe.

Henri studied the law because he believed passionately in one justice for all people. But he discovered that all too often in the real world might was right and justice was cast aside. He lived, in France, with immigrant populations and saw how they suffered from discrimination, and his heart was drawn increasingly to work with the poor and defenseless. So he moved to the Brazilian Amazon, where he found himself in the thick of the land wars. He joined the CPT and put his formidable talents to work to defend the defenseless and to prosecute the powerful. He made himself a lot of enemies, and received numerous death threats. But he was, and is, totally unwilling to compromise. "I'm not afraid to die," he declares. "I'm not a young man anymore, I'm a priest. And I don't carry a gun. My weapon is the Gospel."

These days Henri lives in the squalid little town of Xinguara in the south of Pará. It is an area where impunity would reign unchallenged—if it weren't for Henri and his colleagues in the CPT. One of them is called Aninha. Many people take her for a nun, which she isn't, but she has the single-minded dedication of a woman with a vocation. Her vocation is to work with the downtrodden. A sociologist by training, Aninha grew up in a large rural family and has an intuitive understanding and sympathy for the poor and the suffering, together with the militancy and passion of one who lives for a cause. "I love my work," she says. "I see it as a way of living out compassion. Sharing the suffering of the people and doing what I can to change it, to transform it. Living with them like we do, and sharing their pain makes you realize that it really is possible to transform not only people but also the whole system. You dream about it. Dream about bringing an end to suffering, injustice, and discrimination. And you draw your energy from each small victory."

Among those who are coordinating the CPT campaign against slave labor is another French Dominican, Brother Xavier, whom we met in chapter 1 at the Araguaína bus station. Fifty, athletic, blue eyed, and with a keen analytical mind, Xavier is a man with a passion for righting wrongs. A dynamo of energy, he can be found organizing pilgrimages, speaking at conferences, visiting and encouraging the landless, thinking, planning, strategizing, and making as much noise as he can about slavery. His mission is to nag the government officials who are working to eradicate it, to warn the peons who are most vulnerable to it, to support its victims and their families, and to publicize the issue and disturb people like you and me until we are forced to do something about it. Xavier is also a computer fanatic who makes the most of modern technology to keep in touch with the outside world. A formidable combination of brains and charm, he can persuade almost anyone to do almost anything . . . while still thinking it was their own idea.

One of Xavier's colleagues is Trindade, an attractive woman of forty who has the honey brown skin and black curly hair typical of the region. Trindade started out as a secretary with a group of CPT lawyers, but that wasn't enough. She decided to acquire her own legal skills. "What I wanted to do was to defend the men and women who work on the land. I wanted them to understand that the law isn't something to be afraid of, it's a tool they can use in their struggle to attain citizenship," she told me. "So I went off to Mato Grosso to work in the prelacy. It was a real privilege to work with a church that was totally committed to the poor and was transforming lives. I got involved in the land struggle and all sorts of human rights issues. And I learned that it's not easy being a professional woman. You still have to be better than a man. There's no margin for error. You have to be technically proficient, politically correct, and completely savvy. You can't be ingenuous. What keeps me going? My friends and family. The fact that I value myself and my work. And the knowledge that God is a liberator."

CPT field staff may dream of social justice, but they share the lives and everyday troubles of the weak, the dispossessed, and the enslaved. It's not just a job, more a way of life, and it takes a terrible toll on private lives. Airton (who told us about Zezinho de Codespar) describes it as an evangelical and militant option, where you have to give up a lot because of the demands of your work. Amarildo (who works in Tucumã) has this to say: "First of all it's an extraordinary privilege to be able to see Brazil through the eyes of the rural workers, those who live in the poorest parts of town and those who are on the edge of society. Then I'd say that if you are going to do this sort of work—and it's a tough assignment—you need to have four motivating factors. You need to be passionately political, seeking to do your utmost to transform society while fighting tooth and nail for those who work on the land. You need to be a bit of a prophet, too. We're called to denounce evil and injustice wherever we see them. And to announce the new world of peace and hope and dignity for all people. Then there's the question of ethics. Simply put, we seek to do good to all men. And lastly, you need to be a poet. You can't explain everything by reason. You have to leave room for poetry and romance. Only thus can you support the solitude, the exhaustion, and the frustration that mark our lives. Somehow we have to balance these points: politics, ethics, prophecy, and, most of all, poetry."

My own feeling is that you have to be a saint or a lunatic to survive the relentless pressure of work and the everyday diet of misery and despair. It's a twenty-four-hour commitment, seven days a week, under grindingly difficult conditions, heat, dust, and constant travel along hideous roads, in an atmosphere of mistrust and suspicion where a lot of people would rather you went away and left them in peace, and a significant number would rather you were dead.

Yet they have their victories. They'll work painstakingly on the minutest details of lawsuits, and sometimes they'll see justice done. They'll join in the celebrations in tiny wooden churches far out in the countryside or on the edges of scruffy little towns; they'll rejoice with the community over the birth of a new baby or the wedding of a young couple. They know that change is slow, and they'll celebrate it when they see it: in the successful working of a farmers' association or a group of women, in all the small and subtle signs that people are beginning to take responsibility for themselves and standing up against violence and repression.

But we must not be lulled into thinking that things have settled down, that violence is diminishing, that Amazônia is finally becoming "civilized." As communications improve and a message from Xavier in Araguaína can reach the computer of his colleagues in Paris within a matter of seconds, so the ranchers can contact one another within minutes to warn each other, for example, that the police are on a raid. Government officials may have access to smart new vehicles as they drive onto the remote ranches to carry out labor inspections, but if the *gato* wants to hold them up he can fell a tree across the road while he moves his workers out of reach.

The CPT has international exposure and international backing; it has offices in Xinguara and Tucumã and Marabá and Araguaína—as well as across the country; it is understaffed and overworked and it does miracles. But it is not alone. Across the region, across the country, and across the continent, people are beginning to become aware of the wrongs that we do to one another, and starting to think about basic human rights: the right to go to school, to have access to health care, to have a decent place to live. Rights for indigenous people, for children and women, the rights and responsibilities of citizenship and a better understanding of the political process. The right to earn a fair day's wage for a fair day's work.

And for those of us who have the education to be able to read this book, the money to buy it, and the interest in the subject, there is one question that we must put to ourselves. Now that we know that some of our fellow humans are living in slavery, being discarded like unwanted garbage when their use is over, what are we going to do?

10

The Landless Movement

An Alternative for Landless Workers?

If you were on the track of the largest and most successful popular movement in South America, probably the last place you would expect to find it would be in genial, disorganized Brazil. Yet that is where it is. The Landless Movement (MST), which first began to take shape as a result of land occupations in Rio Grande do Sul in 1979, now enjoys a wide measure of support from overseas. It even turns a profit. And it sends shivers down the spine of the government. The MST is all about agrarian reform, and the reason that we are looking at it in the context of this book is that for landless rural workers it provides a viable alternative to falling into slavery.

Although Brazil is the only country in South America never to have had a full-blown nationwide revolution, it has generated some serious popular movements, most frequently in connection with access to the land. The Peasant Leagues (founded by Francisco Julião) that sprang up in the sugar-growing areas of the northeast in the mid-1950s represented peasants in land disputes and posed a serious potential threat to large landowners. This had the government worried, and allegations of communist involvement provided the excuse for a 1964 military coup and subsequent period of violent repression. But repression breeds revolt, and as military power began to wane three institutions in the country started to flex their muscles: the church, the trade unions, and the Workers' Party (PT). The church had already set up a network of base communities, bringing the church to the people and providing a safe place for discussing social issues that often extended into the political arena. The emerging trade unions were sheltered and supported by the CUT, the central union of workers, and were becoming ever more vocal and more effective in serving their members. And for the first time the masses had their own political voice in the Worker's Party, which had its beginnings in political action by the Union of Metal Workers, São Paulo, starting in 1978.

Each of these organizations supported the idea of land reform, but they weren't the ones who were actually doing it. Hence the need for the principal actors to form their own movement. The mission of the MST is to support the landless in their struggle for land reform. They recruit people who are interested in living and working on their own plot of land, they organize camps and lead land occupations, they negotiate with the relevant government agencies, and after the land has been "won" they make sure that their members have the wherewithal and the skills to be able to manage it. Most importantly they imbue members with self-confidence and a sense of mission—the feeling that they needn't always be victims but can take control of their lives.

Even among those who do have their own piece of land, it's very common to go out and do seasonal jobs for other larger farmers. And since Xavier is involved in a campaign to try to educate rural workers about slave labor, he spends a lot of time telling them how to avoid it. Xavier is a popular figure with the local MST leaders, and when they invited him to give a talk in one of their camps I asked if I could go along, too.

We start out from Araguaína in the ancient pickup that belongs to the CPT. Its brightly painted wooden body is decorated with the slogans of the month: THIS IS THE YEAR OF THE JUBILEE;[1] NO TO PAYMENT OF THE EXTERNAL DEBT. As we rattle off down the potholed highway south, the roar of the engine makes it hard to talk and I find myself falling into a stupor engendered by the heat and the long, straight, featureless road. Suddenly we swerve off onto a dirt track heading toward the Araguaia River, through fields of white floppy-eared cattle. We are heading for an enormous ranch, illegally appropriated by a former state governor, never put into production, and subsequently occupied by the MST. The rancher, who had paid little previous attention to his property, immediately applied for an eviction order and the MST moved out, one step ahead of the police. Undaunted, they set up a roadside camp just outside the fence.

At a narrow bridge we come to a checkpoint where fifteen policemen are camped beside the river, keeping an eye on the comings and goings in the MST camp. They carry out a cursory inspection of the car but do not attempt to stop it. A mile or two farther down the road we get our first view of the camp: a long row of black plastic and palm-leaf shelters on either side of the

Tricky Bridge

road, two or three deep, with guard posts at either end. The guards are armed with nightsticks, and are polite but businesslike.

Xavier drives us slowly the length of camp, through the guard post at the other end, and off into a small clearing where the initial occupation had taken place. You can still see the signs of the MST camp—drainage ditches, holes for the latrines, a few stout poles that had formerly been part of the shelters. Xavier tells me they occupied the site at three in the morning. Eight busloads of them. Everything was so meticulously prepared in advance that within two hours of their arrival they had erected their living quarters and were having their first meeting. When they heard of the eviction order they moved their camp outside the fence line, but there was an unspoken understanding that they would go in again if their demands were not met. The government had promised agrarian reform, and they felt that their role was to agitate until it happened.

We drive back and leave the car in the shade. One of the camp leaders is called for, and he greets us politely and leads us to the assembly room. A large airy structure made of stout saplings with low log benches on all sides, it is currently housing a meeting of the coordination committee. Each person introduces himself and shakes our hands, and we sit a little apart while they finish the business of the day. I glance around the room and note the variety of age and dress. A young man in camouflage pants and a Che Guevara T-shirt, a middle-aged man in a smart black cowboy hat, an old man with a white beard and a baseball cap, and a handful of women. I get the impression that these people know where they are going and know how they are going to get there.

The meeting ends, and people start filing in for the session on slave labor. Xavier has taped up some large placards on the walls. They show men with empty faces, black plastic tents with rows of hammocks, hard-bitten overseers, and fields of blackened tree stumps. One of the younger men reads out from a list of names, each a *fazenda* that has been involved in slave labor.

Abaete	*Alvorada*
Acapu	*Ana Paula*
Acapulco	*Aragarças*
Agropec	*Araguari*
Água Viva	*Arizona* . . .

The men sit gravely listening. Every so often there is a murmur as someone recognizes a name or remembers an incident. Another man takes over and this time he reads from a shorter list—the list of *fazendas* that have been indicted on several occasions.

Alvorada	*Colorado*
Bannach	*Estrela de Maceio*
Belauto	*Fartura* . . .
Brasil Verde	

Xavier explains that the current system of punishment isn't being effective; fines are seldom imposed and rarely paid. The ranchers are hiding behind the *gatos* and evading responsibility, only two have ever been convicted,[2] and neither of them was jailed. Xavier reads out the list of their names; members of powerful clans that rule with impunity.

Jairo and Geraldo Andrade	*Mutran family*
Antonio Barbosa	*Lunardelli family*
Luis Pires	*Murad family*
Miguel Resende	*Quagliato brothers*

Slowly the discussion gets under way, defining, analyzing, reflecting. It touches on the mechanisms of luring the workers with false promises, the question of debt, the terrible working conditions, the violence, the inability to leave. Of perhaps sixty men in the room each one has a story to tell, and for many it is the first time that it has been told. But here they are among their *companheiros* and as confidence builds up, the stories begin to come out. The common factor is that they hadn't recognized slave labor for what it was, hadn't known what to do about it, and hadn't had any alternative. Now they have, and as the stories wind on they discuss possible strategies for spreading the word so that their friends and families won't get drawn into the same situation.

Twelve o'clock is lunchtime, and we are taken off into a tent where the camp coordinators live. Twenty or thirty people are standing around, heaped plates in hand, and the discussion ranges over a variety of topics: the possibility of getting more food from the mayor of the nearest town, the pharmacy that has promised a supply of medicines, the school they are planning to set up, the work gang that is being put together to do some fencing for a friendly rancher, the state of the negotiations over the land they want, the rancher's refusal to contemplate selling, their suffering, their hopes and dreams.

Aparecida, in her thirties, blond, worn but still pretty, offers to show me around the camp and explain how everyday life can function with somewhere between nine and twelve hundred people living in close quarters on the roadside.

"We live in groups of twenty families," she says, leading me down the steep bank among the orderly rows of tents. "Each group has its own well and latrines. We do our washing down in the river. The groups have their own representatives, and we also have committees who deal with health and hygiene and education. Oh yes, and with information. It's important to keep our *companheiros* informed on our progress and keep in touch with what's going on outside the camp. And there's the animation group—they tell us what is happening in other camps, and remind us what we're fighting for. We sing songs and encourage each other. Because it can be difficult, you know. Sometimes we're short of food, and there's always a level of uncertainty, and sometimes we get afraid. Like when the rancher sends his gunmen driving along the road firing their guns into the air. We have to keep our spirits up. And of course we have to have security guards on duty twenty-four hours a day.

"I'm working in the supplies committee. No, we don't grow any food in this camp. We haven't got any suitable land, although we do have a few small vegetable plots down by the river. So we have to go round asking for donations. The government gives us some food, and one or two of the churches, and there's even a rancher who lives nearby who sends us a bit of meat once in a while.

"At the end of the day we all get together to hear the news. We talk about the workers' struggle, and we think about some of our heroes like Che Guevara and Chico Mendes and Karl Marx. It's important to understand that we are part of something much bigger than ourselves, and that way we see that even if we have to go through hard times now, in the end we shall get what we are fighting for: a piece of land for ourselves and our children so that they can live a decent life. We're fighting to make Brazil a better place to live. So that families don't have to live in the *favelas* and their children don't have to live in the street. We're fighting for the young people so they won't get mixed up in drugs and prostitution and ruin their lives, so they can have a piece of land to grow their food, and can live decently and buy the things that young people want, and not have to steal."

Aparecida's eyes are shining, and I can see that she has caught the vision.

"So you're happy here?" I ask.

"Goodness me yes!" she answers roundly. "Mind you, there was a time when I despised the landless movement. That was when I was living with my husband before he got killed. I could never have imagined myself living in a black plastic tent by the side of the road! But I didn't understand what it was all about. I was perfectly happy where I was. And then he was murdered and I was left on my own trying to raise three kids. I had to move to the town and take in washing. It was hard, I can tell you. There was never enough money. One of the children would need a pair of sandals, or some medicine, and I was working harder and harder and I never could get out of debt. And then I sat down and thought about the landless movement and I figured things couldn't possibly be any worse than they were already. So I put my name down and here I am."

I wish I could hear more, but it's two o'clock and people are making their way toward the assembly room for the afternoon session. Aparecida and I squash ourselves into the corner of the room, which already holds nearly a hundred people. I settle on the floor and look around. They are a mixed bunch, in appearance, color, and age. Each one introduces himself and says a word or two, and I learn that they come from all over the country: São Paulo, Minas Gerais, Maranhão, Goiás. They'd been small farmers, sharecroppers, squatters, laborers, people who did odd jobs or sold things on the sidewalk. Many of them had worked in the gold mines.

Tonhão, in his mid forties and very self-possessed, speaks for himself and his twenty-year-old son. They were both stuck in the jungle on separate *fazendas,* both terrorized by gunmen, both succeeding after several attempts at running away. A man in a red T-shirt tells us the story of Zezinho de Codespar when the peons were burned to death. A skinny old man with a straggly beard was on a *fazenda* way north of the Amazon River where all the peons went in by air and the managers spoke Spanish. He'd seen a man flayed alive and had been so frightened that he had run away through the forest and walked for thirty days until he came to a settlement. By the time he got there he was more dead than alive, but he told the police and they went in and rescued the workers.

Someone tells the story of Fazenda Santo Antonio when the *gato* had refused to pay and the peons had staged a revolt and gone after him with their machetes. A tough old cowboy in a green-and-yellow shirt with a bright blue hat tells how he worked with cattle for three years and never received so much as one calf in payment. A bearded black with round gold glasses takes notes in the corner. Everyone agrees that slave labor exists, even if they hadn't recognized it. The important thing is to be aware of the dangers. To talk about it with friends and family. To encourage people to join the union so they won't be alone. Never to take a job without knowing where they are going. Leaving word with their families. Knowing who to contact when things go wrong.

The day ends with the general assembly. As the sun hangs low in the sky and smoke rises from a hundred cooking fires, men, women, and children stream to the central meeting point, carrying their sickles, hoes, and machetes. Someone gives an account of the seminar, someone else talks about the work gang that is to leave tomorrow at dawn, they sing a couple of songs and then disperse to their tents. The CPT Toyota is surrounded by at least fifty people clamoring for a ride to town. Good-humoredly Xavier points out the space limitations and after some hard bargaining the lucky ones climb aboard and the rest wave us good-bye.

As I sit squashed in the front between Xavier and a pregnant woman with two small children, I reflect on the events of the day. Cliché or not, it really seems almost too good to be true. The MST has created a society where everyone is valued for himself, where women and children, young and old have an equal say, where the notoriously carefree Brazilians are living under the discipline of a boot camp and yet seem united, purposeful, and self-confident. It was clearly a lot better than the alternatives. Here was a group of people who had been sharecroppers or squatters, or had never owned any land. Some of them had had periods of relative stability until something had pushed them over the edge. They had lost their jobs, or their land, or their health, or their families. Others had drifted from one job to another, from working on the ranches to working on construction to trying their luck in the gold mines. All of them had ended up landless and desperate. And they had been given a glimmer of hope, the prospect of having a piece of land so that they could feed their families. It was a dream that made it worth their while to live in a plastic tent, to invade a *fazenda* in the night, to construct another plastic shelter, to be moved out, to set up on the roadside, and to wait for another chance. Some of them would lose heart and drop out. But others would hang on and make it through. They would face camping out for months on end, enduring cold, rain, hunger, and uncertainty. They would face policemen and *pistoleiros,* and constant fear. I could see why the government was nervous.

11

The Vila Rica Commission

One Town's Attempt to Deal with Debt Bondage

V ila Rica, Mato Grosso, is an unattractive little town, and
it's a grindingly long, uncomfortable journey to get there.
But it has a special place in the story of modern slavery,
for it was here that the local people set up a commission to find
out what was going on, and to do something about it. Ricardo
and I want to find out what they have done, so together we board
the bus in Redenção and settle down to one of those interminable Amazon journeys that leave you stiff, sweaty, and dazed.
When we finally haul into the bus station after innumerable hours
spent swerving wildly around potholes and inhaling generous
quantities of dust, we don't care where we are; we simply want
to get off the bus.

We make our way, via an elderly taxi, to the parish house. It's
a simple wooden structure with a warren of small rooms furnished with hard wooden beds and hammock hooks; out back
there's a chapel, a very small room that serves as a library, and a
brave little bed of vegetables. It's hard to grow vegetables in the
Amazon—they are always getting eaten by something or other—
so every shoot of young green lettuce is to be lovingly watered
and carefully savored. Brother Sebastião bustles up, hospitably
provides us with cold drinks, and introduces us to Sister Aurora.
Smart, feisty, Sister Aurora takes us in hand. Her severe demeanor
hides a soft heart and an acute intelligence. She is anxious for
us to meet the mayor. "Oh yes, of course you'll want to hear
about the commission," she says, smiling, "but it's effectively

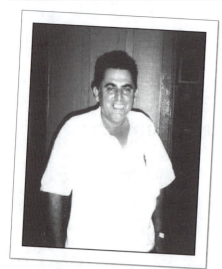

The mayor of Vila Rica

been disbanded under the current mayor. I think you should start by meeting him, to help you get a bit of background."

Leonídio Benedito Chaves, the mayor, is a rotund man nearing fifty, with a puffy face. He's a man with a core of steel; I wouldn't care to cross him. Like so many of the large landowners, the mayor presents himself as a medium-sized landowner, and like most ranchers he blames the labor problems on the *gatos*. "They don't pay the peons, and everyone loses out. It's a serious problem." Many of the ranchers these days, he says, are managing without the *gatos* and doing their own hiring. He's doing it himself.

"These days I do my hiring direct," he tells us. "Everyone knows me, I've been working here since 'eighty-five. You can ask about me in any of the bars around town. No one will speak badly of me. I pay every week; never had a problem. I don't do the work at the expense of the peons. I feed them well and treat them right. And I take out an insurance policy in case of accident.

"This isn't an area of large ranches." Of course, the mayor himself has many thousand hectares, and wicked tongues say that he never actually bought his land . . . "The jobs here are small—clearing pastures, that sort of thing. And I use locals to work for me. In fact I prefer to use family men, people I know. I don't like to use migrant workers. They only give trouble. It's the liquor that does it. Then they start to fight and before you know where you are somebody's dead. That's why I never allow any liquor on the *fazenda*. You can't afford to lose control of the workers. But I make a point of feeding them well. It's like a car. If it's out of fuel it won't go."

We ask the mayor if he thinks it possible to comply with the labor laws when hiring large numbers of peons on short-term jobs.

"Well," he says, sighing deeply, "I'll be honest with you. It's very difficult. Half of them have no papers, you see. Some of them want to work today but tomorrow they don't. You'll get a guy who works fine for a week or two and then just pushes off. You can't secure the labor.

"Here's the way I see it. In the old days there was peace in the countryside. It was when they invented all these labor laws that everything changed. They started talking about all these rights that had never existed before. And the result was twenty years of confusion and conflict."

The mayor stirs himself and shouts for a jug of orange juice. We're sitting on the shady veranda of his modest house, and a line of supplicants is building up outside. He waves at them graciously, and lights himself another cigarette.

"This area," I start, gratefully swallowing the orange juice, "it must have been very tough when you first arrived."

"It was," says the mayor. "It's an isolated area. Abandoned, really. Miles from nowhere. It's a natural hangout for outlaws. Even today violence is part of the culture. It's the culture of the frontier. You can steal a bunch of cattle and slip over the border and vanish into thin air. And drugs! That's a big problem for us. They ought to make this area a priority. Not worry themselves about São Felix do Araguaia. We're the ones on the front line.

"But don't go thinking this is like something out of the Wild West. Vila Rica is a serious town. Full of serious people. Oh yes, they've had their problems. At the time of the great migrations, when the people came in from the south. But things have settled down now."

Back at the parish house we talk to Sister Aurora. "Don't believe a word he says about things settling down," she laughs. "It's a frontier area all right, and there are plenty of people who are up to no good. No good at all. Of course it's partly a question of culture. You couldn't exactly call these ranchers liberals. I'm going to take you to meet Sônia. She was the chairman of the commission. And the interesting thing is that she is the daughter of one of the ranchers. A typical rancher of the old school. It was because of what happened on his place that the police came in. And Sônia found herself mediating between her own family and the peons. Talk about a rock and a hard place!"

Sônia is forty, glamorous. Well coiffed and manicured. Dressed in a tight black short-skirted Lycra dress. Long wavy hair. Bright lipstick. We arrive unheralded, and Sônia starts off reluctantly, pleading memory lapses. It's all water under the bridge and her life has moved on. But as she gets into the story she gathers confidence, and slowly the picture emerges of a courageous woman in a tight spot.

"Well it was all a long time ago," she begins, "after we'd been hit by the Federal Police. They suddenly showed up in town, without any warning, and started accusing us of all sorts of terrible things. Said that the peons on the ranches were living like slaves. Talked as though we were criminals. It was all most unpleasant. Of course the ranchers were upset. Naturally. So we decided we'd better get together and discuss the whole thing. In a civilized fashion. Clear up any little misunderstanding and get the whole thing sorted out.

"I was involved from the start. There'd been a problem on my dad's *fazenda* and the peons were in a really bad state. They had been abandoned by the *gato,* and several of them were really sick with malaria. It was all news to me; I'd never even set foot on the place. Somebody came to my office and told me all about it and I just said, Okay, let's go see what's going on. That's the way I am, see? If there's something wrong I want to fix it. Well, we discovered that the peons hadn't been paid at all. Worse still, there wasn't any money to buy food. It turned out that one man had been killed in an accident when they were clearing the forest, lots of them were sick, and they were living on rice and water. It was a terrible thing.

"It wasn't my dad's fault. He had paid up front but the *gato* had done a runner and left everyone flat. I must say that the police weren't at all sympathetic. They just said that they didn't care whether my dad had already paid or not, the fact was that the peons hadn't had their money and that he'd have to pay them. A bunch of peons showed up at his office to demand their money, and my dad got so angry that he made himself ill. He's got a heart condition, and can't take any strain.

"Naturally the whole town was upset. Divided right down the middle. On the one hand were the ranchers and their union and on the other were the workers and their union. I was the chairman of the town council and we had a meeting straight away and agreed that something must be done. So we decided to form a commission to look into the whole question of labor relations. We couldn't have the town in a state like that. After all, we'd always been such a united little community. We threw the commission open to all parties. There were representatives from the town council, the church, and both the unions. All the factions involved.

"We thought to ourselves, let's just sit down and see if we can sort this out. We felt we needed to get a clear perspective on what was happening on the *fazendas.* The police had succeeded in putting the whole community at loggerheads, and we couldn't leave it like that.

"And it's hard for people from outside to understand what is going on. It's a question of culture, you see. The Feds came in all heavy handed. No, they didn't handle it well. Their arrival was a shock to the whole community. Because we hadn't really known what was happening. Most ranchers very seldom actually went to the *fazendas*. They hired the *gatos* to do the work. They never knew that some of the *gatos* were cheating the peons. It was none of their business, they just wanted the job done. And then all of a sudden the police showed up out of a clear blue sky, insisting that it was all the fault of the ranchers! Well, they didn't see it that way at all. And then the Labor Department explained that the ranchers were responsible, had been all along. So naturally they felt that everyone had suddenly turned against them. I mean, it wasn't as though they had done anything wrong. And there's the police telling them they've got to do this and they've got to do that, and they've got to look after the peons if they get malaria. People were always getting malaria, that wasn't anything new.

"We members of the commission, we weren't against anyone. We saw our job as being simply to listen to people, and not to judge them. We set up a process whereby the ranchers and the *gatos* could negotiate. Our objective was find a space for everyone to get together and see what could be done. And I think we were pretty successful."

As we walk out into the hot sun, Sister Aurora tells us that the commission only lasted for a couple of years. Then there was a change of administration and it lapsed. Her guess is that the ranchers managed to squash it. But it was remarkably successful. The commission did manage to show the ranchers that they were responsible for their workers, and that was a huge step in the right direction. "I'll show you a newspaper cutting about Sônia's dad," she says with a grin. "You wouldn't want to tangle with him, I can tell you."

I check out the article[1] and study the photograph. Sônia's dad looks very large and very angry. "I'm up to here with peons,"[2] he is quoted as saying. "From now on I'm going to mechanize my entire operation."

As I sit in the parish house that evening and write up my notes I reflect that Sônia must indeed be an extraordinary woman, and exceptionally courageous. Her urge to sort things out must have infuriated her father. I wonder if that relationship has been patched up, or if, more likely, her family threw her out. I decide to go back and find out more.

I track her down the next evening just as she is finishing her day's work, and she invites me to accompany her on her evening walk. We take a long circuit around the garbage dump, out into the countryside, and then back to the gas station.

"Did you know that this town is famous for the work you did with that commission?" I say without preamble as we stride along a dusty path between dusty fields.

"Is that so?" Sônia opens her eyes very wide.

"It certainly is," I answer, "and it sounds like you were a bit of a heroine. After all, it must have required a lot of courage on your part . . . "

Sônia smiles. "Well I won't pretend it was easy," she says, "but I do believe that you have to do what you have to do, come what may. And at the time it just seemed the obvious thing."

"Could you tell me about it?" I ask. "What was the sequence of events, how you felt at the time, how you feel now?"

Sônia hesitates for a fraction of a second, and then takes a deep breath. "It was like this," she says. "I was sitting in my office one evening when they came to tell me there was a problem on the *fazenda* and that somebody had called the Feds. Something about a group of peons who hadn't been paid. It was the police chief who called me out. Well I didn't hesitate. I didn't have anything to hide. I'm like that, I'm a very open person. I said: All right, let's go see what's going on. When I went in and saw what a state those peons were in I knew we'd have to do something.

"The police tried to get after my father but he wasn't well, he had high blood pressure and he never could cope with strain. So I told them I'd deal with it. He didn't see why he should pay the peons since he'd already paid the *gato,* but I finally persuaded him. After all, they'd done the work. So I called in Raimundo the overseer. He knows everyone. I said: Here's what we'll do. We'll call the peons one at a time and see who worked and who didn't. Because there's always some good-for-nothings who pretend they've been working when they've never been near the place.

"So that's what we did. We had them in one by one, and they told me how long they'd worked, and if Raimundo confirmed that then I paid them and made them sign. The Labor Department people were there, too; it was all open and above board. But my dad took it very badly. It's hardly surprising.

"It was after that that we set up the commission. I'd like to say that part of the commission's job was to orient people. We discovered that the peons had been lodged in rooming houses and had run up debts. So we advised the ranchers not to give out advances to avoid the business of debt. Sometimes they had to, though. Every rule has its exception! We encouraged the men to register with us if they were looking for work, so that we could monitor their movements. We thought that it would put things on a more solid footing, but some of the peons refused. They had no papers, you see, and some of them had criminal records. Some were fugitives from justice. It's only to be expected in a border area like this. And then of course the *gatos* didn't like it. They'd got a little deal going with the women who run the rooming houses, and they didn't want us to interfere."

We cross a small country road and then turn back toward the town. "The commission consisted of the ranchers and their representatives and the workers and their representatives, isn't that right?" I inquire.

Sônia nods.

"Both sides must have felt they'd been wronged and tempers must have been high," I venture.

Sônia smiles.

"So however did you manage to get the two sides together?" I finish.

Sônia stops abruptly and turns to face me. "Look," she says, "it's never easy to change things. We had to believe that it would work. Don't you see?"

"And did it?"

There was a long pause.

"Things were never the same again," she says passionately. And she isn't just thinking about the commission.

Sister Aurora is intrigued when I tell her of my conversation with Sônia. "Her memory tends to be a little selective," she tells me. "But there's no doubt that she's a brave woman. And now I think you should go talk to the man from the rural workers' union. He'll give you a different angle."

I have the distinct impression that I am being managed. Very well managed too.

The union leader is called Rowilson and, judging from his stomach, he has done well by himself. He lives in a neat little house, and while we talk to him his wife is doing the family wash out back. We arrange ourselves in a row on the plastic sofa, which is strategically placed to give the best possible view of the heavy wooden dresser, crammed with an assortment of kitsch.

"They want to know about the commission," announces Sister Aurora. "So I took them to Sônia's place and now we've come to you."

"So she told you the story of her father's *fazenda*?" Rowilson squints at us. It's difficult to conduct a conversation when we're sitting in a row like guests at wedding in India. "Nossa Senhora da Fátima. I never got to go there myself. But it was a terrible situation. The peons were living on a diet of rice and water, and a lot of them were sick.

"They did their best to keep visitors out. Chained the gate and padlocked it. The police had no choice but to take it off its hinges. And then when they got to the house there was no one there. Sônia's brother was the manager and he'd run off into the woods. When he finally showed up he did his best to make sure that no one found anything, and it was only by chance that they came across the labor camp. There were somewhere around thirty peons there, and every last one of them sick and undernour-ished. The police decided to take them all out there and then. When they got to town they all went in a body over to Antonio Delgado's place and demanded their money. But he wouldn't even talk to them, so they had to go and call Sônia.

"Sônia had to negotiate with her own father, and that was a tough call. She's a smart woman, and she'd never have got her-self into that situation if she hadn't been pushed into it. It must have taken a lot of guts.

"We'd been hearing stories about slave labor for years. But we could never put our finger on anything. Like that story of the fire over in Pará that killed all the peons. Back in 'eighty-eight or 'eighty-nine. Or the story of all those peons who disappeared over on Romão Flores's place. We were never able to verify any-thing there either. Of course it's a huge ranch: a hundred thou-sand hectares or more. We kept hearing rumors, but we'd never actually been able to get any concrete proof.

"The first real proof was from the Ana Paula ranch. Back in 'ninety-five, it was. One of the peons' wives managed to escape and she went and told the priest what was going on. She said that things were so bad that a whole lot of peons had run away, with the *gato* after them. One of them was her husband, and the *gatos* caught him and tied him up. The priest told us and we called the labor people in Brasília, and they sent in a team of inspectors. They arrived at night, and we had a briefing meeting and they left at four in the morning. The woman went in with them, and they found her husband still tied up. And they got all the peons out of there and brought a lawsuit against the rancher.

"Of course the whole town was buzzing. There were national repercussions and the ranchers were furious. They thought it was a put up job by the Workers' Party and the church. But once the first case had come up then we started hearing about others.

"Well, we reckoned we must get together and sort something out. The object of the commission was to clarify the situation, not to condemn anyone. We involved all parties: the ranchers' union, the workers' union, the church, the Labor Department, and the town council. We had several meetings of the whole commission, including the government people and the ranch-ers. Of course some of the ranchers were against it, but what would you expect?

"After the government people had left we had to figure out how to keep going. We had several meetings of the whole commission, but a lot of the decisions were taken internally by a small group. Three or four people whom we could trust. We had meetings of this inner clique to decide if the situation warranted calling in the people from the labor office. We had to work in utmost secrecy. We couldn't trust the ranchers. Half of the time they wouldn't talk to us anyway. The owner of the Ana Paula ranch lived in another state, for example. Sônia's dad refused to have anything to do with us, and we couldn't get onto his *fazenda* to talk to the peons. It was too dangerous. And there were other cases where it was a question of life and death.

"Yes, the commission was a success. We did a good job and changed a lot of things. No, I wouldn't say that we changed the culture. Not the culture of the ranchers. They don't change their spots so easily. But it's the peons who have changed. They won't accept bad conditions any longer, and they're much more aware of their rights. They're getting a lot more active. For example, they're not afraid to go and tell the church or the union if they're being badly treated. And that's a big change, believe me!"

"He's quite right," Sister Aurora confirms when she hears our account of the conversation with Rowilson. We're sitting in her airy kitchen with its latticed wooden walls overlooking her flower garden, and drinking cups of delicately flavored lemongrass tea. "About the peons, I mean. They are getting much more involved. It was a good thing, that commission, even if it was thrust on all parties concerned. They'll all tell you it was their idea but in fact the idea came from the government inspectors. It was quite an achievement, getting both sides to sit at the same table—even though they all kept their secrets and never really trusted the other side. I think the main lesson that everyone learned was that the ranchers couldn't just go on having everything their way and taking no responsibility for what was going on out on the *fazendas,* and the peons learned that things could be different and that they could take charge, to some extent, over their own lives. That's a tough lesson, because it implies taking responsibility for themselves. But it's all about being citizens of Brazil and children of God, isn't it? All of us equal in His sight."

12

A Case History

Slavery Through the Eyes of a Peon and His Wife

Outh of Vila Rica the road runs straight as an arrow for more than six hundred kilometers to Barra do Garças, and there's not a whole lot on the way there . . . as Ricardo and I discover to our cost when our borrowed vehicle develops a puncture and subsequently proves to have neither jack nor wheel brace. It is a bakingly hot morning, we are plagued by swarms of sweat flies, and we're left sitting under the sparse shade of the only tree within sight long enough to make us irritable with ourselves and with each other.

But God is good and eventually a truck driver materializes out of a cloud of dust, fixes us up, and sends us on our way for what turns out to be a surprising interview with a twist to its tail. We are on our way to talk to Domingos Pinto Fonseca, who was involved in one of the more notorious of the recent cases over in the Xingu region: on Fazenda Maciel Two.

We were given approximate directions, and it's not yet midday when we track him down on a long dusty trail in the middle of nowhere. Domingos and his family live in a simple house made of saplings with an earth floor. The front room is furnished with two of the ubiquitous plastic sofas—hot, slippery, and uncomfortable to sit on—and a table on which reposes a blue spotted cloth and an open Bible. A water filter sits in the corner of the room, small items like toothbrushes are casually tucked into the thatch of the roof, and a handful of scraggly chickens keeps wandering in, only to be shooed out by the nearest person. Domingos is a skinny little man who looks older than his fifty-something years. He has an impressive mustache that is too large for his face, and exceptionally bushy eyebrows. His wife, Zilda, pops in and out of the kitchen, which is separated from the front room by a flimsy sheet, and several small children are impartially shooed out along with the scraggly chickens.

Domingos settles down on a wooden stool to tell us his story. "I'm not from here," he starts, "I'm from Goiás. But I've worked all over, Tocantins, Mato Grosso, Pará. Worked on so many *fazendas* I can't remember all their names. Half of them I never knew anyway. Some of them were okay, others weren't. There were some that wouldn't even let you leave if you were owing. Quite a few, in fact.

"Why did I go? Well, I wanted to work, didn't I? I'm not one to sit around and starve to death, oh no. I wanted to go with my friends. And I made money, oh yes. All those weeks in the forest and suddenly you're free as a bird with a little money in your pocket. You can buy whatever you want: a pair of boots, a new pair of jeans, a hammock. A drop of liquor . . .

"But you were asking about Maciel Two. It must have been 'ninety-nine when I was there. The *fazenda* is over in Tucumã, and the *gato* who took us in was Antonio Avelino. I've worked with him before. He was a good man; I had no complaints. It was a big job and there were a lot of us in there. There were a hundred

Domingos and family

eighty-nine of us went in, in six buses. A big group, hey? Oh yes, he gave me an advance. Sixty *reais* it was. I bought a hammock and some boots. No, we didn't pay the bus fare. What was the food like? Nothing special but it was all right. The cook traveled ahead of us and when we arrived the food was all ready.

"When we got to the turnoff the buses couldn't go any further, and we all had to get out and wait for the truck. But we had to wait a long time because it had got stuck. It finally arrived and picked us up and took us almost all the way in. Of course we had to keep pushing, and finally it got bogged down so badly that it couldn't go any further. So we all got out and walked.

"That evening there was a discussion among the men. None of us were happy about the terms. They'd offered us ninety *reais* an *alqueire* under the *cativo* system for every *alqueire* we cleared. You know what that is, don't you? It means they pay a better rate, but we have to pay for own food. The other system is called *livre*. They pay you less but they supply all the food. So the deal was ninety *reais* an *alqueire* divided among the whole team, Saturdays and Sundays off, and free meat. When we saw the place we had to work, well, we knew at once that the money wasn't enough. It was thick jungle and it would take us several days to clear an *alqueire*. Divide ninety *reais* by the members of your team and discount all your food and you'd end up working for nothing. A lot of the men told the manager they weren't going to stay, and he wasn't too pleased, I can tell you. He told us he'd go off and find some more peons: real men who weren't afraid of hard work. But when he brought them in they didn't want to stay either! Mind you, you couldn't just walk off the job. Not with all those *pistoleiros* hanging about. They told us that if we wanted to leave we'd have to go on our feet, since they couldn't be running peons backward and forward all the time. They had work to do. In the end things got so bad that they put a guard post on the road. But they couldn't stop people from leaving, even if they had to walk every step of the way. And one of them was so mad that he called in the Feds.

"The first we knew about it was when we heard this tractor. I thought I must be dreaming, because there wasn't any road. Well, I climbed up a little bank by the river to get a good look and I saw them, a whole lot of policemen sitting on a tractor! They brought a large lady who turned out to be their chief, of all things.

Her name was Valderez. And she said to me, Get your stuff together because we're going to get you out of here. Well, there were lots of other gangs of peons scattered around in the forest, and they told us to go and tell them. At that point there were maybe a hundred men left. The big lady got us out of there, and she made sure that we all got our pay. She told us that the working conditions weren't fit for human beings, but she didn't have to tell us that; we knew it already! A lot of the guys were sick. Scratches and cuts and bites. Malaria. And foot rot. We were working up to our knees in mud half the time, our boots rotted, and we had terrible problems with our feet.

"Do you know something? I was never afraid. I'm not afraid of dying, and I'd never run away. The ones who ran away were the gutless ones. They didn't have the guts to pay for their food. I mean, if a man owes, he has to pay. They should have settled up at the very least. If they didn't like the terms they should have asked for a raise. If they didn't want to work they should have said so."

His wife, Zilda, bursts through the curtain from the kitchen to join the conversation. "That's the trouble with Domingos!" she says angrily. "He's as honest as the day. He committed himself to the job and he wasn't about to run out. But he had a terrible time. He ran a thorn deep into his foot and the nurse took it out without anesthetic. There was a man called Wesley who ran the canteen and he was a thief . . . "

"He was all right," interrupts Domingos. "I was in charge of getting the food for our team, and he always noted everything down in his little book."

"Did he tell you how much things cost?" I inquire.

"Of course not!" says Zilda with a note of scorn in her voice. "They never do. Only when it's time to settle up, and then they charge what they please. You told me so yourself." She turns to Domingos indignantly. "He never weighed things properly. He used to dole out rice by the handful. One handful, one kilo he used to say. The only thing he did weigh properly was the meat. And as for that *gato* Antonio Avelino! He said he'd pass on your money, but he never sent a penny. I tried to call him I don't know how many times, and I could never get him. And me stuck out here with no money. It was enough to drive us to despair."

Domingos:	(obstinately) "I told you like it is. The *gato* never did me any harm. He said he'd send money to the families if we wanted. I was going to send some, but then the Feds came in."
Zilda:	(to us) "We were practically starving to death. I was about to sell my furniture."
Domingos:	(to us) "I got my advance. Sixty *reais* it was. I didn't ask for more. I don't like to be in debt."

Zilda snorts, and Ricardo leaps into the breach before the conversation can degenerate into bickering. "Domingos," he says with a wide smile, "can you describe a typical day on the *fazenda*? What did you do?"

Domingos:	(surprised) "What did we do? Well, we got up at five, we worked all day, and then we went to bed. That's to say I was the one who got up at five because I had to cook the lunch. The others got up a little later."
Ricardo:	"What did you do in the evenings?"
Domingos:	"We used to sit around and talk. Sometimes we'd play cards. On Sundays we'd have football games. No, I don't play myself, I'm too old. But I used to."

"Did you mix with the overseers?"

"Well," says Domingos, "there were three guards. They used to carry revolvers. No, they didn't play football with us. Neither did the manager. In fact, he didn't talk much to us at all. He told us what the job was and left us to get on with it. Five hundred *alqueires* it was. Dense forest to be cleared. We must have done about half when the Feds came in.

"Like I said, some of the guys were afraid of Bibiano. He was the supervisor, and he always carried a gun. But I liked him. And he liked me because I was a good worker. He never had to tell me anything more than once. If it hadn't been for the Feds we'd have finished another section. And then I was going to send you some money." He glances at Zilda but she refuses to catch his eye.

Domingos explains that he never liked to take a large advance. That way he wasn't obliged to stay if he didn't like the job. But no, thank God, he never had to run away.

Ricardo:	"If the *gato* told you a lot of lies would you run away?"
Domingos:	"Sure I'd leave. No one would kill me. It's all a lie, this story of killing peons. Except if they're owing, of course. If a man owes money and runs away then of course they have to kill him. It's obvious."

Zilda bursts into the conversation. "I want to tell you something," she says vehemently. "It's about the *fazenda*. Maciel Two. Do you know who it belongs to? It belongs to my father's family."

Ricardo:	(startled) "What?"
Zilda:	"Jeová Pimentel is the man who owns it, and I was raised by his family. My mother gave me away when I was two. It was Jeová's grandfather Joaquim who raised me. I lived with them in Goiânia."

Ricardo and I exchange startled glances as Zilda presses on.

"Yes, I don't look like the daughter of a rich rancher, do I?" she says defiantly. "But I consider them my family. Although they treated me more like a servant than a daughter. I did all the cooking, cleaning, and washing. They didn't treat me like an equal. I had to do all the work, and I was always the last to eat. They never once bought me any new clothes, and I didn't get any schooling. Second grade, that's as far as I went. They only got me my birth certificate on my wedding day and I overheard them say they must register me under my father's name otherwise I might want my share of their money.

"But I must say that I am grateful to them because I learned a lot. I consider them my family. There was one time when I got really sick, and I called them and told them I was coming down to see them. But I didn't want to ask them for money to pay my fare, so it took me another six months before I had saved up the money. When I got there I had to have surgery and they paid for everything. All done privately.

"But now it's all different. Since the police went into the *fazenda*. Domingos was one of the people who testified and my family was furious because they thought we should have been on their side. A few months back I called Jeová's family and they said that as far as they were concerned I might as well be

dead and they never wanted to see me again. I never expected to
hear that. It made me cry.

"Jeová was convicted, you know. But he never went to jail.
And I don't believe he was guilty. It was all the fault of the *gato*.
He got it wrong from the start. He took all the peons in before
the land was even divided up into lots, and they had to stay in
there eating their heads off for almost a month before they could
begin work.

"I was worried about my old man. He can't read or write; he's
a real country bumpkin, what does he know about the world? I
thought he'd never get out of there alive, I tell you. I talked to
Rodolfo, he's Jeová's cousin. I told him to tell Domingos that I
needed him back here. But he never came. Just stayed there
working himself to death without pay."

Domingos:	(resentfully) "After we got onto the *fazenda* we all had a meeting and we finally agreed about the money. It wasn't much but it would do. And nobody ever told me you wanted me to go home. Anyway I wouldn't leave till I paid off my debt."
Zilda:	(glaring at him) "You just listen to me, old man! You went there in January and left me with sixty *reais*. I called Rodolfo and begged for more money. I said I couldn't manage here on my own and I needed you back. And they said they'd tell you but you never came . . . "
Domingos:	(even more resentfully) "I was going to send you some money when I had finished the next contract. It was all agreed. But the police came in."
Zilda:	(furious) "If they hadn't come in you'd never have got anything, you old fool!"

Things are getting distinctly uncomfortable when we are saved
by a short sharp tussle that breaks out between two of the dogs.
In the subsequent flurry of shushing and shooing out, the tension is broken and we all laugh.

Zilda looks at Domingos in exasperation. "Let me tell you one
thing." She turns to us. "When my old man came back from there
he was half crazy. Thin as a rake. Good for nothing. I had to get
some medicine to calm him down. Mind you, I never wanted

him to go in the first place. I said to him: Old Man, don't go. I'll sell my things in town to buy some cows, and we'll do all right. But he's obstinate as anything. He would go. He said he'd make more money that way. But he never did."

Domingos tells us that he left the *fazenda* with 503 *reais*— money he certainly wouldn't have gotten if it hadn't been for the intervention by the police. I was later able to check his account against their report.[1] Its stark format made the story sound even more chilling. They started with the bald facts.

The name of the *fazenda* is Maciel Two. There is some confusion as to who is the owner; the title deed states that it is Jeová de Souza Pimentel, whereas he says the property belongs to his cousin Haroldo. Haroldo later claimed that the *fazenda* had formerly belonged to him, but that he had sold it to his cousin and now owned the adjoining property.

Such confusion over the titling is a convenient way of avoiding responsibility, and since we are talking about not working ranches but patches of virgin jungle, it is all too easy to cloud the issue of where the boundaries are located. In the case of Maciel Two it is very likely that neither party has legitimate title, since the *fazenda* lies in an area claimed by the Parakanã Indians.

The inspectors managed to locate 180 peons who had been there for three months without pay. They later discovered that almost twice that number had previously been working there, but that many of them had already left. In the early stages the workers were not physically prevented from leaving, but they were effectively held prisoner by the extreme isolation of the *fazenda*.

The peons stated that they were badly treated, badly fed, and frequently sick. They pointed out that the price quoted before they started work was not the same as the price offered when they reached the *fazenda*. They said they were supervised by armed guards, and that the manager Rodolfo always carried a rifle. They complained that the food was expensive, the water unfit to drink, and conditions were terrible. One of the people who made a statement was Domingos. He told the police that the work was tough and there was a lot of sickness. He was particularly indignant about the fact that after they had been rescued by the police the peons had to walk forty-five kilometers on foot in order to get out. He felt that the state governor should have sent a plane.

There is, by the way, a story behind this. Federal inspectors had routinely advised state authorities of impending inspections, but the practice had been recently discontinued due to the fact that it had been impossible to maintain secrecy, and many operations had been aborted. Therefore when federal officials had requested assistance from the state in the matter of evacuating large numbers of peons, the governor had indignantly refused.

The team had quite an adventure getting in. The *fazenda* lies 180 kilometers from Tucumã along an atrocious road, full of immense potholes. Their cars were constantly getting bogged down in the mud, and when it happened for the umpteenth time at one A.M. they decided to stop for the night. Fortunately there was a house nearby, and the owner, Gaucho, appeared out of the night to offer them shelter. Some people stayed in his house and others slept in the car. The next morning they managed to reach the *fazenda* headquarters, only to discover that the manager Rodolfo wasn't there, having allegedly gone off to collect his family. Two of the workers told them they wouldn't be able to get to the labor camps except by tractor.

They then went to find the *gato* and discovered that he had run off into the forest. They inspected the canteen and took possession of the account books. Every transaction had been entered, but there were no prices marked in. They also inspected the sick bay, noting that its inhabitants were in a lamentable state.

They finally managed to get to the camps by tractor, where they found 180 men living in miserable conditions, lodged in decrepit plastic shelters with no sanitary facilities and thick mud everywhere. All the peons without exception wanted to leave, and the inspectors undertook to provide transport—at the *fazenda*'s expense.

Since Rodolfo was due to return imminently the team decided to await his arrival, but he never showed up. So they made their way out, with extreme difficulty, escorted by the tractor.

When they reached Tucumã they called Jeová's house in Goiânia, and were told that Rodolfo would be arriving the next day—which he did. He was accompanied by Haroldo, who stated that he was the owner and that he would settle up with the peons.

A brisk discussion ensued about the amount of money owing to the workers, and there was considerable delay in obtaining the cash.

The Federal Police later arrested Jeová, although he maintained stoutly that the area where the jungle had been cleared was not on Fazenda Maciel Two but rather on neighboring Fazenda Santa Inês, which belongs to his cousin Haroldo. The question of who owned what remained shrouded in confusion, and although there was a map that showed Maciel Two and Santa Inês as being two sections of the same property, Jeová claimed to know nothing about it.

The *gato* did produce a contract signed by Jeová, but Jeová said he was the intermediary, and not the owner of the property. He admitted that he had not received permission from the federal environmental authority for clearing the forest.

Rodolfo Silva Pimentel claimed to have been the manager of Maciel Two since September 1998. He stated that the property did indeed belong to Jeová, and that his cousin Haroldo was the owner of Fazenda Santa Inês. He said that he had been helping out on Santa Inês because Haroldo had been sick and unable to work there himself. He agreed that conditions were difficult, and said that he visited the work camps every second week. He stated that the men bought their food, tools, medicines, and clothes from the canteen (managed by the *gato*) and explained that the high prices were to cover freight costs. He confirmed that the *gato* had received the money to pay the peons, and said that he was not aware that they had not received anything.

Haroldo Vieira Passarinho confirmed that he was the owner of Fazenda Santa Inês where the peons had been working, and stated that he had not been on the *fazenda* for several months due to illness. He had been the previous owner of Maciel Two and had sold it to his cousin Jeová. He had been told by other ranchers that Antonio Avelino was a competent *gato* and that is why he had hired him. He had paid him two-thirds of the price of the contract in advance, and was unaware of the fact that the peons had not been paid. He stated that there were two vehicles on the *fazenda,* one belonging to Antonio Avelino and the other to Jeová. Either of these could be used for transport if necessary. After some initial discussion he agreed to pay all the peons.

Antonio Avelino confirmed that he was the *gato,* that he had been hired to work on Haroldo's *fazenda,* and that Rodolfo was working as the manager. He'd never had any trouble with the police or with the environmental department. He stated that the canteen was run by his nephew Wesley and that all supplies were charged to the peons. He also said that if anyone wanted to leave he could take them to the road—a journey of up to four hours—and from there they could get a bus. He stated that he didn't know Jeová, but did know that he was the owner of Maciel Two.

Antonio Avelino subsequently vanished. There is a case pending against the *fazenda* for illegal deforestation, illegal lumbering, disregard of labor laws, enticement of workers, fraud (citing the two maps in existence, one of which designates Jeová as the owner and the other Haroldo), and slave labor. The land reform agency planned to expropriate the *fazenda,* but was unable to do so when they discovered that it was on Indian lands. Haroldo was later fined R$123,165.10 for labor infractions, but the money has not yet been collected and the outstanding debt has now been passed onto federal debt collectors.

To the inhabitants of Tucumã, the case of Maciel Two became a nine-day wonder. For several days Antonio Avelino, Rodolfo, and Haroldo swaggered around the town attempting to discover who had blown the whistle on them. The Labor Department was hard at work making sure that the peons were correctly paid. With cash in their pockets, the peons enjoyed a brief moment of glory.

But the excitement would quickly fade, the police and government inspectors would go home, and the bars, brothels, and rooming houses would gear up once again. The town would revert to business as usual, and before long another *gato* would show up to take the peons off to work on some distant *fazenda* of the interior.

13

Volkswagen's Model Ranch

What Went Wrong

azenda Rio Cristalino, property of the Volkswagen company, was a model ranching project. As well it might be when you look at the money that went into it. But it wasn't just money; it was state-of-the-art technology, allied to a lot of hard work, and rightly or wrongly they achieved miracles. For a time.

Situated in the south of Pará, in pretty and well-watered hill country, the ranch covered 140,000 hectares and ran 46,000 head of cattle (the projection for 1988 was for 106,000). Unlike the majority of SUDAM-funded phantom ranches, Cristalino was established quickly and managed efficiently. The first tree was cut in September 1973, and within twenty-two months they had established enough pasture to run twenty-one hundred head of cattle.[1]

In its publicity material the company prided itself on the fact that the presence of a firm such as Volkswagen would bring innumerable benefits to the area, by generating taxable income, complying with the labor laws, signing work contracts, registering the contractors, and introducing fair and safe labor practices.

Padre Ricardo described the administrative complex as "a little Brasília in the Amazon." There were offices, garages, workshops, laboratories, a butchery, a bakery, a weather station, a health post, a guest house, a club, a swimming pool, and football pitches. Electricity was generated from two wood-burning steam engines using off-cuts from the timber from their sawmills, they made their own bricks, they ran a supermarket that supplied subsidized meat and milk, and they gave their staff free vegetables. They had a primary school and a fleet of buses, and they ran literacy and sewing classes for the women. Their program of stock improvement relied on insemination and selective breeding, they made silage and hay, and the herd management was entirely computerized. It was a model operation. At any rate on the surface.

But all was not what it seemed. Far from the comforts of the administrative centers were the work camps where the peons lived in plastic shelters and labored to pay off their debts, guarded by gunmen. It was the traditional system of casual labor, and among the managerial staff there would have been few who worried their heads about such things. They had a job to do.

There had been dark rumors emanating from the *fazenda* for some time, and in 1981 José Camilo da Silva made a statement to the CPT[2] complaining of the treatment he had received. From the moment that his group of workers had been stopped and searched at the guard post, José had begun to feel uneasy. "I told my companions that I was afraid they were up to something," he declared, "and we didn't like it any better when we got into the camp. In fact we decided to leave. Well they didn't stop us, not at first. We must have walked 40 kilometers before they came after us, and they told us we'd better get back otherwise they'd start shooting. We were all sick with malaria and by that time we could hardly stand up. But somehow or other we managed to crawl back, and fell into our hammocks. Next thing that happened was that they cut our hammock strings and made us get up and walk past them, and then they started shooting at our feet. After that they made sure that there were gunmen watching us all the time, they worked us seven days a week, and sometimes they didn't even give us any food. Well, I got so ill I had to go to the hospital and the doctor said I might as well go home, because he couldn't do anything for me. I asked the *gato* for my money but I never got any. Not one cent."

Two years later a bunch of peons arrived at the CPT[3] with terrible stories of workers being bought and sold like cattle, of beatings, sexual humiliations, and illegal detention. "It was just like being in jail," one of them said. "Working from sunrise to sunset seven days a week and expecting to be killed at any minute."

The man who got drawn into this whole story without realizing quite where it would lead him was Padre Ricardo. "They called me in because I was the local CPT coordinator," he told me. "There had been rumors about Rio Cristalino over the years, but Cristalino was a particularly delicate case because it belonged to such a large, powerful company and we couldn't go throwing accusations about just like that. We had to have proof.

"When we got the statement from the peons who had managed to escape, we finally had something to act on. We couldn't tell the police, otherwise they'd have alerted the *fazenda*. So we decided to tell the recently inaugurated state governor, Jáder Barbalho. His electoral campaign was based on promises to fight crime in the countryside and to support human rights. But none of it was true. Although he had agreed to give me a hearing in the state capital, he went off to Brasília without any warning. So I took one of the peons with me all the way to Belém—more than a thousand kilometers—on a wild goose chase. Despite that, we sent word to his staff and tried to catch up with him in Brasília. We traveled another two thousand kilometers and then we learned that he was no longer in Brasília but had left for Rio de Janeiro! Well, at that point the only thing to do was to hold a press conference and spill the beans. Well, I thought it would make all the headlines. After all, it was a *big* story and should have made quite a splash. There was a large international company accused of using slave labor, by one of the victims. Plus there were probably another eight hundred slaves in there at that very minute.

But you have to remember that at the time the press was still largely controlled by the government, and they weren't about to pick a fight with a heavyweight company like Volkswagen. In the end the story didn't get a lot of coverage in Brazil, but it did have huge repercussions in Germany and it made a lot of people very upset, including the directors of Volkswagen Brasil in São Paulo."

One state deputy, Expedito Soares, stood up in the assembly and accused Volkswagen of using slave labor. The company denied all accusations of wrongdoing, stated unequivocally that the wages and benefits that it paid to its staff were exemplary,[4] and invited the state deputy to visit the *fazenda* and see for himself.

A commission of deputies, union leaders, and journalists was put together and in July 1983 they left São Paulo for the *fazenda*, accompanied by a group of senior officials from Volkswagen. The deputies had sent word for Padre Ricardo to be at hand, and when they got to the *fazenda* they insisted that he join the commission.

The commission's report[5] made some strikingly inappropriate criticisms. They noted, for example, that the *fazenda* was very large and that it did not make the best possible use of its soils since all the cleared areas had been put under pasture. They criticized the fact that each section of the *fazenda* was run as a separate entity, complete with its own installations and equipment, and referred to the existence of section chiefs as a form of repression. They criticized the salary differences between the professionals and the workers, and they criticized the principal objective of the company: the production of beef for export.

Exactly the sort of comments that a large corporation might expect to hear from a bunch of union leaders with an imperfect understanding of either the workings of big business or even the basic principles of cattle ranching.

But as the commission dug deeper they began to discover more. Two of the cowboys reported that a certain Antonio had attempted to leave the *fazenda*—which had a system of guard posts that required you to have a pass before you could leave—and had been pursued by one of the security guards, beaten up, and handed over to the police. The company confirmed the story and said that Antonio had indeed been turned in because he carried a gun, which was forbidden, as well as being against the law. Authoritarian, perhaps, but hardly illegal.

When the commission investigated the system of employment they learned that apart from the three hundred regular staff, the *fazenda* employed casual labor to the tune of five hundred in the dry season and up to one thousand in the wet season. Casual labor was hired and organized by a series of *gatos,* chief of whom were Chicô and Abilão—both known as notoriously hard taskmasters who didn't hesitate to use violence. Abilão told the commission he had to be tough on the workers because they were a bunch of lazy good-for-nothings who were quite likely to take his money and disappear into the forest. He maintained that his overseers carried guns as a safety precaution. Chicô told them he carried a gun because he moved around the *fazenda* with large sums of money as well as supplies.

The commission visited a neighboring town to meet some of the peons who had formerly worked on Cristalino. Most of them were reluctant to speak, but one or two brave souls described life as on the *fazenda* as "a real jail sentence." They talked of how the peons lived in shelters and were bitten to death by mosquitoes and often sick, and they told dark stories of workers who had disappeared.

Ricardo filled me in on the visit. "Naturally the company was very anxious to impress us by showing us all the wonderful things they had done, the beautiful lawns, the nice buildings, the school, and the club," he told me. "But we didn't want to see the buildings, we wanted to see the peons, and they made sure we never got anywhere near them! It was only by chance that we ran into one of them, and he was looking terrible because he had malaria. You can imagine my surprise when he came up to me, seized me by the arm, and said, 'Are you the padre?'

"I nodded, and then he whispered into my ear, 'You must save me!'

"'Save you from what?' I said, in surprise.

"'Get me out of here!' he said. 'I've been working ten months and they won't let me leave because I owe them money. And now I've got malaria.'

"I called over the other members of the commission as well as the *fazenda* staff and asked him to repeat what he had just said. He was very nervous, but he did repeat it. Well, the manager, Bruegger, was furious. He said to me, 'What sort of a priest do you think you are? I'm every bit as good a Catholic as you are, but you're completely and totally biased. You'll swallow whatever the peons tell you but you'll never listen to our side of the story.'

"We managed to get several statements from the peons, in spite of the fact that the company officials did their best to keep them right away from us. In fact we ended up with more on the company than we had when we arrived. But we weren't smart enough to get to the bottom of things. The team from VW were really clever, they kept diverting the conversation, and we ended up wasting time on stupid little things. I myself was young and accustomed to defending workers on questions of land disputes. I wasn't really equipped to discuss labor laws and criminal procedures, and those members of the commission who were better prepared weren't tough enough. We were extraordinarily ingenuous.

"That night Herr Bruegger gave us a wonderful dinner; a real banquet it was. At the end he got to his feet and announced that he wanted to give me a present. I remember feeling incredibly embarrassed, and deciding that whatever it was I couldn't possibly keep it. But it turned out to be a chalice made out of Brazil wood: a beautiful thing. I stood up and thanked them and then I said that . . . I was going to ask them for two more things! Well of course there was a dead silence and everyone was embarrassed. But I pressed on and I said, right there in public, that what I really wanted to do was to go talk to the peon whom we had seen earlier. I wanted to hear more of his story. And in addition to this I wanted Herr Bruegger's solemn promise that the peon would leave the *fazenda* safe and sound and be taken to Barreira do Campo. Well that was like a slap in the face to Herr Bruegger. He told me he'd put me in touch with the peon but he couldn't answer for his life, since he was so sick. Anyway, after dinner they did take me to find him. By that stage he was in the hospital on a drip. I told him that Herr Bruegger had guaranteed that he could leave, and I asked where he lived. He told me he came from Porto Nacional in Tocantins. Well, as it happened, the bishop there was a very good friend of mine and I asked him to be sure and give the bishop my regards—then I'd know that he had got safely home. But he never got in touch, and I'll always have that doubt in my mind. As to whether he ever left the *fazenda* alive.

"On the first day of the visit when the commission was coming to collect me, they met Abilão, one of the chief *gatos*. He was driving a pickup with a group of peons in the back, and they noticed that one of them had his hands tied. Abilão told them the guy had run away and they'd brought him back because he was owing.

"I told Bruegger later that I thought the system of casual labor was immoral and he laughed. 'Padre,' he said, 'give me the name of one single *fazenda* in the south of Pará that doesn't work this way.' 'Well,' I said, 'unfortunately I can't. But in any case all the *fazendas* that use the system are in the wrong, and that includes Rio Cristalino.'

"Later on the CPT brought a case against the *fazenda* on behalf of the four peons who had escaped.[6] They were claiming their pay, and in the end they got it. Fourteen years later, can you believe? At the first hearing the judge threw the case out and ordered the peons to pay expenses. By the time they managed to place the blame on the *fazenda* it didn't even belong to Volkswagen any longer! But they got their money in the end."

In August 2000 Ricardo and I set off to find out what had become of the peons. We ran one of them to earth in the little settlement of Canabrava, Mato Grosso. It's a village of mud houses thatched with palm leaves, huddling under huge shady mango trees. It could be anywhere in Africa.

His name was José Ribamar, and he had recently moved onto a *posse*—a piece of land to which he hoped to acquire squatter's rights in due course. He'd called some of his friends to a work party to help him clear the thick bush. It was a long way out of town, and it was more by good luck than good management that we finally found him.

Ribamar is in his mid-thirties. Dark, with an exceptionally fine mustache, he looked to me like a classic *pistoleiro*. He led us to the chicken house, where we sat on stools and conducted our conversation against a continuous soporific cackle from the chickens.

"I was seventeen when I went to Cristalino," he told me. "I was hired by Batista, who is the brother of Chicô. He told me the job was in Pará, and said that there was good money to be made. As much money as we wanted. I remember thinking to myself: If it's as good as all that, how come he has to look for workers so far away? There were fifty peons on our truck, and they stopped us at the entrance to the

José Ribamar

fazenda and checked us all out for arms and liquor. And they gave us a blood test for malaria. They didn't waste time, they put us to work right away. We were five on my team, and Zeca was the boss. We took it in turns to do the cooking. I remember that the food was very expensive, and that was a worry. It cost almost twice what it cost at home, and we couldn't even go hunting because we had no guns. We lived on rice and beans and manioc flour with a bit of meat. After we had been there for a while we started hearing stories about people disappearing or getting beaten up. One day I overheard Batista boasting to Chicô about how he had bought us, like a herd of cattle. I got really scared when I heard that. There were armed guards around the place and people said you couldn't leave until you had paid your debt, and you'd never pay your debt because they cheated you over settling the accounts. We heard all sorts of things. They told us there was a woman who was raped in front of her husband. They said he got so mad that he went after them, and then they caught him and beat him up so viciously that he lost his mind. And nobody ever saw him again. They told us that another peon was beaten up and left naked tied to a tree in the forest. We began to be afraid that we'd never get out of there. Maybe they'd shoot us in the back. Maybe they'd burn us to death and throw our bodies in the river."

Ribamar's mother is still indignant when she remembers the story. "He was far too young to go off like that," she said angrily. "Barely seventeen. I never wanted him to go. We'd heard all sorts of stories about life on those *fazendas*. All that talk of malaria and people getting killed, well it worried me. I was convinced I'd never see him again. I cried and cried. No, I didn't forbid him, how could I?"

"I wanted to make a bit of money," added Ribamar. "I wanted to see the world."

"I said to my boy," said Dona Dâlva, appealing to me as one woman to another, "I said, Riba, better you don't go. But he went anyway. I couldn't stop him. They must have been gone for five or six months. We heard nothing, except stories that no one gets out of there alive. If they don't die of malaria they get killed."

"How did you manage to get away?" I turned to Ribamar.

"We hitched a ride with a government agronomist," he told me. "Of course he couldn't take us past the guard post, so we walked round it, through the forest."

"When they got back they were thin as rakes," said Dona Dâlva. "Yellow they were. From spending so much time in the forest. Not a good drop of blood left in their bodies. Still, they were lucky to be alive. When you think of what might have happened . . . "

Fazenda Rio Cristalino

Meanwhile down on Fazenda Rio Cristalino they never quite succeeded in balancing the books. It was hardly surprising, after making such a massive investment. Ten years of losses, together with the continuous trickle of bad publicity and the righteous indignation of some of the shareholders in Germany, led to the decision to sell to the Brazilian firm of Matsubara. They bought it for a song, and made a point of emphasizing their record of good behavior regarding compliance with the labor laws. But they couldn't make it pay, and in 1997 the *fazenda* was auctioned off by Volkswagen, which still held the mortgage on the property.

It was bought by a couple of Brazilian businessmen, Eufrásio Pereira Luiz and José Marcos Monteiro, but by this stage it was too far gone to be easily recoverable. Pastures need constant maintenance in the Amazon or they deteriorate into intractable scrub. Rumor has it that the new owners encouraged a group of landless to invade, hoping that the *fazenda* would then be scheduled for agrarian reform and they could get title to the land. On 2 August 1998 the order was given for expropriation— against a payment of forty million *reais,* which was exactly twice what its new owners had paid for it. The rural workers' union in Santana discovered that Eufrásio Pereira Luiz had already pulled the same trick on one of his properties in Mato Grosso.[7] It was a remarkably simple way of turning a good profit.

In February 1999 seventeen hundred landless families from the area moved onto the *fazenda* and started cultivating the land. Unfortunately for them, in November of that year somebody discovered uranium on the property, and the federal government promptly revoked the expropriation order on the grounds of national sovereignty—without, however, taking any steps to relocate the new settlers. Despite the prevailing state of uncertainty the settlers, who had already had their first harvest, were determined to hang on. But their numbers were small and the estate was large, and there were plenty of other people who saw a golden opportunity to lay hands on a piece of land, or a fortune in timber. Former employees of the company who had quietly been letting off large areas of the remaining pasture for grazing now began to depredate the forest reserve for valuable timbers. Estate buildings were sacked and property stolen, bands of gunmen began to roam about freely, and the settlers were reduced to a state of fear and trembling. Rival groups of settlers moved in to get a slice of the action. Gold miners came swarming in and posted no fewer than 120 separate claims. The federal Department of Mining and Energy decided that they only needed access to some four thousand hectares; the rest of the estate could be used for the purposes of agrarian reform.

By this point the situation on Fazenda Cristalino was completely out of control, and the owners of the estate decided to petition to reinstitute their property rights.[8] The rural workers' union immediately weighed in, requesting that the expropriation order be upheld on the grounds that the existing settlers were using the land productively, and the estate was therefore fulfilling its social function. They hastened to point out, however, that the settlers were being threatened by gangs of armed men, and they formally requested police protection. Their request was echoed by the judge from Santana in a letter dated 11 February 2000 addressed to the police chief in Redenção, in which he described the situation of lawlessness, with conflicting groups of squatters, miners, and lumbermen controlling separate pieces of turf and terrorizing the rightful inhabitants. Names mentioned include Chico da Kombi, Zé Fiscal, and Santilho, all of them notorious in the area. The judge also stated that liquor, arms, and drugs were being trafficked freely, and large areas of forest reserve[9] were being cut illegally. Many of the squatters had given up in despair, but those who stuck it out were squabbling among themselves. Malaria was rife in both its *vivax* and *falciparum* forms,[10] and violence was running rampant. A disastrous ending for a model ranch.

One of the people who has been closely involved with the settlement of small farmers on Rio Cristalino is the leader of the rural workers' union in Rio Maria, Carlos Cabral. His mission is to settle as many landless families on Cristalino as he can. But one of his problems is that he has fought with the workers' union in Santana, and they are supporting a rival group of settlers. Forty, thin, tense as a coiled spring, Carlos is a man marked to die. A man with a charmed life, he has already survived one assassination attempt. I meet him in the hot little wooden union building in Rio Maria, where he works with his brother-in-law Orlando Canuto—another man who narrowly escaped death when he and his two brothers were abducted in April 1990 by men posing as federal policemen. His brothers were both murdered, but Orlando miraculously escaped.

Carlos rapidly sketches out the situation on Cristalino and tells me that they hope to send up to three thousand families onto the land. He already has fourteen hundred registered families on his books, but is deeply concerned that those who settle should be genuinely landless people and not speculators. He is also worried about the group that was allegedly bribed to move onto the *fazenda*. They are members of a small landless movement based in Brasília and nobody in Pará has ever heard of them.

"I went down to Brasília to check them out," he told me. "They were a new organization who wanted to get one project off the ground that would give them a high national profile. I wouldn't be at all surprised if there weren't some larger farmers in their midst—it does happen.[11] Well, I looked at their project and it was certainly well designed. But outsiders know nothing about the realities of life here in southern Pará. They want to farm it collectively. You can't do that without doing a lot of work with the people first. Here in Pará the culture is completely different; it's every man for himself and to hell with the rest.

"We weren't opposed to them joining us. But we did feel we should be in charge. After all, we've been fighting for land ever since 1979 and we've lost a lot of lives. We registered all our families, and then they moved in, but it wasn't smooth going. Far from it! The truth is that we weren't properly organized, we were bickering among ourselves and the government was stringing us along. They're supposed to provide all sorts of support, technical and financial, but they hadn't done a thing. Probably because of the uncertainty about whether the land was really going to be expropriated or not. So the settlers didn't feel at all secure, and most of them were starting to get thoroughly demoralized. Food was a worry, although fortunately the first harvest was excellent, and that gave us enough to be going on with. But the most serious problem is security. Can you imagine what it's like with all those families scattered across the *fazenda* without any kind of support? The place is huge; eighty kilometers from one end to the other, and it's like a battlefield with gunmen running around all over the place. We finally advised them to move out. We pointed out that it was far too dangerous for them to stay. But of course they don't want to leave after all that hard work. Everything they have is in there."

That evening I returned to the union to chat to some of the settlers who were living on Cristalino. They were a mixed collection: two teenaged boys, several men in their twenties and thirties, a middle-aged couple, and an old man with a bristling white mustache. They were all ardent supporters of Carlos. The old man was their spokesman. "We have been in there for more than a year now," he told me, "and we've had our first harvest. The land is good. I got ten sacks of rice and twelve of corn. And I've planted manioc—I've got five thousand plants in the ground. But if the security situation doesn't improve we really will have to leave. There are all sorts of bandits and criminals in there, and sometimes they go around shooting the place up.

"Of course, it's all to do with the question of who the land belongs to. The government talks of expropriation, but they've done nothing. So it's a free-for-all. People like us, people who really need the land, why, we're in the minority. The owners of the *fazenda* have got no control over the place. In fact it's my opinion that they're scared to show their faces. So all sorts of people have moved in, to try to get a piece of the action. They're stealing the timber, they're selling off huge chunks of land, they're renting out the pastures, they're nothing more than a bunch of thieves. Thieves and criminals. And they know perfectly well that the police daren't come anywhere near the place. The more confusion the better, as far as they're concerned. The last thing they want is to have the place expropriated and handed over to people like us."

"Either they kill us or we kill them," said one of the younger men passionately. "This is the biggest land conflict in the south of Pará. And the ones who are causing the trouble are the land grabbers. Some of them are the *fazenda* staff and some of them came in from outside. Of course, the smart ones have made their money and got out, but there are still lots of people trying to get in on the act. It's not as if they really need the land. They're speculators, that's what they are. Taking land from families who really need it. Well, we're not going to let them get away with it. We'll fight them if necessary. We're not going to be the ones who leave."

"I'm only leaving in a coffin!" shouted the old man.

"There'll be fighting," persisted the young man. "There'll be deaths. You'll see."

As I walk back through the darkened streets of Rio Maria I reflect on the case of Rio Cristalino. The waste of money and energy and enthusiasm. The terrible things that took place in the distant forests. The managers in their comfortable houses and the directors in their city apartments. The shareholders back in Germany who created a scandal when they heard about the slaves. The total inability of the successive owners to manage an operation of such complexity. The naked greed of the *pistoleiros* and the land grabbers. The defenseless settlers holing up on their little plots while their representatives squabbled among themselves.

The lives that have been lost and will be lost. And the land itself, reverting to jungle.

If it hadn't been for all the scandal, would Cristalino still be a model ranching operation? Did Herr Bruegger the manager really know what was going on? What about the company directors in São Paulo? If they had known, couldn't they have devised a better way of handling their migrant labor? Could they not have saved the ranch? Would the ranch truly be more productive in the hands of small farmers, and if so what were the steps that needed to be taken to make sure that they could live in safety? Suppose that the government came up with some scheme to settle the former victims of slave labor; if given the opportunity, would they accept? Would they make something out of it? At this late stage, when so much has already been lost, what is the way forward? Will the jungle win in the end? I can't sort out the rights and wrongs of it all. The peons live such precarious lives. Padre Ricardo sums it up in the following poem.

> I'm a short-term worker,
> Captive in the freedom of the forests
> Held fast in the long days
> With no roots.
> Boat without a rudder,
> Life without a past,
> Short-term worker
> On a short stretch of road
> On a short term of life.

14

Model Ranch 2001

A State-of-the-Art Ranch Is Accused of Slavery

O nce upon a time there was a family of Italian descent who lived in the state of São Paulo. They were hardworking, they were visionaries, and they made a lot of money. They founded their fortune on planting sugarcane and making it into alcohol, they'd expanded into the cattle business in São Paulo, Paraná, and Goiás, and they dreamed of establishing a presence in the great empty lands of the north.

There were three sons—Roque, João Luiz, and Fernando—and each of them went looking in a different direction. In 1972 Roque flew up and down the rivers in Pará until he found what he was searching for. On the western bank of the broad beautiful Araguaia River, Roque found a rich rolling land that he felt in his bones would be good cattle country. It was an area that was being opened up for settlement, the government was supplying easy financing, and Roque felt that the time was right. He took a careful compass reference, loaded a Caterpillar truck onto a river barge, and headed off to his promised land.

Today the Quagliato holdings in the south of Pará cover 160,000 hectares and run an immense herd of cattle. Well might they choose for their motto "Transforming Pará into cattle country." Their model operation uses state-of-the-art technology and produces some of the finest cattle in the world. Lots of people think you can't ranch successfully in the Amazon, but the Quagliatos seem to have found the secret. I decided to go and see for myself. So I called the ranch office, and was warmly invited to visit one of the *fazendas* belonging to the Quagliato Group. My host? Roque Quagliato, the man who made it all happen.

Fazenda Rio Vermelho is just off the road that links Marabá and Redenção. As you drive through the ranch gate, through neatly kept pastures dotted with fat white cattle, you could be in Texas . . . if it weren't for the palm trees that invade the pastures and the silhouette of the forest on the skyline.

Although it is a Sunday there is plenty of activity in the ranch office, where I am met by a visiting vet from São Paulo who has come to give an insemination course. "This is Brazil's largest cattle operation," he tells me proudly. "Possibly the largest in the world. We're running between a hundred thirty-five and a hundred fifty thousand head. That requires a hundred trained inseminators. The biggest team anywhere."

A hush falls on the room as Roque Quagliato enters, attended by a small delegation. In his early sixties, he is a man with a presence, comfortably built, with an impressive mustache and a large Stetson. Well spoken, affable, authoritarian, he never has to raise his voice and never has to say anything twice. His side-kick Oskar Bollen is the ranch manager, a vet by training. Close-cropped blond hair and bright blue eyes, his job is to field any awkward questions. He doesn't speak unless spoken to. Quagliato's nephew, Beto, is an animal husbandry specialist. He too has an affable manner. A tough trio, highly professional. I wouldn't want to cross any of them.

Roque Quagliato leads us into his private sanctum. It is a classic rancher's office, with deep leather armchairs, ornate western saddlery, silver harness, photos of champion cattle, and professional magazines in Portuguese and English. Roque is a hands-on rancher who knows every detail of his operation. He paints a graphic picture of the pioneer past when they slept in hammocks under a roof of thatch, talks knowledgeably about herd management, sketches out his plans for pasture improvement, waxes enthusiastic about the future of the area in terms of beef exports, and, like any good farmer, jumps to his feet and invites me on a tour of the ranch.

We climb into an air-conditioned double-cabin pickup and take a look at one of the self-contained administrative units. Each unit has its headquarters, staff housing, corrals, barns, and airstrip. The houses are neatly painted up, and furnished with the trappings of rural respectability: TV, fridge, gas stove, plastic sofa, artificial flowers. The staff and their families chat easily with the boss, but respectfully.

Apart from the permanent staff of cowboys, tractor drivers, mechanics, office staff, pilots and veterinarians, the *fazenda* hires teams of short-term workers for seasonal jobs such as pasture maintenance and fencing. We swing past their housing—tall, airy brick buildings that contain kitchen, bathrooms, a large dormitory, and living space. A row of hammocks hangs neatly in the dormitory, personal possessions are draped over string lines, and a shelf along the side holds several radios and boom boxes. The kitchen is presided over by the cook who is in the process of serving lunch. Eight or ten peons are sitting at a trestle table, tucking into a substantial meal. They come from all over—Piauí, Maranhão, Goiás, and Bahia—and most of them have worked on the *fazenda* several times.

As we drive through the pastures, Roque explains that he is in the process of switching over to intensive pasture management, which will require putting more stock on less pasture on a rotational system. He is justifiably proud of his level of technology. "We are doing embryonic transfers as well as insemination," he tells me, "and we've developed a breed of Nelore/Brangus that is ready for slaughter in just over two years. That's a real breakthrough and should almost double our productivity. And talking of productivity, I think it's time for a spot of lunch." He points the car toward a patch of thick forest. "This is where I built my house. I wanted it to be right in the jungle."

The house looks like something out of a magazine article. A long, low building open on all sides, it is simply and comfortably furnished and surrounded by an emerald-green lawn with a dazzling swimming pool. Scarlet and blue macaws perch in the trees, uniformed menservants bring iced coconut water, and lunch is laid out Brazilian-style on the long polished table. I feel as if I am on a movie set.

A place fit for a king, the ranch did indeed host King Gustav of Sweden on a private visit in 1986. His wife, Silvia, is sister to Roque's sister-in-law. A beautiful ranch, one of many, all run in a highly professional manner, with a genial owner. Yet Fazenda Brasil Verde, one of these beautiful *fazendas*, is the subject of a 1998 petition against the republic of Brazil to the Inter-American

Commission on Human Rights. The charge: *negligence in failing to bring to justice and punish those responsible for repeated use of slave labor on Fazenda Brasil Verde.*

Complaints of slave labor have been brought against Brasil Verde in 1988, 1989, 1992, 1993, 1996, 1997, 1999, and 2000.[1] The *fazenda* is one of the most serious of all the repeat offenders, and in 1999 João Luiz Quagliato was convicted of a criminal offense in connection with the labor laws, although the sentence was subsequently suspended.

The first complaints date from December 1988/January 1989 and were directed against *gato* Zé Manoel, known as Velho Mano.[2] Velho Mano had recruited a bunch of peons in Arapoema, Tocantins, including two underaged boys, Iron Canuto da Silva and Luiz Ferreira da Cruz (Neguinho). After several months with no news, Iron's parents set off to discover what had happened to him. They came across the *gato* by chance, and he told them that the boys had run away. He said that he had gone after them, and that in the course of an argument Neguinho had struck him with a sickle. He had fired his gun after them, he continued, and had not seen them since.

Iron's mother wanted to go find the boys, but Velho Mano did everything he could to dissuade her. He told her that the road was terrible, the workers were deep in the forest, and the boys were not there anyway. Undeterred, she traveled to the *fazenda,* where the manager denied all knowledge of the affair and asked her to leave. She managed to locate the *gato* once again, and this time his story was a little different. He denied shooting at the boys, and maintained that they had taken their money and gone off to the mines. Back in Arapoema, Iron's parents heard rumors that the two boys had been murdered. Their bodies were never found.

Adailton Martins dos Reis was also working on the *fazenda* and stated that Velho Mano was extremely violent, dragging people by the hair, loosing his dogs on them, and not allowing anyone to leave.[3] He added, "We were often hungry, he kept humiliating us, and I heard him many times threatening to shoot the peons." In order to pay off his debt and be permitted to leave, Adailton had had to sell all his possessions to the *gato:* a mattress, a hammock, two axes, two pots, two plates, and two spoons.

As a result of these statements, Superintendent Carvalho of the Federal Police from Marabá did, reluctantly, order an inspection to be carried out on Brasil Verde. But he pointed out that he couldn't do anything until after Carnaval (February 1989), and anyway it wasn't his responsibility since he was assigned to drug investigations. His heart was not in the matter, and even by the customary lax standards of the Brazilian police this inspection was extraordinarily perfunctory. No statements were taken from the peons, nor from the manager, no list was made of who was working there, no request was made to check the contract between the *gato* and the workers, no search was made for arms, and the account books (which register the debts contracted by the peons) were not confiscated. The police were told that the two boys had run away to Fazenda Belém but made no attempt to verify this statement. No further action was taken, and the matter rested there. Their report[4] concluded that they could find no evidence of slave labor.

The ranch managers admitted that workers often ran away, principally when they owed money; noted that one of the *gatos,* Zé Bigode, was holding six peons who had not been paid; and stated that the peons were always complaining about the low price paid per hectare, but the fact was that they had no option since they couldn't find any better-paid work anywhere else. The police noted that the peons were being recruited in the local towns with promises of work in the *fazendas* and told that they would not be required to pay for anything, and that there were recruiting agents who hung out in the bus stations and were paid in cash for each peon that they delivered. Although statements about low salaries and infringements of the labor laws indicated that the peons were indeed being kept under conditions of slavery, the police did not even initiate an inquiry.

A further complaint was lodged against the *fazenda* in 1992 by the CPT,[5] saying that no progress had been made in the case of the two boys Iron and Neguinho and pointing out that there was evidence of the continued practice of slave labor. The police took no action, on the grounds that they had carried out an inspection three years earlier.[6]

By 1993 the *fazenda* was in trouble again, and this time an inspection was carried out by the state labor department. Brazilian

law states that all workers must be registered and be in possession of a signed working contract, but inspectors found forty-
nine workers with no documents, as well as several more whose
documents were not in order and who wished to leave. Once
again they did not classify conditions as characterizing slave labor,[7] although they did send a stiff letter to João Luiz Quagliato
raising several points of law. Each point was carefully rebutted,
item by item. They asked him for a copy of the contract between
the *fazenda* and the *gatos*. He supplied it. They asked the value
of the contract and he told them. They asked questions about
living conditions for the peons, and he told them the answers.
They asked whether the *fazenda* would continue to use contract
labor and he said they would. They asked if there was a chance
of better salaries and he replied that the salaries paid were perfectly fair. They asked what steps the *fazenda* had taken to stop
the *gatos* breaking the law, and he replied that they had not broken the law.

In his letter João Luiz stated, "We utterly deny any allegation
of slave labor. All workers on the ranch have complete freedom
to come and go and are never reduced to conditions of slavery."
He added that accusations of slave labor had never been proved,
and any allegation to that effect was purely malicious. He said
that it was common practice to use short-term workers for pasture maintenance, denied that the pay was laughable, and confirmed that the peons did indeed run away, usually just after
they received an advance. As a result of the police raid the *fazenda*
was charged with enticement of workers and disregard of the
labor laws, but not with the crime of slave labor.

Meanwhile the CPT had been continually attempting to get
some action on the case of the two boys who had disappeared in
1989, but the attorney general's office said that the case was time
expired.[8] They did criticize the action of the police and pointed
out that both the fact of holding workers without payment and
the fact that so many workers were obliged to run away would
have justified opening an inquiry into the possible presence of
slave labor as well as infractions of the labor laws, but said that it
would be difficult at that late stage to carry out a proper investigation. In 1996 the case was shelved.

In March 1997 José da Costa Oliveira stated[9] that he and his companions had been contracted by *gato* Raimundo to work on the estate but had never received any money and added that he and fifty companions had been hidden in the forest and forbidden from moving around the *fazenda* because there was an inspection in progress. He also said that he had been threatened with death if he brought any complaint.

Antonio Pereira da Silva said he'd seen the *gato* threaten and humiliate workers, and Valdemar Veloso Silva stated that they were not allowed to leave while they were owing. Alfredo Rodrigues from Piauí said that his team of eight was earning ten *reais* per *alqueire* cleared. It took them between one and two days to clear one *alqueire,* leaving them with approximately one *real* per head per day before discounts. He said that when they arrived they had to sign a letter of resignation, which meant that if they were later sacked the owner would not have to pay them a series of benefits required by law. He said that the guards were armed and that the peons were humiliated and sworn at by the supervisors. He added that if the supervisor was not satisfied with the quality of their work they were forced to do it again. Despite his complaints Alfredo returned to the *fazenda* four years later, and on that occasion he was rescued once again, this time by state labor inspectors.

In the Ministry of Labor's report[10] on the inspection of Fazenda Brasil Verde carried out between 21 and 30 April 1997, they state that the peons were lodged in miserable conditions and were forbidden from leaving the *fazenda* while they were in debt to the owner, under threat of death. Labor inspectors also discovered blank IOUs which had been signed by the workers, as well as signed statements giving notice to leave their employment, also blank.

João Luiz Quagliato indignantly told a journalist from the *Folha de São Paulo,* "There has never been slave labor on my *fazenda.*" Despite his protests, this time the Attorney General's office did take action, bringing criminal charges against the owner, the manager Antonio Alves Vieira, and the labor contractor, Raimundo Alves da Rocha. The *gato* was accused of slave labor, holding the workers against their will, and interstate recruitment by the use of fraudulent promises. The manager was accused of slave labor and fraudulent recruitment. But since there was no evidence that João Luiz was aware of the existence of slave labor on his *fazenda,* he himself was charged only with certain infringements of the labor laws.

Mr. Quagliato's lawyers argued the toss for nearly two years before accepting the verdict. Since João Luiz was a first-time offender sentenced to less than one year in jail, his sentence was suspended on condition that he kept his record clean for the following two years and donated food parcels to a charity for the same period. The cases against both manager and *gato* are still current; they are being tried for several different crimes, including that of slave labor. Even so, the *fazenda* was obliged to take steps to improve the accommodation, constructing the vastly improved lodgings that were noted in the course of subsequent inspections. They also altered their hiring practices, concentrating on bringing peons from the dirt-poor state of Piauí, where unemployment was high and wages low. The ranch manager commented to a journalist that "the folks from over there are easier to manage."

By that stage it had been nearly ten years since the first accusations of slave labor at Fazenda Brasil Verde had been leveled and although further accusations were subsequently brought against the *fazenda,* no attempt was made to reopen the case against João Luiz. It is worth noting that five other *fazendas* belonging to the Quagliatos had also at different times been accused of slave labor: Fazendas Primavera, Califórnia, São Carlos, Rio Vermelho, and Santa Rosa.

In 1998, after being denounced once again for slave labor, João Luiz Quagliato told the *Folha de São Paulo* that he was the victim of injustice. The attorney general from the Labor Office in Marabá noted that while Mr. Quagliato might deny all wrongdoing the fact remained that working conditions on his ranch had improved enormously.

At this stage—on 23 November 1998—the Center for Justice and International Law (CEJIL) and the CPT denounced the Republic of Brazil to the Inter-American Commission for Human Rights in Washington, D.C., specifically in connection with repeated accusations of slave labor directed at Fazenda Brasil Verde. The charges against the republic were: *not investigating the practice of slave labor in connection with the 1988 disappearance of the two boys, the existence of subhuman working conditions, and the fact that the peons were working to pay off their debts and threatened with death if they wished to leave.* The plaintiffs stated that Brazil was in contravention of the American Declaration of Human Rights, the Universal Declaration of Human Rights, the Supplementary Convention of the United Nations on the Abolition of Slavery, and the 1995 Convention of the World Trade Organization. While such denunciations would not have implied criminal sanctions—since at the time Brazil had not signed the international treaty recognizing the jurisdiction of the international court in Sao José, Costa Rica—they do nonetheless carry considerable weight as moral sanctions, and a serious country such as Brazil cannot afford to be exposed to public condemnation for such negligence in failing to protect its citizens.

Meanwhile, back on Fazenda Brasil Verde, the Quagliatos were soon in trouble again. In 2000 a spectacular raid was carried out by inspectors from the state labor department accompanied by a television journalist. They found eighty peons from Piauí, including Alfredo Rodrigues again. The story told by Antonio Francisco da Silva (who was underaged) and Gonçalo Luis Furtado[11] was all too familiar. He and his friends had been hired by *gato* Meladinho, given an advance, and taken by bus, train, and truck onto the *fazenda*. On arrival they found another group from the same town; eighty in all. The *gato* took their work contracts, saying that he would sign them—incidentally altering Antonio's date of birth so that he no longer appeared to be underaged. The peons complained of working eleven-hour days and of poor food; said that they were supervised by the *gato* as well as by an armed guard; and stated that when they asked to leave, the *gato* punched Antonio, and the manager recommended that they be tied up for two weeks and beaten every day. They were finally able to leave, but only after the *gato* had taken their hammocks, clothes, and shoes in payment of the "debt." (The lawyer for the Quagliato group, Flávio Guimarães, told me a different version of the story. He maintained that the *fazenda* would not employ Antonio and Gonçalo because they had not passed the required medical exams, and anyway they were underaged. He stated that the working contracts had not been signed and the workers had not been paid because they had only just arrived on the *fazenda,* and pointed out that several of the peons had previously worked for Brasil Verde.) By the time the labor inspectors arrived, both the *gato* and the manager had fled.

The inspectors did note some significant improvements. Plastic tents had been replaced by wooden buildings—even if they did leak in the rain. The men were wearing boots instead of flip-flops, and hats to protect them from the sun, and all the paperwork was in order. Despite all this, every single peon, without exception, asked to be sent home. The state labor attorney had no doubt that what was happening constituted private imprisonment, forced labor, and slave labor. Yet he did nothing. Why?

Despite repeated allegations of slave labor—a criminal offense punishable by a jail sentence—the only people to be tried for the crime were the manager and the *gato*. João Luiz Quagliato was awarded a two-year suspended sentence, on condition that he kept his record clean. Yet in clear contravention of the law, no action was taken against him when he was twice accused of breaking the environmental laws (1999) as well as of further infringing the labor laws (2000). Curiously enough, in May 2000 the state labor attorney brought a civil case against him, which was settled by an agreement in which he recognized that the blank IOUs signed by the peons had no legal validity and also undertook to further improve labor conditions on the *fazenda*. He also agreed to dispense with the use of *gatos* and sign working contracts for the new recruits in their hometowns—effectively acknowledging his responsibility toward them from the outset.

One of the finer points of the law that particularly annoyed Roque Quagliato was the stipulation, imposed by the Labor Department, that the *fazenda* must provide drinking fountains for the workers. He told me indignantly that when he had visited the Labor Department in Marabá he had been forced to drink water out of a communal glass. It was this type of demand that stung him into saying that he was being picked up for trifling offenses, adding, "The law is very demanding, and we need more flexibility in order to be able to comply with it." He singled out the presence of the Federal Police on labor inspections as being particularly disagreeable, and fellow rancher Maurício Fraga heartily agreed, saying that the ranchers were being treated like bandits.

As a result of what he undoubtedly felt to be persecution, Roque Quagliato, together with his friends Maurício Fraga and José Coelho Victor, initiated a series of discussions with Labor Ministry officials. These led to the drawing up of a further agreement on 9 April 2002, which stated that any future inspections of their *fazendas*—and they owned twenty-three properties among them[12]—would not include the presence of the police. "We are law abiding citizens and there is no need for all this apparatus," they said. The deal was struck with attorneys from the Federal Labor Tribunal, state and federal labor inspectors, and representatives from the government's flying squad, and it provoked a violent reaction from the CPT. They wrote furious letters to everyone they could think of, pointing out in no uncertain terms that without the presence of the police both inspectors and peons would feel constrained, and it would be far more difficult to bring criminal charges without having a police chief on the inspection team since successful prosecution of charges implies catching the offender in flagrante delicto.

In July 2001 Roque Quagliato gave an interview to the local newspaper in Xinguara. When asked how it felt to be a big-time rancher, he said frankly that it wasn't easy. While other big businessmen were looked up to as heroes, ranchers were considered to be villains and accused of exploiting their workers. Whereas the truth was exactly the opposite: Large ranchers were in a position to treat their workers well and pay them decent salaries. Furthermore, it was thanks to large farmers that Brazil had the world's cheapest food. He added that in his opinion there was no such thing as slave labor in the south of Pará.[13] What there might be were ranchers who didn't sign work contracts and didn't always pay the minimum wage, but he stated that his group had been so concerned about the situation that they had pounded on the door of the Labor Department in order to be able to come up with an agreement that they hoped would be a model for the rest of the state.

The fact that the Quagliato clan enjoys relative immunity from prosecution—with nothing more serious than numerous annoying citations for infractions of the labor laws—sheds an interesting light on the question of impunity among the powerful families in Pará. Corruption is endemic in the state, at all levels from the top downward, and it is clearly not in the interest of the lords of

the land to have one of their number indicted for criminal behavior. This is especially so in the south of Pará, an area that is
making serious moves toward splitting off and forming a separate state—which would be immensely rich due to the mineral
wealth of Carajás. One of the big names in the South of Pará is
Quagliato, and the family would certainly wield a lot of influence in any future state of Carajás.

Like Rio Cristalino, Brasil Verde is a model ranching operation that embodies vision, energy, talent, hard work, and top-of-
the-line technology. Yet until they are finally brought to book,
its affable owners will continue to run their operation—partly,
at any rate—on the backs of a sullen, terrorized labor force that
works for little more than its keep and can be easily discarded
when it is no longer useful. Which raises the question of model
ranches. Models of what?

15

Black Slaves, White Slaves

"I Used to Be Somebody, Now I'm Nothing"—
What Can Be Done?

I f you and I are concerned about saving the oceans and the rain forests, stopping child labor, going after terrorists, using our purchasing power to buy goods that are fairly traded, and supporting equal rights, we should take a long hard look at one of the most important and lesser-known issues of our time: the issue of slavery. Slavery has always been with us—as has smallpox. We are now on the verge of eradicating smallpox. What are we doing about slavery?

A hidden, insidious evil, slavery today—sometimes classified as "white slavery"—flourishes on the back of violence and greed. Its victims are temporary and disposable. Costing nothing, they have no value, and no links are created between master and slave. In the old days of black slavery in the Mississippi Delta or in Pernambuco, slaves were part of their master's property. Born slaves, they died slaves. In exchange for their labor they were clothed, housed, fed, and doctored. For better or worse they belonged to their master; they worked in his fields, cooked and cared for his house and his family, and bore his children. As international pressure grew to abolish slavery, the price of slaves went up so astronomically that it became cheaper to hire indentured labor from Europe and abolish slavery.

Black slaves belonged either in the house or the field, but today's slaves belong nowhere. Black slaves were owned and used; white slaves are controlled and used. Under the feudal system black slaves were part of a settled order of society, recognized and reinforced by crown and church. Under the capitalist system white slaves are recruited as required, worked as hard as possible, and discarded when their usefulness is past. Social, economic, and geographic conditions in Brazil have always made it an ideal breeding ground for slavery. In the Amazon backlands, the presence of the state is sadly inadequate and the rule of law is the rule of the gun. There is a large reservoir of uneducated, unemployed, hungry migrants who are easily manipulated and controlled. Driven from their homes by poverty and lack of opportunity, they find themselves in a violent land where the rule is every man for himself and the Devil take the hindmost. Uprooted from their communities, they soon find themselves adrift in the world. Many of them are alcoholics, and some are fugitives from justice. Yet they retain their code of honor and forge their own chains: If a man owes he has to pay.

John Donne, the English poet, wrote in the seventeenth century that no man is an island; we are all connected. How much more so in the age of trading blocs, globalization, and the Internet! In the globalized economy, the bottom line is maximum profit for minimum outlay. If we think that what is happening with a slave laborer in the Amazon is none of our business we are wrong. The slave laborer in the Amazon is destroying the forest that helps regulate our climate. He is making the charcoal that may possibly temper the steel in the car we drive. He is clearing pasture for the cows that provide the hamburger we may have eaten yesterday for lunch.

Agribusiness is responsible for 41 percent of Brazilian exports, and we should note that two important sectors of the Brazilian economy, ranching and logging, are also the two principal activities in which the use of slave labor has been detected according to statistics from the Ministry of Labor (see Figure 15–1). Much of the deforestation that takes place in the Amazon is directly linked to the expansion of cattle ranching; still, some is linked to clearing land for planting grain and also, to an extent that is extremely difficult to evaluate, to the illegal extraction and possible exportation of hardwoods. In other contexts the idea of boycotting products directly produced by the sweat of slave labor has been an efficient weapon for helping fight such practices. The campaign against Asian carpets is a case in point.[1] But in Brazil any attempt to trace the inputs of slave labor in the

production of manufactured goods becomes extremely compli-
cated. Wood, for example, may appear as a component of charcoal, which may temper the steel that goes into some of the
products we buy. It may be used in the construction industry
that builds the factories that may make goods for export. It may
be used for fence posts on the cattle ranches that export the
meat that we may eat. Equally it may not, since of the final cost
of meat produced in Brazil, slave labor constitutes a clandestine
component that is probably infinitesimal but is certainly almost
impossible to calculate with any accuracy.

Other economic activities have also been implicated in the
use of slave labor, some of which may have some relevance to
the list of Brazilian exports: cotton, soybeans, garlic, cocoa, field
beans, maté tea, and various types of mining activities. Nevertheless these appear to be sporadic and isolated occurrences,
without the regular systematic character of cattle ranching in
Amazônia. Soybeans, however, deserve particular attention. The
accelerated growth of Brazilian production[2] is largely due to the

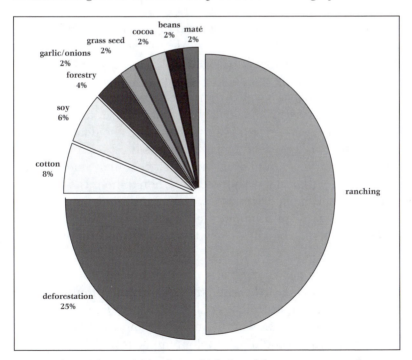

Figure 15-1. Activities from which slave laborers were rescued
(Flying Squad 1995–2001)

recent opening up of new areas for planting on the agricultural frontier in the north, in Mato Gross, Maranhão, Pará, and Tocantins.

As for cattle ranching, Brazil has the largest commercial herd in the world—170 million head—and produces seven million tons of meat a year, of which 10 percent is sold internationally. Brazilian soybeans feed first-world cattle, meat that you or I may eat at some point. The export of Brazilian beef on the bone must by law be certified free of foot-and-mouth disease.[3] Could Brazil perhaps consider certifying its beef as having been produced in a socially responsible manner as well?

It sounds like something out of the Dark Ages: a bunch of poverty-stricken, illiterate men chopping down the forest, hired by trickery, imprisoned by debt, and abandoned when their use is past. Not the sort of thing you would associate with twenty-first-century big business. Hardly what you would expect to find in a country with such elaborate labor laws as Brazil. Yet slavery flourishes because violence is unchecked, starving men need to eat, and business likes a cheap workforce. Money is expensive, in Brazil, social charges on labor are high, and if Brazilian agriculture is to be competitive in world markets—particularly in view of protectionism in northern countries—it needs to cut costs to the bone, opening the door to slavery.

Slavery flourishes because there are no adequate mechanisms to stop it. The victim of slavery does not realize his condition until it is too late. The trap is sprung and he is held fast by isolation, by fear, and by debt. Once he enters the cycle of debt slavery it is hard for him to break away, since a man would rather eat in slavery than starve in freedom. Then there is the question of his pride. If he is driven to escape, many times he will keep silent. He has been ashamed and humiliated, and those who make trouble may be killed. Besides, he will need to work again.

Debt slavery has a long history in the Amazon, but it made a big comeback in the 1960s when the government simultaneously made available large stretches of land and large sums of money. Large numbers of men were required for short periods, and local labor shortages could be supplemented, as was the tradition, from the poverty-stricken northeast. Troublesome labor laws could be circumvented by paying on the basis of production. Or not at all.

By the early 1980s the system had become so widely used that Friedrich Bruegger, manager of Fazenda Rio Cristalino, was genuinely amazed that a naive young priest like Ricardo Rezende would even question it. "Give me the name of one single ranch in Pará that doesn't operate under this system," he laughed. Over the years, the system has become institutionalized. It employs thousands of peons and hundreds of *gatos* and gunmen; it spins off service industries like rooming houses, brothels, and suppliers of food and tools; and it takes up the time of a lot of people who are trying to eradicate it, people like Xavier and Henri and their colleagues. It is also highly profitable.

Although the good old days of government credits are largely gone, there is still money to be made from setting up cattle ranches, particularly if both land and labor cost virtually nothing. These days the frontier has moved to the region around São Félix do Xingu, where a local administration that is widely considered to be corrupt gives free rein to all manner of wickedness, from drug peddling to arms dealing to land grabbing. You don't have to be a mathematical genius to work out what happens to state funding in places like São Félix do Xingu where local government employees on a monthly salary of six hundred *reais* can

Mayor of São Félix

build themselves three-hundred-thousand-*real* mansions in the space of a few years. The prefect of São Félix, who was somewhat vague when I questioned him on the size of his properties, has become a very rich man during his term of office, and there are people in town who claim to have proof of his involvement in massive fraud as well as in the drug trade. This was the man who in one breath vigorously denied the existence of slave labor, and in the next complained that too much government interference in "labor relations" would lead to widespread unemployment.

Land on the Xingu River is being taken up at such speed that even overseas Brazilians know where to get the best bargains. You can find out all about it on the Internet. Much of the land still belongs to the government, and insiders have set up a profitable little racket whereby they will send in a couple of men with chain saws to clear the "boundaries" and sell the land for twenty *reais* a hectare. The new landowners will then hire local *gatos* to turn the virgin forest into cattle pasture. One such is Francisco Donato Filho (Chico Filho), the secretary of agriculture for the state of Piauí, whose case we shall look at in the next chapter. And if you ask why the government doesn't do something to stop this massive land theft, consider this. Government agents in isolated areas like São Félix are easily intimidated and susceptible to corruption, while any federal inspector unwise enough to consider checking out the situation will find innumerable barriers in his path. Hotel rooms will mysteriously be full; he will be unable to find any form of transport. He will be advised that roads are impassable and that his safety cannot be guaranteed, and if he decides to travel by river he will find that there are suddenly no boats available. The president of the union of river pilots in São Félix do Xingu told Federal Police in August 2001 that his members no longer found it convenient to hire themselves out to government officials. Too many of them had been discovered floating upside down in the river. He mentioned a figure of twenty-two.

Interfering with powerful economic interests in a place where there is no law to protect you is a risky business. There's a lot of illegal money to be made out in the Xingu area, and the system of debt slavery suits a lot of people. It suits the rancher because he can get a large piece of land for very little money, develop it with free labor, and end up with a property that is all set to increase in value, particularly if the proposed slaughterhouse ever gets built. It suits the prefect because by attracting more economic activity to his area he will be in a position to attract more state funding—much of which may subsequently be diverted for other purposes. It suits the local shopkeepers because it brings them more custom. It suits almost everybody, and that's one of the reasons why it is going to be so difficult to stamp out.

Sixty percent of all slave laborers in Brazil come from the northeast, chiefly from the states of Bahia, Maranhão, and Piauí. While slave labor can be found across Brazil, from Rio Grande do Sul in

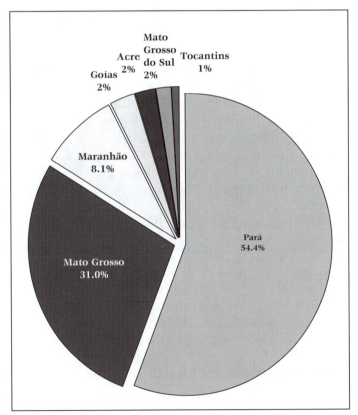

Figure 15-2. States with the highest incidence of rescued slave labor
(Flying Squad, 1995–2001)

the south to Roraima in the north, from Rondônia in the west to Minas Gerais in the east, the bulk of recorded cases are to be found in the states of Maranhão, Pará, and Mato Grosso. Reasons for this are obvious: These are the states on the agricultural frontier, and these are the states most closely monitored by government and NGOs. It is no coincidence that the areas with the highest reported occurrences of slave labor are those where the CPT is most active: Marabá, Xinguara, Sapucaia, Santana do Araguaia, Tucumã, São Félix do Xingu, and most recently Iriri. In areas like Santana and Sapucaia, where the ranches are already established, peons are hired to maintain the pastures and the fencing. In the Xingu they will be required for the more dangerous work of clearing the forest.

Although many peons are afraid or ashamed to blow the whistle on their employers, once in a while they will summon up the courage to do so. They run away because they have been pushed beyond the limits of endurance, and because they realize that they will never be able to work free from the debt. They steal away at night, often walking for several days through the forest, lonely, fearful, hungry, and footsore. Their first thought will be to contact the Federal Police, whom they see as their potential saviors. Sometimes they will talk to the parish priest, or the rural workers' union, or the CPT. If they manage to make the right connections, they may be able to summon the help of the government's flying squad of inspectors, which exists for this very purpose: to check out accusations of slave labor, to make sure workers get paid, and to punish the slavers. Slavery is not only a detestable practice, it is a criminal offense.

The Universal Declaration of Human Rights (1948) states unequivocally:

All human beings are born free and equal in dignity and rights. No one shall be held in slavery or servitude; slavery and the slave trade shall be prohibited in all their forms.

The Brazilian Constitution says:

All people have the right to life, freedom, equality, security, and property (*"Todos têm direito à vida, à liberdade, à igualdade, à segurança e à propriedade"*).

Flying squad at work

But the Brazilian law on slavery is much less direct. Reducing someone to "a situation analogous to slavery" is a common crime, which can be tried by the state courts and is punishable by a prison term. Curiously enough, crimes connected with labor practices such as fraudulently enticing workers from one state to another, disobeying the labor laws, and retaining workers' documents come theoretically under federal jurisdiction, but in practice they are often sent to state courts.[4]

Under Brazilian law, the agencies responsible for investigating allegations of slavery are the Labor Department and the Federal Police. As chapter 4 describes, in 1994 CEJIL and Americas Watch brought a case against the republic of Brazil at the Organization of American States. The charge was that the state had neglected to protect one of its citizens, Antonio, against slave labor and grievous bodily harm. Antonio, as I noted, had been left for dead after trying to escape from a *fazenda* in Marabá belonging to Benedito Mutran. For the first time the situation of slave labor in Brazil was embarrassingly brought to light, and the government reacted with alacrity. In 1995 they set up a flying squad and an interagency group (GERTRAF) to coordinate actions taken toward eradicating forced labor and slave labor. The flying squad operates at the state level and consists of highly motivated and courageous volunteers who come from outside the state in question. Free from local political pressures, they are able to act with impartiality and a certain measure of personal safety as they make their way into the lawless backlands. They are supported by agents from the Federal Police—also from outside the state—whose job is to deal with the criminal aspects of the case, as well as giving cover to both labor inspectors and peons, sometimes in the face of armed *pistoleiros.*

The flying squad has carried out a number of spectacular rescue operations, liberating large numbers of peons from terrible conditions, making sure they get paid, assuring medical care where necessary, and returning them to wherever they came from. They also initiate the process whereby ranchers are fined for labor malpractices and provide the documentation necessary to support criminal prosecutions by the federal attorney general's office.

Despite meticulous planning, many of these operations are stillborn. Sometimes inspectors can't localize the informant, who may have changed his mind and disappeared or may have been silenced. Sometimes the inspectors arrive too late; the peons have either finished the job or been moved on because word got out that the Feds were in town. In some areas there's a conspiracy of silence or noncooperation. In one town they found all doors shut against them. In another they received a telephone call saying that gunmen were coming over to kill them. It's a tough, dangerous assignment, working long hours under difficult conditions in hostile environments. But they do it because they want to see justice done, the criminals brought to book, and the peons treated like human beings.

So far so good, but the courageous and frequently thankless work carried out by the flying squad is often frustrated by the paralyzing slowness of the overburdened judicial system. In the past six years a total of two ranchers have been convicted of using slave labor. Neither of them has gone to jail. Caetano da Silva was convicted and sent down for four years, but he is appealing his sentence at liberty. Antonio Barbosa de Melo, sentenced to two years, had his sentence commuted to supplying food parcels to the poor. In fact the only criminals who landed up behind bars on counts of slave labor were two *gatos:* Chicô (who formerly worked on Rio Cristalino, among others) and Antonio Avelino (the *gato* involved in the case of Fazenda Maciel

Two). Antonio Avelino was later released on the grounds that he was seventy years old. Not too old to be a *gato,* but clearly too old to go to jail.

It is hardly surprising that cases of recidivism are numerous. Fazenda Brasil Verde is one of the principal offenders—together with Fazendas São Carlos, Primavera, Colorado, Rio Vermelho, and Santa Rosa, which also belong to the Quagliato brothers—but there are many more. Fazenda Forkilha (which belongs to Jairo Andrade, he who murdered a gunman by shooting him fifty-six times after cutting off all his fingers one by one) was repeatedly denounced for slave labor, as were several *fazendas* belonging to Jairo's brother Gilberto. One of these was Fazenda Caru in Maranhão, where government inspectors dug up the corpses of several peons. They also found an account book that subsequently acquired legendary status as being the first to clearly mark an entry: "To buying one peon."

The International Labor Organization places Brazil among the nine nations with serious problems of slavery, together with Mauritania, Sudan, Pakistan, India, Thailand, Haiti, Peru, and the Dominican Republic. While it is fair to say that the Brazilian government is making some attempts to do something about slave labor, it is clearly fighting a losing battle. And this is very serious indeed. It is serious because slavery is an evil running virtually unchecked. It is also serious because a heavyweight democratic country like Brazil simply must not tolerate the practice of slavery. Most Brazilians don't know about it, just as you and I didn't know. Among those who hear about it will be those who do not believe, or do not wish to believe. There will be those who accept, reluctantly, that it may be so, but will not know what to do about it.

There are several things that can be done, both at institutional and at personal levels. Let's start with institutional changes. The role of the government here is to prevent, detect, and punish crime. The setting up of the flying squad has gone a long way toward detection, but it is still far too little. The flying squad has opened up the proverbial can of worms and discovered that the dimension of the problem is far greater than anyone could have imagined. There are still huge tracts of territory in Amazônia about which the government knows very little and has virtually no control, and it's a safe bet that as those areas are opened up for development slavery will migrate there, if it hasn't already. Then there is the question of the victims themselves. It is vital that they are able to recognize the process of enslavement, as well as having the courage to denounce their oppressors. *Slavery* is such a harsh word that even its victims are sometimes reluctant to apply it to themselves. There is also a real risk of reprisals, both to the informant and to those who sought to help him. Several cases on record document the story of escaped peons who seek refuge in the local police station, only to be beaten up and returned to their masters. The government does run a witness protection program, but it is still a brave man who will stick his neck out and call the cops. It's a lot safer to keep your head down.

Punishment is a difficult and complex issue. Clearly it is not yet effective. The object of the flying squad is to normalize labor relations and make sure the peons are paid. But they can only bring moral pressure to bear, and can't oblige the landowners to settle up. They can present them with a list of infractions of the labor laws, and impose healthy fines, but again they can't oblige anyone to pay, and both sides know that if it comes to a lawsuit nothing will effectively happen. The police may bring criminal charges, but lawsuits will be tried at state level,[5] and even if convicted the landowners will have little difficulty in wriggling out of their sentences.

The only way to achieve lasting solutions is to hit the landowners where it hurts—in their pocketbooks.[6] Increased fines are not the solution if they are not collected. But there is another option. For several years Congress has been discussing a law that would permit the confiscation of ranches that have been caught out using slave labor. Several ranches have been subject to disappropriation, or compulsory purchase, but to date this has not produced the desired effect of being a serious deterrent. In fact, it has sometimes proved to be a bonanza—witness the government's treatment of Luis Pires (described in chapter 2) and Eufrásio Pereira Luiz of Fazenda Rio Cristalino (see chapter 13).

How are we going to stop slavery? Deep-rooted evils require deep-rooted solutions, and these take time to grow. First and foremost is making sure that everyone involved has a clear understanding of the problem. Landowners need to know what is expected of them; workers and their families need to know how to protect themselves and what to do if things go wrong.

The most effective geographic areas on which to focus are those that supply large numbers of peons, chiefly the states of Bahia, Maranhão, and Piauí. Recognized way stations—such as Colinas, Guaraí, and Araguaína in Tocantins, and Xinguara, Santana, and Marabá in Pará—could also become the targets of preventive campaigns. Workers and their families should be encouraged to find out as much as possible about the forthcoming work contract, with full details of names, places, and expected length of service. A particularly effective strategy has been adopted by the CPT. As part of its preventive campaign the CPT has distributed hundreds of copies of a pocket-sized cartoon booklet illustrating the problem of slave labor and giving some hints for survival, including telephone numbers to call in order to summon help.

But let us not delude ourselves: Until employers are shamed or forced into improving conditions for their workers, until the workers are prepared to stand up for themselves, until society at large is prepared to condemn the practice, slavery will continue. And who is the victim of slavery? He is more than just a nameless migrant worker, he is somebody's son, somebody's brother, somebody's husband. Someone, somewhere, knows his name and waits for him to come home.

It's a big problem, but it can be solved, and the single biggest step we can take is to publicize the issue. Think about it, talk about it, bring it to the public eye. You who support UNICEF and the World Wildlife Fund, think about supporting Anti-Slavery International, Free the Slaves, Human Rights Watch, and the CPT. Human rights violations affect all of us, and slavery should be at the top of the list. Make sure that people understand that we're not talking about the Deep South in the 1800s. We're talking about stolen lives, here and now. Is it really acceptable to us that a society like ours, with all its resources, all its knowledge, all its humanity, should permit the existence of slavery while we walk free?

16

Into the Enemy's Camp

On the Road with the Flying Squad

The spearhead of the Brazilian government's fight against slavery is the flying squad of labor inspectors, established in 1995 to investigate accusations of slavery.[1] The flying squad operates at the federal level and consists of ad hoc groups of labor inspectors and Federal Police drawn from a dedicated body of volunteers, none of whom lives or works in the state where they are operating. This provides a measure of independence from local pressures and some degree of personal safety—reinforced by the presence of the police—but this is, nonetheless, a delicate and dangerous operation and a tough personal choice. While on mission they spend long hours in difficult conditions, confronting hostility and suspicion on the part of the landowners and sometimes from the peons themselves, and they can count on no support from state authorities, who are often jealous of federal encroachment on their territory. In addition to this, they are frequently the target of criticism from their home workplaces. Section chiefs, fearful that they may not achieve their work targets, are often unwilling to let them go on open-ended missions, while some of their colleagues accuse them, not always in a friendly manner, of indulging in "rural tourism."

After some persistence I received guarded permission to accompany the group on one of its missions, but it was made clear to me first that the Federal Police would be under no obligation to guarantee my safety, and second that my presence on the ranches could legally be construed as trespass, if the ranchers should happen to be present at the time of inspection. So it is with some trepidation that I present myself at the rendezvous point, fully aware that my presence might be regarded by some members of the team as an intrusion, if not a downright nuisance.

We meet in Redenção, the town where they used to land the planes on main street. More recently it has been the scene of a massive demonstration organized by the ranchers against the government inspectors. One of the labor inspectors, Ricciotti, tells me about it on the second day of the trip. "The flying squad has a history and a reputation," he says, as we sit in a sidewalk bar across from the hotel, "and our reputation has been hard earned, let me tell you. All these towns are hostile, and we've been threatened on several occasions. Back in 'ninety-eight the ranchers closed this place down. One of the inspectors from the environmental agency had been murdered, and the government had sent in a massive team—to mark their territory. Well, we were unlucky enough to turn up just after they had left, and emotions were running high. In fact we heard that they were going to run us out of town. There were stories that they were planning to burn our vehicles. So we beat a strategic retreat to the next town, but not before negotiating a meeting in the town hall for the following day. The deal was that there would be twelve of us and twelve of them. When we got there they had packed the house. There were over a hundred of them and they were after our blood. The mayor opened the meeting by saying that labor inspections were leading to unemployment, and the coordinator of our group stood up and said that the south of Pará was known to be a center of *pistolagem.* At that point the sky fell in; the president of the town council was so angry that he hurled his notebook onto the floor and things turned very nasty. If it hadn't been for the Feds we'd never have got out of there in one piece. We'd have been well and truly beaten up, at the very least."

The mission that I join consists of five labor inspectors, one of whom is a doctor, and five members of the Federal Police, one of whom is a police chief. Their job is to investigate accusations of slave labor on several different *fazendas,* and I discover on the first day just how delicate and complex the job will prove to be. Officials from the local Labor Department and Federal Police were not warned of the team's arrival, in an attempt to preserve maximum secrecy. Nevertheless the arrival of three cars with out-of-state license plates is in itself ample warning to the inhabitants of the town, although they cannot know which are the target *fazendas*. We set off in close convoy to investigate one of the complaints, heading for the town of Santana do Araguaia, some two hundred kilometers south on the road to Mato Grosso. Distances are immense, while speed and secrecy are of the essence, and I am glad to be in the backseat as we hurtle off down the potholed road across the gaping bridges on a mission that is to prove fruitless. The informant has vanished.

Intensive detective work that night produces another informant, and so we set off the next morning bright and early down the same road. We stop thirty kilometers short of the town and take the entrance marked for Rio Cristalino, the ranch that formerly belonged to Volkswagen. The tarmac gives way to a dirt road, and we drive at high speed through clouds of swirling dust across impossibly narrow bridges with scarcely room for one car to pass. We pass the guard post, through the ruined pastures, past the looted buildings of the headquarters, and I remember the bands of rival gunmen and loggers, glad to be in the company of the Feds. But there is little sign of life, only a small herd of cattle being driven along the dusty road by a couple of cowboys with whips of plaited leather, and patches of newly burned forest sporting newly erected wooden shacks where some of the squatters are maintaining a precarious hold on the land. The landscape is shrouded in smoke and dust. It is the burning season.

Burned forest: Rio Cristalino

Suddenly the car slews off down a small track and heads toward the distant hills, bucking and skidding over the road. A huge area of forest reserve has recently been cleared and burned. The police strap on their guns, and the level of tension increases dramatically. The Land Rover pulls off into the burned area, but it's not long before progress is halted by huge logs across the road. Is it an ambush? We pick our way warily on foot through the desolate land, but the expected shots do not materialize. An hour later, hot, sweaty, and covered with ash, we see the first signs of the workers' camp. It has been recently abandoned, and so has the next one, twenty minutes farther on. There are all the signs of recent and hasty evacuation: a pile of old batteries, discarded boots, and empty bottles. We expect to find several hundred peons, but we arrived too late; did they get word of the blitz, or have they simply finished the job? We drive on through patches of brilliant green high forest, alive with butterflies, to inspect another large area of burned forest. Not a peon in sight. I ask the name of the *fazenda*. "Rio Cristalino," says the informant. "Sector Eight." So this is one of the parts of the *fazenda* that was illegally sold off, illegally burned, and employed slave labor. I wonder what Herr Bruegger would have thought.

Our car is driven by Paulinho from the Labor Ministry; the other two passengers are Freire, one of the federal agents, and Paulo, the chief of police. We talk about the work of the flying squad. "It's all about human rights," says Paulinho as the car skids dangerously through the deep sand, righting itself in the nick of time to cross a rotting narrow bridge. "And citizenship. We're restoring the peons' citizenship."

"What citizenship?" I wonder aloud. "What measure of citizenship do the peons have?"

There is a silence, and Paulinho catches my eye in the driving mirror. "You're right," he says ruefully. "Maybe it's more a question of conferring citizenship. Dignity, self-respect. Freeing them from fear. It's particularly important that the informant comes out well. He's put his life on the line, after all."

"What about the rancher and the *gato*? What is your attitude toward them?"

"We're here to normalize working relationships," he says earnestly. "We don't think of it in terms of punishing people. We don't want to create any sort of hostility; we simply want the bosses to understand what is expected of them."

Two days later we find ourselves heading down the same road. Four days into the mission with nothing to show for it, and frustrations and tensions are beginning to emerge. One of the team members overslept, there was confusion about our meeting point, one of the drivers had forgotten to fill up his tank, there was no fuel available, and fraying tempers were not improved by a particularly nasty lunch of greasy chicken and cold beets in a flyblown roadside stop. We turn off once again onto Fazenda Rio Cristalino and drive at high speed for three hours. The informant appears to have lost his way. One of the police yells at him, and Paulinho leaps to the rescue, calmly talking him through the options until he can orient himself. He directs us along a small logging trail, and two hours later we come to a small camp. The police jump out of the cars, brandishing their submachine guns, and four peons cower in the forest as the team closes in. The camp consists of one small, rough structure of logs, partially covered with plastic. A plank across the dirty stream provides the washing area. There is a whining of mosquitoes, and I cravenly hope I won't come away with a case of malaria. The peons' meager possessions are draped over wooden poles, a pair of muddy jeans, a shirt, two towels. A pot of beans is bubbling on the log fire but food supplies are running low, and work has been halted for several days. The peons are visibly nervous and have clearly been told that the police mean trouble, but they slowly regain their confidence and ask to be taken out.

The next day there is a group meeting, and Claudia the coordinator attempts to restore the flagging morale of the team. "We expected to find forty peons, and we found four," she tells us. "But we can't evaluate our success in terms of numbers. The ideal will be when we come on a mission and don't find any, because there aren't any. But we have a long way to go before that! Now let me tell you what the next target will be. I had a call from Brother Henri in Xinguara and he says there's another case over in the Xingu. Sixty peons abandoned in the forest and apparently the place belongs to a state deputy from Piauí. Now for those of you who don't know, it's a dangerous area. The Federal Police went there last year and found the whole town closed against them. Nobody would give them a hotel room. They were all left out in the rain. We'll need to be well prepared, so I'm going to send someone to buy us some supplies. Everyone should take a hammock. We'll leave first thing tomorrow, and we'll stop off in Xinguara and talk to the informant. He's being sheltered by the CPT.

"In the meantime I'll take a car back to Santana and we'll see if we can track down Edmilson, the *gato* from yesterday's *fazenda*. I'm sure he can't have gone far. Paulinho will stay here and take the statements from the peons we brought out yesterday, and I want everyone to be ready to leave at six-thirty sharp. And next time we go in, I want us to be careful how we approach the peons. Remember they are wounded people and they've probably been told that if the Ministry of Labor comes nosing around they'll lose their jobs. Let me repeat that São Félix is a city of spies. It's a small town and word gets around."

I have the feeling that the team needs to have something solid to show for their efforts. We have been on the job for the best part of a week with little success. I also sense that they are under increasing pressure in the face of a new determination on the part of the local ranchers to frustrate their efforts. This new attitude is clearly demonstrated by the agreement recently concluded between government officials and three powerful local ranchers, Roque Quagliato, Maurício Fraga, and José Coelho Victor, an agreement that effectively guarantees the failure of any inspection by stipulating that the Feds won't enter any of their twenty-three *fazendas*. The accord provoked howls of protest from the CPT, and the beleaguered flying squad urgently needs to prove that it is still an effective force in the battle against slavery.

So it is with a renewed sense of determination that we assemble early the next morning to face the atrocious road to São Félix, a road that is a nightmare of dust and potholes at the best of times, and virtually impassable during the rains. Even with the best of available vehicles and some highly skilled driving it takes us most of the day to reach São Félix, a distance of 289 kilometers. From the outset it is clear that the town is determinedly hostile. São Félix is an abandoned river settlement that dates back nearly a hundred years and has a long history of bloodshed. Over the centuries the town and surrounding area have been the scene of violent conflicts and power struggles, as one cycle of exploitation succeeded another. In the early years of the last century the area was run as a private fiefdom by Colonel Tancredo, who controlled the rubber trade with a rod of iron, trading on his own terms and ruthlessly exploiting the luckless rubber tappers. When that trade collapsed, most of the population left and those who remained were reduced to a subsistence lifestyle. The currency was the .44–caliber bullet; one bullet bought a kilo of meat or a kilo of salt, while two bullets were required for the hide of a wild pig. The next focus of economic activity was the trade in Brazil nuts, followed, during the Second World War, by another brief rubber boom. Then came the trade in hides and skins, followed by Operation Amazônia and a sudden uncontrollable influx of migrants into the area. The link road was put in from Xinguara, and new settlements sprang up overnight. Signs were erected in neighboring settlements touting São Félix as the best land in the Amazon, and large numbers of settlers came pouring in looking for land, or timber, or gold. And still they come, attracted by the huge areas of virgin forest where there is land for the taking and no significant presence of the state to curb the wildest excesses.

The current state of play in São Félix is that anything goes. The town is run by a prefect who is under investigation for gross corruption and has twenty-one court cases pending against him, while the backlands are the scene of an orgy of land grabbing, illegal logging, drug dealing, money laundering—every conceivable sort of wickedness, including the use of slave labor. It's a town where you never sit with your back to the door and are careful what you say, a town where a minority of the citizenry is making ridiculous amounts of money, where there is neither water nor drains, and where you can't trust the police. It is the town we visited at the beginning of this book when we met Albertino the escaped slave laborer in the hospital, and where the rooming houses are brimming with crowds of peons waiting to find jobs hundreds of kilometers away in the forest.

São Félix is where the road ends, and from this point the only practical way to travel is by river. There is precarious access to the settlements by roads that are nothing more than glorified logging trails, but the only way to get to our target area is by river. It is the end of the dry season and the river is low and dangerous, full of rocks and rapids. During the wet season the river is navigable by barge, but the only option currently available is the motorized canoe locally known as the *voadeira* (flying boat). There must be fifteen *voadeiras* tied up on the riverbank, but for some reason there isn't a single one available. One after another the pilots shake their heads: They have a problem with their engines, they have another job to do, they have a touch of fever . . . It's the president of the river pilots' union who finally lays it on the line. "I'm a law-abiding man myself," he says, "but let me tell you something. The people downriver don't appreciate visits from the government. Pilots who hire out their boats tend to wake up floating upside down in the river. I've lost too many pilots, and I can't afford to lose any more."

The case that we have come to investigate involves a large piece of land some three or four hours downriver where the virgin forest is being cleared for pasture. The owner's name is Chico Filho, and he is from the state government in Piauí. A former state deputy, he was now state minister of agriculture. His family owns several other *fazendas* in several different states, and he doesn't at all like being accused of using slave labor—hardly the sort of image that a minister of agriculture wishes to present to his constituents. The story is this. He hired *gato* Claudionor from Xinguara to clear the forest and leave the land ready for planting. He was in a hurry to get the job done on time, and it is entirely possible that he neglected the tiresome chore of getting permission from the environmental department.

Gato Claudionor took sixty peons into the deputy's *fazenda*, conveniently collecting them from a rooming house in Xinguara that belongs to his wife. They had immense difficulty in reaching the deputy's land, and from the start they worked against time. First you have to clear the vines and undergrowth, then cut the trees, and then leave them to dry out before you do the burn, and if you aren't on schedule you'll miss the planting season and lose all your work. Claudionor reckoned that he wasn't given enough men to get the job done on time. Chico Filho reckoned it was all the fault of Claudionor, so he swooped down and abruptly ordered work to cease. Furthermore, he refused to pay for the work that had already been done. He removed the radio, so there was no form of communication, and simply abandoned the peons to their own devices. Many of them had been sick with malaria, no medical assistance had been provided, they were running short of food, and they had no option but to make their own way back to town, carrying their sick companions with them.

Inspectors' day

We find the peons in the hotel belonging to the Goiano, and they are in a sorry state. Several of them are very drunk indeed, others have malaria, and Ceará has hurt his arm. The doctor in the hospital told him to take some antibiotics, but he could only afford to buy two pills. "I didn't have very much money," he mutters, hanging his head. Maria the cook butts into the conversation. "He hurt his arm when he fell off the truck," she says. "It was when we were coming off the *fazenda*. Some of us were so sick that we couldn't walk, and then a logging truck came along and the driver said we could climb up on top. And Ceará fell off. I told him, I said, 'Ceará,' I said, 'You ought to have that arm looked at. It's my belief you've broken it.' I went with him to the hospital and they took an X-ray, but all they did was give him a shot. That's not going to mend a broken arm, is it?"

The peons line up to tell their stories. Most of them describe themselves as migrant workers. They come from Maranhão or Piauí, or Bahia, or Minas Gerais, but none of them has been home for ten, twelve, or twenty years. Bit by bit we piece together the story. They were hired in Xinguara and traveled to the *fazenda* by bus and then by riverboat. The job was difficult, but they were used to that. Their chief complaint is that they were abandoned in the forest with no medical help and no transport. Worst of all they hadn't had any meat. Oh yes, they could always catch fish, but when you're working hard like that fish doesn't have the vitamins. A man needs meat. And the meat hadn't been properly salted, so it had rotted.

What they can't understand is that the rancher came in and told them to stop work just like that. He'd arranged for them to clear 150 *alqueires,* and they did the preliminary clearing of 139. But they only just got started on the tree felling. The terrain was particularly difficult, and they simply weren't able to work any faster. On the one hand the rancher said he wouldn't pay them until the job was finished, and on the other he ordered them to stop work. They can't see the sense of it. And they want their money.

"Don't worry, we'll get you your money," the team reassures them. "And as for your bill at the hotel, it's the deputy who will pay that. We've been in touch with him and he is sending his lawyer over tomorrow to sort things out. Meanwhile those of you with malaria should go to the hospital and get blood slides, and you can get started on your treatment."

I talk to the *gato,* Claudionor. He is dressed in a fine hat, pointed boots, a belt with a big buckle, and a green T-shirt emblazoned with the inscription HAPPINESS IS KNOWING JESUS. "I want to tell you two things," he says. "This whole job has been nothing but trouble. Ever since the beginning. First of all I didn't have enough men to do the job. We started too late. And there were problems with money from the start. The deputy kept telling us he'd send us this much but he always sent less. Too little, too late. Working conditions were the worst I've seen. The place was full of malaria. It was a nightmare getting in. One of the boats overturned in the rapids and we lost a lot of stuff. And then all of a sudden he turns up on the *fazenda* and orders us to stop work. Just like that. Says he's not going to pay. 'You didn't do the job right,' he says, 'And I'm not paying.' Well of course I was horrified. What was I going to do about the peons? And all the bills at the supermarket? 'Do as you please,' says he, 'It's your problem.'"

Meanwhile the inspectors are painstakingly proceeding with the work of getting statements. What is your name? Address?

Mother's name? How many days did you work? What was the deal? Did you receive an advance? Did you receive any salary? A peon with a beaming face seizes me by the arm and leans toward me confidentially, smelling strongly of liquor. "Let me tell you something," he says happily. "It's just as well you turned up. We'd never have got our money otherwise. Mind you, I wouldn't have the courage to denounce a state deputy. I've known of several cases of informants who call the police, get their money, and end up with a bullet in the back. It's very dangerous round here, you know."

We are lodged in the best joint in town, the gloomy, ill-lit Hotel Jacaré. The name means "crocodile," which is somehow appropriate. It is clean and the rooms are air-conditioned, which grants some relief from the sullen damp heat and the smoky air generated by the burning forest, but the management is economizing by putting in low-wattage lightbulbs, and no soap is provided. A young man in a checked shirt and jeans lounges around all day listening to every conversation, and the manager launches into a long litany of complaints. Things are expensive and difficult to get, staff are unreliable, there's no water supply and no drains. Why, the town has only just been connected to the main electricity. Thank goodness you can get television, that's about the only thing to be said for the place.

Claudia embarks on the lengthy and frustrating business of attempting to contact the deputy on the antiquated telephone system, while Paulinho and Francisco set up an improvised office in one of the bedrooms and calculate the moneys owed to the peons. Ricciotti darts in and out of the hospital, checking on the malaria screening and setting Ceará's arm, and the Feds spend a lot of time chasing up those who have not yet made statements.

Rumors fly thick and fast. A long list of supplicants turns up at the door wanting help over all manner of unrelated cases. Claudia finally manages to raise the deputy on the phone. First he says that the land doesn't belong to him, and then he says it does. No, of course he won't pay. Well, maybe he will. Eventually his lawyer arrives in a plane, piloted, curiously enough, by a Federal Policeman. Negotiations drag on in an atmosphere of ill will and mutual mistrust. Another group of peons turns up from the deputy's place. They have just arrived, and the lawyer refuses to accept their claims, because the bill is now getting too high. A call comes from Brasília. News has come in of a second case, several hours upriver. Will it be possible to go check it out? I set off across town to see whether I can raise a boat. The nuns give me the name of a boatman who agrees, in innocence, to take five people. I hope devoutly that no harm will come to him. On the way back I drop in at the Xingu Lodge, which is reputed to have the best food in town. To my surprise I discover that the place is run by a foreigner. Mid-sixties, with a shock of white hair, he looks like a character from Hemingway or Graham Greene. He operates a fishing camp upriver, he has a magnificent collection of orchids, and I suspect that the full story of his life would occupy many a convivial evening, and many bottles of beer. "I've been here fourteen years," he tells me, "and there's always something going on in this place, let me tell you. Used to be a trade here in jaborandi leaves for eye medicine, and that led to some pretty vicious little fights. Then there's the loggers, the land grabbers, and the drug smugglers. You've heard about our prefect, I take it? This place is a nest of corruption. Land grabbing, illegal logging, money laundering, you name it. The Feds were here a couple of years back on the track of a ring of drug traffickers. They used to deal the stuff direct with Suriname. The Feds caught one of the local pilots just as he was landing and they asked him what he was carrying, and he looked at them and said straight out, 'Cocaine,' can you believe it? There are a lot of killings round here. Bodies going to the cemetery on a daily basis. But nobody knows who killed them, or why. Or if they know they're not saying."

Meanwhile the new case is heating up. The police find the *gato* João. Visibly nervous, he promises fulsomely to come back with all the documentation, and then does a runner upriver. We set off in hot pursuit, police chief Paulo, federal agent Walber, Francisco the labor inspector, informant Japonês, and me. The speedboat heads off up the broad beautiful river, through rocks and rapids and numerous islands. Japonês has underestimated our journey time by 100 percent, but fortunately we have taken a lot of fuel aboard. As we pull away from the city the tensions fall away and we find ourselves relaxing and enjoying the trip.

We are heading toward Kayapó Indian territory, and I do not see the expected signs of devastated forest. On the contrary we see very few signs of life; several barges steam down the river pushing giant floating logs, we pass the occasional small clearing, and once we pass an area of pasture, although there are no cattle to be seen. Late in the afternoon we dodge behind an island and head for the shore. As we approach we see a boatload of men pulling off from the bank. Walber and Paulo rise to their feet in unison, brandish their submachine guns, and order the boat in to land. For a brief moment I wonder if there will be a shootout, but the other boatman thinks better of it, and as we land we see the distraught figure of the *gato* João running down to the river's edge.

The Feds take charge and march him off to his living quarters to search for arms and chain saws. We inspect his tent. He has a small store of food, a few medicines, a hammock, and a water filter. Francisco and I follow Japonês through the high forest to the peons' quarters. Despite the evidence that many people have recently left in a hurry, there are still some left, as evidenced by the pressure cooker bubbling away over the fire. A dirty stream provides washing water, but they are taking their drinking water from the river. Adalberto the *subgato* embarks on a long and unconvincing story about how well he treats the peons, while Japonês goes off into the forest to find the chain saw operators. The light is fading and they are already on their way home, lugging the heavy saws. They opt to come out with us. Meanwhile the police have had no luck in searching for arms but they have discovered some more chain saws hidden in the bush. You are supposed to register your chain saws, but very few people bother to do so. Somehow we manage to cram everyone into the two boats and set off, perilously overladen, down the shallow river as the red sun sets over the surrounding hills. The night is inky black, but the boatman navigates his way confidently down the river, and despite a few alarming coughs from the engine the fuel miraculously sees us back to town.

The week drags on. The lawyer invents excuse after excuse and finally leaves town without paying. The Feds tell me they are powerless to stop him from going. The peons are beginning to lose heart, because the owner of the rooming house is threatening to put them all out into the street. A painted lady with a raddled face and high spiky heels hovers anxiously around to see if she will be paid. She has supplied more than three hundred meals to the peons, and she can do no more. She is owing at all the stores. Claudia shuts herself in the room that we share and embroiders compulsively. Some of the Feds are showing signs of restlessness and announce that they wish to leave. It would be too dangerous for the rest of the team to stay without them. Even Paulinho is feeling the strain and complains of a headache. The deputy is openly defying the government, and such a thing has never happened. In truth, they cannot force him to pay up. Paulo the chief of police takes statements for a police inquiry but everyone knows that if the case should come to trial it will be all but impossible to find any of the peons to testify.

Seldom have I had such a feeling of impotence. It seems as if all the cards are stacked against us. All the statements have been taken, all the calculations made, yet by law there is no way to oblige the ranchers to pay up. The days roll on, and finally Claudia makes the decision to leave. There is nothing more to be done. This is the first time that the flying squad has been faced down, and it has created an alarming precedent. Everyone is thoroughly demoralized, the peons are furious, there is a trail of debts across the town, and nothing has been achieved. It looks like the ranchers are developing a new strategy, and the team will have to change its tactics. With heavy hearts we load the cars and prepare to face the hideous road. "This place reeks of blood," mutters Francisco as he slings his bag into the back of the car.

Just as we are leaving I spot the white VW Beetle belonging to the CPT in Tucumã. Padre Danilo and Brother Carlinho have come down to see what can be done, but Claudia holds out little hope. I later hear their story. They arrived to find the town in an uproar. Rumor had it that once the team had gone the deputy would settle up with the peons on his own terms—which is exactly what happened. Danilo and Carlinho spent a frustrating week negotiating with the lawyer who finally returned, and flatly refused to allow them to attend the settlement, threatening to walk out if they attempted to come anywhere near. They sat across the street in impotent fury while the lawyer calmly paid each peon a trifling sum and made sure he signed several receipts—one of which was blank. He categorically refused to pay the bill at the hotel, with the result that by the time the peons had settled up they were left with nothing. Worse still, they felt that the government too had betrayed them. "These people came from Brasília and they couldn't help us," said one of them. "If they can't help us, who can?"

It is a question that we all ponder many times. Faced with such determination and in a context of total impunity, what is to be done? However dedicated to their job, the flying squad cannot afford to sit around indefinitely. Once they are gone, business will continue as normal. The peons urgently need to find work, the *gatos* will make their rounds, and the ranchers will continue to invade and destroy the forest, with ever-increasing confidence as they discover that they can defeat the government.

I leave my new friends in Xinguara; their way lies north, while I must go south. It is not the triumphant outcome that we expected, and we are all a little subdued. I have a lengthy journey ahead, to reflect on what I have learned from my trip. There is no doubt in my mind that there are people in the Brazilian government who are serious in their attempts to wipe out slavery. This is largely as a result of the continuous, unrelenting pressure brought against the government by local and international NGOs, principally the CPT, Americas Watch, and CEJIL. They had denounced the government of Brazil to the Organization of American States on two counts of slavery: the question of Antonio, who had been shot in the back of the head while attempting to flee from Fazenda Espirito Santo, and the repeated denunciations of slave labor on Fazenda Brasil Verde. The second case remains unresolved, but in the case of Antonio the government is negotiating an agreement to indemnify the victim, as well as making an official undertaking to take new steps toward fighting slavery. According to the terms of the agreement, the government will recognize its responsibility in not being capable of preventing slave labor because of legislative and administrative deficiencies and commit themselves to the following measures:

- confiscating *fazendas* involved in the practice of slavery;
- redefining the crime of slavery as subjecting someone to work through the use of threat, violence, or fraud;
- sharply increasing the penalties for slavery, including longer jail sentences and higher fines;

- creating a specialized group within the Federal Police to accompany the flying squad;
- instructing the attorney general's office to accompany closely all cases involving slave labor;
- creating a far-reaching publicity campaign using the mass media to alert people, especially those in the states with the highest incidence of slavery (Pará, Mato Grosso, and Maranhão) and most intense recruitment for slavery (Maranhão, Tocantins, Piauí, and Bahia).

A solid set of measures, if they can be gotten through Congress,[2] but it must be remembered that there are many members of Congress who are landowners themselves or represent landowning states and thus have no interest in altering the status quo. Like environmental protection, slavery is too important an issue to be left solely in the hands of governments. If slavery is to stop, it is we who must make sure that it does.

Like the fight against terrorism, the fight against slavery will be both long and hard, because there are so many people who make a profit from it. It will be a fight on many fronts. Since there are two root causes—the large body of unskilled unemployed migrant labor on the one hand, and the constant demand for a pool of easily manipulated people on the other—the fight to end slavery will require a two-pronged attack. First society must provide education, training, access to the land, and whatever it takes to permit people to live in safety and earn a decent living. Second the system of punishment for offenders must be made to work. Complex labor laws must be simplified, and law enforcement officials must be given all the support that they need to make the system workable for both landowners and rural workers. Most importantly, we, as members of the human family, must be prepared to stand up and say that we are not prepared to tolerate slavery.

There are precedents for us to follow. Nations have succeeded in throwing out dictatorial regimes, putting a stop to torture, bringing in legislation to protect environmental and human rights, and it is a battle that we must carry on until people everywhere can live their lives in freedom. The bottom line is that it depends on people like you and me. Do you remember Albertino and Batista, the escaped slaves whom we met at the beginning of this story? Shortly after I met him, Albertino had his arm amputated, which meant that he could no longer work. But he did receive a working contract, which meant that he was able to draw a disability pension, and didn't starve to death. Batista, on the other hand, was unwilling to press charges against the land-owner and returned home. He remains one of the thousands of men caught up in slavery, from which very few will be lucky enough to escape. The vast majority will be condemned to re-peat the cycle over and over again until they die—worn out with unremitting toil, weakened by fever, maybe with a bullet in the back. If we, together, will take a stand against slavery, if we will support all those like Xavier and Henri and Claudia and Paulinho who are working to put a stop to it, then in the end we shall succeed, and no one will have to die on the distant *fazendas* and be buried in an unmarked grave while someone, somewhere, waits for him to come home.

It is up to us.

Free at last!

Notes

Introduction

1. British organization based in London founded in 1839 to combat slavery.
2. Kevin Bales, *Disposable People,* University of California Press, 1999.

1. The Chain of Slavery

1. In this context a squatter is someone who lives and works on the land but doesn't have title.
2. One hectare is 2.471 acres.
3. In 1968, during the military dictatorship, a small band (between sixty and seventy) of urban guerrillas moved to an isolated area of southern Pará to train for guerrilla warfare and prepare for the return of democracy. Between 1972 and 1974 the Brazilian army waged three campaigns against them, using forces that numbered up to fifteen thousand men, finally defeating them in January 1975.
4. Originally from Spain, Pedro Casaldáliga has been bishop of the prelacy of São Félix do Araguaia in Mato Grosso since 1971. A passionate proponent of social justice, he has many times been threatened with death. In 1972 he published a document titled "Amazon Church in Conflict with the Large Landowners," drawing attention to the plight of the landless peasants and those in debt slavery.
5. *O Liberal,* 27 March 1999.
6. R$1, one Brazilian *real,* is worth approximately forty cents U.S.
7. See John Hemming, *Red Gold,* Macmillan, London, 1978.
8. After the decline of the Roman Empire, chattel slavery in Europe was replaced by the institution of serfdom. By the early years of the fifteenth century, however, the practice of taking slaves from Africa had begun to take root, increasing along with improved shipping and access to lands that required large amounts of labor.
9. In his report *Voyage dans le nord do Brésil, fait durant les années 1613 et 1614.*
10. Under the sharecropping system the landowner and the sharecropper divide the harvest between them.
11. In 1876 Henry Alexander Wickham smuggled seventy thousand rubber seeds from Belém to the Royal Botanical Gardens at Kew, London. They were grown very successfully, and the rubber seedlings were later

sent to Malaya to become the basis of the rubber plantations that subsequently destroyed the Brazilian rubber trade.

12. President of the rural workers' union in Xapuri, Acre, Chico Mendes defended the rubber tappers who were being threatened with expulsion from their customary lands. He succeeded in allying their cause with that of the environmentalists and attracted so much attention internationally that he became the victim of death threats on the part of the ranchers. Despite having police protection he was murdered on 22 December 1988.

13. "Money from the Forest," *Veja* magazine, 22 August 2001.

14. Gilberto Dimenstein, *Meninas da Noite* (Girls of the Night), Editora Ática, São Paulo, 1992.

15. *"Apesar de Você"* (In Spite of You), Chico Buarque, 1971.

2. Links in the Chain

1. Under Brazilian law a *fazenda* that is not fulfilling its "social function"—is not productive—can be subject to compulsory purchase.

2. *"Incra pagou a superfatura"* (Incra pays over the odds). *O Liberal,* Belém, 22 December 1999.

3. The Occupation of Amazônia

1. E. O. Wilson reckons the figure at between seven and ten million.

2. Starting in 1926 Henry Ford twice attempted unsuccessfully to grow rubber at Fordlândia and Belterra in Pará. In 1945 he abandoned his attempts and sold out. In 1967 Ford's compatriot Daniel Ludwig bought an immense estate at Jari and invested heavily in trees that produce cellulose. But he too was defeated and sold.

3. These roads were christened respectively the Belém-Brasília and the BR 364, later known as the Trans Cocaina.

4. In 1965 the U.S. Air Force made an aerial survey of Amazônia, and the Hudson Institute's Great Lakes Plan was completed in 1967. The largest lake was projected to have an area of 240,000 square kilometers (the size of the United Kingdom).

5. Marcos Kowarick, *Amazonia Na Trilha do Saque,* Editora Anita, São Luís, 1995.

6. *Principal Socio Economic Indicators from Colonization Projects for Agrarian Reform,* 1992, FAO/UNDP.

7. Kowarick, *Amazonia Na Trilha do Saque.*

8. Under Brazilian law squatters could acquire some rights over the land if they had lived and worked there uncontested for a period of time.

9. The army conducted extensive maneuvers in 1970 and set up five military bases in 1972.

10. The Second National Development Plan 1975–9.

11. Source: EMBRAPA (Brazilian Agricultural Research Institute).

12. Paulo Fontelles, a lawyer, worked as adviser to the CPT in Conceição do Araguaia. Subsequently elected state deputy, he was murdered in 1987.

13. Source: 1996–7 census, taken by IBGE, and quoted in *Novo Retrato da Agricultura Familiar: o Brasil Redescoberto,* INCRA/FAO, 2000.

4. Debt Slavery: The Bosses

1. Kevin Bales, *Disposable People,* University of California Press, 1999.
2. *Debt Bondage,* 1998, Anti-Slavery International.
3. Africa too had an extensive history of enslaving its people.
4. The real numbers are hard to estimate. According to figures from the Ministry of Labor, for every worker rescued from slave labor another three remain undiscovered. The CPT estimates for the year 2000 that the total number of victims of slavery could be as high as fifteen thousand (see Chart 4–1).
5. *O Dia,* 23 August 2001.
6. *Veja,* 14 April 1993.
7. In 2001 a bill to simplify the labor laws was sent to Congress. In Brazil such bills can take a long time to work their way through the system, and in order to overcome this barrier and simplify existing laws a draft was approved that envisaged the possibility of altering the rules through negotiations between the two sides.
8. Years later Jáder Barbalho became the leader of the Senate. But as rumors of his involvement in huge financial scandals started to come out, and a campaign was mounted to impeach him, he resigned (in 2001) before he could be removed from office.
9. *Folha de São Paulo,* 18 November 1991.
10. *Folha de São Paulo,* 19 November 1991.
11. The case was brought by Americas Watch and CEJIL, the Center for International Justice and Human Rights.
12. *Estado de São Paulo,* 5 November 1994.
13. Joseph Hanrahan, bishop of Conceição do Araguaia, had long suffered from intestinal problems. In 1993 he died of intestinal thrombosis. When Jairo Andrade claimed to have poisoned him, his body was exhumed, and the pathologist said that while he did not discard the hypothesis that the bishop may have been poisoned, he could not, at that stage, discover any traces in the body.
14. Brian Kelly and Mark London, *Amazon,* Robert Hale, London, 1984.

5. The *Gatos*

1. *Diário de Cuiabá,* 3 March 1991.

6. The Peons

1. Under the *cativo* system workers get a higher wage and have to pay (often exorbitantly) for their food, tools, and clothes. Under the *livre* system wages are lower but food is included.
2. Report by the flying squad of federal government inspectors on the raid carried out on Fazenda Estrela de Maceió in February 1998. For more on the flying squad, see chapters 15 and 16.

3. CPT archives.

4. Report by the Goiânia Town Council, 17 August 1996, sent to the CPT.

5. Indictment by the federal prosecutor, Belém, January 1992.

6. *Estado de São Paulo,* January 1980.

7. Alison Sutton, *Slavery in Brazil,* Anti-Slavery International, London, 1994.

8. Interview, Human Rights Watch, Marabá, 29 November 1991.

7. The Women

1. Pureza talked to Bala on 10 March 1995. "A Procura de Abel," *Tempos Novos,* February–March 1995.

8. Violence

1. *Caros Amigos Especial* 5, 1999.

2. In July 2002 Pantoja and Oliveira were both convicted and received very long sentences which they are appealing.

9. Resistance

1. Under the auspices of Pope John XXIII, the Second Vatican Council (1962–65) articulated the new theology in a document titled *Gaudium et Spes.*

2. The Latin American bishops had two conferences, Medellín (1968), and Puebla (1979) to discuss how to live out the new theology.

10. The Landless Movement

1. The Bible tells us that the Children of Israel were commanded by God to celebrate the Jubilee every fifty years. In that year all debts were to be pardoned and lands redistributed. The campaign of Jubilee 2000 proposed applying these precepts to pardoning the external debts of poor countries.

2. Caetano da Silva and Antonio Barbosa. The former is appealing his sentence. The latter received a suspended sentence.

11. The Vila Rica Commission

1. *Folha de São Paulo,* 24 May 1998.

2. Antonio Delgado, Sônia's father, was known for his short temper. He was murdered in 2001.

12. A Case History

1. *Operation Tucumã, Inspection Report,* March–April 1999, Ministry of Labor/Mobile Inspection Group.

13. Volkswagen's Model Ranch

1. Cristalino publicity material put out by the public relations department of VW Brasil.

2. This statement made on 1 July 1981 was witnessed by Ricardo Rezende and Ana Maria Guimarães of the CPT.

3. José Ribamar de Souza (whom we later interviewed), Francisco Resende de Souza, José Libório, and Pedro Valdo.

4. Letter to Gernot Wirth from VW Germany, 7 September 1983.

5. "North of Brazil, Where Violence and Injustice Reign, Report of a Visit to Rio Cristalino, 5–7 July 1983," Expedito Soares.

6. The CPT brought the case on behalf of José Ribamar de Souza, Francisco Resende de Souza, José Libório, and Pedro Valdo. On the first hearing in 1984 the workers lost, but they won on appeal (24 March 1986) although they did not receive damages. In 1989 the case was moved to another judicial district, and later on the papers disappeared. After repeated complaints from the CPT the documents were found in 1995 and the damages were recalculated. In 1997 when the *fazenda* was auctioned by VW—who held the mortgage—the plaintiffs finally received damages, fourteen years later!

7. Letter from the Rural Workers Union of Santana do Araguaia to the Minister of Land Reform, dated 10 September 1998.

8. The claim was filed on 23 November 1999 by Eufrásio Pereira Luiz and José Marcos Monteiro, plus their respective wives.

9. Under Brazilian law all landowners must reserve a percentage of their land under forest cover.

10. In a letter to the state governor dated 12 May 2000, the Rio Maria rural workers union states that 80 percent of the one thousand families of settlers were suffering from malaria. By July 2000 the percentage had risen to 85 percent.

11. While land reform is directed at the landless, it is not unusual for people who already own land to sign up.

14. Model Ranch 2001

1. CPT archives.

2. Telex from the diocese of Conceição do Araguaia and the CPT to the Federal Police, 28 December 1988.

3. Statement to the CPT.

4. Report on an inspection carried out by the Federal Police on Fazenda Brasil Verde 24 February 1989.

5. CPT letter to Federal Assistant Attorney General Álvaro Augusto Ribeiro Costa, 18 March 1992.

6. Statement made by police agent José Fortes de Carvalho from the Federal Police in Marabá on 9 July 1992.

7. Letter from the state secretary for labor, Pará, to the attorney general's office, 2 August 1993.

8. Report on case 08100.001318/92–19 by the attorney general's office, pp. 71–75, Annex 1, talks of the "impossibility of punishing those responsible."

9. Statement made by José da Costa Oliveira to the regional superintendent of the Federal Police in Pará, Marabá, 10 March 1997.

10. This was the only inspection carried out by the flying squad. All previous and subsequent inspections were carried out by state labor officials, who were unable to institute criminal proceedings since they were not accompanied by the Federal Police.

11. Statement made to the CPT Marabá, 10 March 2000. It is interesting to note that the peons' statements were not taken by the police, who sent them to the CPT office instead.

12. The Quagliato *fazendas:* Rio Vermelho, Quamasa, Califórnia, Primavera, Colorado, Pedra Branca, Itauba, São Sebastião, Brasil Verde, São Carlos, Santa Rosa, Canaxuê, Marca Erre. *Fazendas* belonging to José Coelho Victor: Santa Lúcia, Rancho Alegre, Cachoeirinha, Levi Pará. *Fazendas* belonging to Maurício Pompéia Fraga: Porongai 1, Porongai 2, Uirande, Monte Azul, Rita da Cássia, Sinhá Moça.

13. According to statistics from the Ministry of Labor, more than four hundred rural workers were freed in 2001 from *fazendas* in the south of Pará alone. On 21 October 2001 TV Globo, in its program *Fantástico,* showed fifty-five workers who had been freed several weeks earlier from Fazenda Estrela de Alagoas, Xinguara, in the same district as the Quagliato *fazendas.* The workers had been held as slaves.

15. Black Slaves, White Slaves

1. The Rugmark campaign was begun several years ago in response to growing concern about the use of child labor in the manufacture of carpets, principally in India and Pakistan. The idea was not to prejudice the carpet manufacturers, but to influence consumers to restrict their buying to products certified by the campaign. The certificate was given to producers who committed themselves not to exploit child labor, to cooperate with independent inspectors, and to contribute 1 percent of the purchase price toward a fund destined to rehabilitate the children. Today 30 percent of the rugs sold in Europe carry the Rugmark.

2. The production of soybeans in 2001 was 41.5 million tons, three-quarters of which was sold internationally. Brazil is already the world's second biggest producer of soybeans. The area planted in 2002 has expanded by 14 percent. Source: USDA.

3. Eighty percent of the Brazilian herd is raised in areas certified free from foot-and-mouth disease, and since 99 percent of Brazilian cattle are pasture fed, the risk of mad cow disease is qualified by the International Organization for Epizootia (April 2001) as "negligible"—on the order of 1 percent of probability.

4. Articles 197–209 of the Penal Code list such crimes, which belong to the category of "crimes against the organization of work" and come under the jurisdiction of the federal courts (Art. 109, VI of the federal Constitution). Yet the bulk of interpretations, based on a decision by the Supreme Court, consider that these crimes should be tried by state courts, maintaining that "the federal courts shall judge cases which affect those institutions

that defend worker's rights, and not crimes committed against certain groups of workers." See the decision handed down by Dra Ednamar Silva Ramos, substitute federal judge, Palmas, Tocantins, 19 December 2001.

5. In December 2001 a federal judge in Marabá, Pará, declared himself incompetent and returned to the Pará state courts all the ongoing cases that involved slave labor.

6. This fact was recognized by the President of the republic, Fernando Henrique Cardoso, himself a respected sociologist. When the inter-ministerial group GERTRAF was set up to eradicate slavery he stated: "When accusations of slavery are proved, most slavers simply pay their fines and carry on. Legal sanctions aren't harsh enough. We have to hit these folks where it hurts; in their pocketbooks. The government will no longer give loans or subsidies or roll over debts for these unscrupulous ranchers and businessmen, nor will we allow them to participate in bidding for public contracts."

16. Into the Enemy's Camp

1. As a response to complaints against the Brazilian government first raised at the Organization of American States in 1992 the government set up, in 1995, an interministerial group dedicated to eradicating forced labor (GERTRAF) as well as the flying squad of government inspectors.

2. Many Brazilian laws are defined by the Constitution and require constitutional modifications before they can be changed. As a result none of these measures had been enacted by mid-2002.

Bibliography

Bales, Kevin. *Disposable People,* University of California Press, 1999.

Burns, E. Bradford. *A History of Brazil,* Columbia University Press, New York, 1980.

Dimenstein, Gilberto. *Meninas da Noite,* Editora Ática, São Paulo, 1992.

Esterci, Neide. *Escravos da Desigualdade,* CEDI, Rio de Janeiro, 1994.

Freire, Gilberto. *The Masters and the Slaves,* University of California Press, 1986.

————. *The Mansions and the Shanties,* University of California Press, 1986.

Hemming, John. *Red Gold,* Macmillan, London, 1978.

Kelly, Brian and London, Mark. *Amazon,* Robert Hale, London, 1983.

Kowarick, Marcos. *Amazônia/Carajás, Na Trilha do Saque,* Editora Anita Garibaldi, São Luis, MA, 1995.

Mendes, Chico. *Fight for the Forest,* Latin American Bureau, London, 1989.

Revkin, Andrew. *The Burning Season,* Collins, London. 1990.

Rezende Figueira, Ricardo. *A Justiça do Lobo,* Editora Vozes, Petrópolis, RJ, 1986.

————. *Rio Maria, Song of the Earth,* Orbis, Maryknoll, NY, 1994.

————. *Quão Penosa é a Vida dos Senhores* (thesis), Rio de Janeiro, 1999.

Sutton, Alison. *Slavery in Brazil,* Anti-Slavery International, London, 1994.

Sento-Sé, Jairo Lins de Albuquerque. *Trabalho Escravo no Brasil,* LTr, São Paulo, 2001.

Thomas, Hugh. *The Slave Trade,* Simon and Schuster, 1997.

Toneto, Bernadete. *Frei Henri des Roziers,* Salesiana, São Paulo, 2001.

Ure, John. *Trespassers on the Amazon,* Constable, London, 1986.

Veliz, Claudio. *The New World of the Gothic Fox,* University of California Press, 1994.

Brazil, Authorized Violence in Rural Areas, Amnesty International, London, 1988.

Direitos Humanos no Brasil 2001, Rede Social de Justiça e Direitos Humanos/ Global Exchange, São Paulo, 2001.

Dossiê sobre Violência de Policiais Civis e Militares, Impunidade, Fuga de Presos e Trabalho Escravo no Sul do Pará, CPT, Xinguara, 2000.

Estudos Avançados 38. Universidad de São Paulo, São Paulo, 2001.

A Experiência do Grupo Especial de Fiscalização Móvel, Ministério do Trabalho e Emprego, Brasília, 1999.

Long Night of Waiting: The Struggle for Human Rights in Brazil, Brazil Network, London, 1998.

O Peão entra na Roda, o Pião, CPT/Centro Ecumênico de Documentacão e Informacão, Rio de Janeiro, 1983.

Rural Violence in Brazil, Americas Watch, New York, 1991.

The Struggle for Land in Brazil, Americas Watch, New York, 1992.

São Félix do Xingu, Uma História de Vai e Vem, Paróquia de São Félix do Xingu, 1988.

Terra e Trabalho Escravo, Centro de Estudos Sociais Aplicados, Universidade Federal Fluminense, R.J., 2002.

Trabalho Escravo no Brasil Contemporâneo, CPT/Loyola, São Paulo, 1999.

Trabalho Escravo nas Fazendas do Pará e Amapá, CNBB, Belém PA, 1999.

Violência no Campo, A Luta pela Terra no Sul e Sudeste do Pará no Ano de 1999, CPT, 1999.

Resources

The American Anti-Slavery Group

198 Tremont Street, #421
Boston, MA 02166, USA
Tel: 1 800 884 0719
Website: http://www.anti-slavery.org

Main issue areas
Activism, campaigning, releasing slaves.

Working languages
English.

Resources available
interactive archive, (iabolish.com) press releases.

Amnesty International

99–119 Roseberry Avenue,
London EC1R 4RE,
England.
Tel: 44 20 7814 6200
Fax: 44 20 7833 1510
Email: info@amnesty.org.uk
Website: http://www.amnesty.org.uk

Main issue areas
Human rights abuses, prisoners of conscience, campaigning, advocacy.

Working languages
English, French, Spanish, Arabic.

Resources available
News releases, publications, bookstore.

Anti Slavery Society

Thomas Clarkson House,
The Stable Yard,
Broomsgrove Road,
London SW9 9TL,
England.
Tel: 44 20 7501 8920
Fax: 44 20 7738 4110
Email: info@antislavery.org
Website: http://www.antislavery.org

Main issue areas
Collecting information on slavery/trafficking/child labor, campaigns
and advocacy, education.

Area of activity
Worldwide

Working languages
English

Resources available
Online news releases and publications, library, photos, publications,
videos, microfilm, links, exhibitions.

CCEM: Comité Contre Esclavage Moderne

31 rue des Lilas
75019, Paris.
Tel: 1 44 52 8890
Fax: 1 444 52 8909
Email: ccem@imagenet.fr
Website: www.ccemm-antislavery.org

Main issue areas
Works with slaves within France. Advocacy, information, rescue, lobbying, legal help.

Working language
French

Resources available
Publications, lobby groups.

CSI: Christian Solidarity

Zelglistrasse 64
PO Box 70
CH 8122 Binz (Zurich)
Switzerland
Tel: 41 1 980 4707
Fax: 41 1 980 4715
Email: csi-int@csi-int.org

Main issue areas
Anti-slavery campaign in Sudan, disaster relief, children.

Working languages
English, French, German

Resources available
Lobbying, press releases.

Free the Slaves

1326 14th Street NW,
Washington DC 20005, USA
Tel: 866 324 (free)
1 202 588 1865
Email: info@freetheslaves.net
Website: http://www.freetheslaves.net

Main issue areas
Dissemination of information on contemporary slavery, activism, campaigning.

Area of activity
Worldwide

Working languages
English

Resources available
Online news archive and documentation.

Human Rights Watch

350 Fifth Avenue, 34th floor,
New York, NY 10118–3299, USA
Tel: 1 212 290 4700
Fax: 1 212 736 1300
Email: hrwnyc@hrw.org
Website: http://www.hrw.org

Main issue areas
Advocacy, investigation, education. Main fields of interest are: children's rights, HIV/AIDs, international justice, prisons, refugees, women's rights, academic freedom, freedom of speech, drugs, arms.

Area of activity
Worldwide

Working languages
English, Portuguese, Spanish, French, Russian, Arabic, Chinese.

Resources available
Online news releases, publications, bookstore, film exhibitions, photo essays.

The Pastoral Lands Commission
(Comissão Pastoral da Terra)

Rua 19, No 35,
Centro,
Caixa Postal 749,
74001–970, Goiania, GO.
Brazil.
Tel 55 62 212 6466
Fax: 55 62 212 0421
Email: cptnac@cultura.com.br
Website: http://www.cptnac.com.br

Main issue areas
Land tenure, advocacy, documentation of human rights abuses, slave labor.

Working languages
Portuguese, some English.

Resources available
Publications (in Portuguese).

The Robert. F. Kennedy Memorial

1367 Connecticut Avenue,
Washington, DC 20006, USA
Tel: 1 202 463 7575
Fax: 1 202 463 6606
Website: http://www.rfkmemorial.org

Main issue areas
Human rights center, human rights awards, book and journalism awards,
fellowships.

Working languages
English.

Trocaire

Maynooth
Co Kildare
Ireland
Tel: 1 629 3333
Fax: 1 629 0611
Email: info@trocaire.ie
Website: http://www.trocaire.ie

Main issue areas
Emergency relief, development, advocacy, campaigning, education.

Working languages
English.

Resources available
Press releases, library.

UN High Commission on Human Rights

Office of the High Commissioner for Human Rights,
8–14 Avenue de la Paix,
1211 Geneva 10,
Switzerland.
Tel: 41 22 9917 9000
Website: http://www.unhcr.ch

Main issue areas
Human rights, international law, war crimes, discrimination, asylum, trafficking.

Working languages
English, French, Spanish.

Resources available
Legal instruments, databases, publications.

Index

About the Author

In 1989 Binka Le Breton and her husband moved to an iso-lated corner of southeastern Brazil to set up a farm on the fringes of the rain forest. Over the years they have learned how to work with the trees, the animals, the weather, the local community and each other. Their technology now ranges from the oxcart to the Internet, and in 2000 they opened a rain forest conservation and research center that is visited by scores of foreign research-ers as well as hundreds of Brazilian schoolchildren. They are carrying out important work on land management issues with the recognition and support of several international authorities in the field, including staff from the Smithsonian Institution, Yale Forestry School, and Partners of the Americas.

Le Breton spent fifteen years as a concert pianist, playing in all sorts of offbeat places throughout the world. Between con-certs she took an external degree in English from London Uni-versity and taught English to foreigners in Nairobi, Jakarta, New Delhi, Recife, London, and Washington, D.C. When she moved to the rain forest she started to write books based on her travels and research in Brazil.

Her published works include *Voices from the Amazon,* Kumarian Press, 1993, *A Land to Die For,* Clarity Press, 1997, *Todos Sabiam,* Edicoes Loyola, São Paulo 2000, *Rainforest,* Longmans, London, 1997 and *Vidas Roubadas*, Edicoes Loyola, São Paulo, 2002.

 Also from Kumarian Press...

International Development

Advocacy for Social Justice: A Global Action and Reflection Guide
David Cohen, Rosa de la Vega and Gabrielle Watson

Dealing with Human Rights: Asian and Western Views on the Value of Human Rights
Edited by Martha Meijer

Going Global: Transforming Relief and Development NGOs
Marc Lindenberg and Coralie Bryant

The Humanitarian Enterprise: Dilemmas and Discoveries
Larry Minear

War's Offensive on Women:
The Humanitarian Challenge in Bosnia, Kosovo and Afghanistan
Julie A. Mertus for the Humanitarianism and War Project

Environment, Gender Studies, Global Issues, Globalization, Microfinance, Political Economy

Bringing the Food Economy Home: Local Alternatives to Global Agribusiness
Helena Norberg-Hodge, Todd Merrifield and Steven Gorelick

The Commercialization of Microfinance
Balancing Business and Development
Edited by Deborah Drake and Elisabeth Rhyne

The Hidden Assembly Line
Gender Dynamics of Subcontracted Work in a Global Economy
Edited by Radhika Balakrishnan

Mainstreaming Microfinance
How Lending to the Poor Began, Grew and Came of Age in Bolivia
Elisabeth Rhyne

Running Out of Control: Dilemmas of Globalization
R. Alan Hedley

Shifting Burdens: Gender and Agrarian Change under Neoliberalism
Edited by Shahra Razavi

The Spaces of Neoliberalism: Land, Place, and Family in Latin America
Edited by Jacquelyn Chase

Where Corruption Lives
Gerald Caiden, O.P Dwivedi and Joseph Jabbra

Visit Kumarian Press at **www.kpbooks.com** or
call **toll-free 800.289.2664** for a complete catalog.

 Kumarian Press, located in Bloomfield, Connecticut, is a forward-looking, scholarly press that promotes active international engagement and an awareness of global connectedness.